Praise for
Nature's Pathways to Mindfulness
John Harvey

"The deep learning and motivation sparked by *Nature's Pathways to Mindfulness* arise from the wealth of welcoming paths that John Harvey lays before us. Harvey synthesizes the science behind nature's impressive effects on our wellbeing. He explores a bevy of gateways into mindfulness, from sit spots and forest bathing to guided walks and bird-watching. He enhances each path with intimate and colorful windows into his own sojourns. Most importantly, he writes for a wide range of readers—those who might have trouble sitting still or might respond best to time on water; those who crave routine, need to be indoors, or relish adventure. Harvey's book artfully balances the analytical, the instructive, and the intuitive. It will help you find your path and give you a healthy nudge in a good and enriching direction."

KATHERINE HAUSWIRTH, author of *The Morning Light, the Lily White: Daily Dips into Nature and Spirit*

❧

"Many people report feeling good after being out in nature, but few know exactly why. John Harvey takes scientific research and combines it with his own intimate and careful observations to show why contact with nature can restore health and is vital for our continued physical and mental wellbeing. But Harvey doesn't stop there. He also teaches readers how to get the most from their contact with nature, which, in turn, can be life changing."

MICHAEL P. GADOMSKI, naturalist, photographer, and author of *Pennsylvania: A Portrait of the Keystone State* and *The Poconos: Pennsylvania's Mountain Treasure*

"John Harvey teaches us not only how to connect to the wonders and awe of the natural world but why these connections are so vital for our personal wellbeing. Harvey transports the reader into 'sit spots' and other mindful outdoor experiences by sharing rich sensory descriptions of his own experiences that allow us to feel the power of nature. He also provides techniques designed to guide us into deeper relationships with the natural world around us—no matter where we are. Whether on the wings of a tern or listening to the mournful song of a pewee or the flutelike song of a wood thrush, Harvey demonstrates how we can find an uplift to boost our mood or support healing of body and mind by simply taking time to notice, reflect, and appreciate the present moment. In our ever-changing world, we can all benefit from his wisdom."

HOLLY C. MERKER, founder of The Mindful Birding Network, coauthor of the award-winning *Ornitherapy: For Your Mind, Body, and Soul* and *The Power of Birdwatching/ Die Kraft der Vogelbeobachtung*

❧

"In *Pathways to Nature Mindfulness,* John Harvey describes 'tipping points,' moments during nature observation when awareness shifts into the present and away from the created world of thoughts and feelings about past and future. With his 'sit spot' approach, Harvey guides us through a developmental process—we settle in, nature resumes its activity, we drop our habitual present and past obsessions, and we turn to the present. It is a process shared by meditation, but the advantage in nature is that the categories and concepts that support our 'separation' give way to seeing ourselves as being in nature and of nature. We are not only in the present, but in presence. Harvey's book is richly supported with scientific evidence, personal experience, and step-by-step guidance. It is an invaluable resource for those who look to improve their physical, emotional, and mental wellbeing and those who seek personal transformation."

LYLE OLSON, author of *The Meditation Process: Raja Yoga* and *Buddhist Shamatha*

"John Harvey's book is a gem, merging science, practical knowledge, and insight to reveal the spiritual fountain of nature. He takes us on a journey into the natural beauty and harmony of nature that surrounds us and is, in fact, an essential part of ourselves. *Nature's Pathways to Mindfulness* is a manual for recognizing the power of nature to restore our physical and mental balance, harmony, and wellness. Nature is life itself, constantly changing, growing, and healing. We should not fear nature, but open ourselves to the rhythms of adaptability, resilience, and beauty that nature reveals to all who pay attention. Perhaps the most important lesson we learn from Harvey is how much a part of nature we are. Through nature's pathways, we begin to experience and maybe know for the first time that we are an integral part of a vast reality that is filled with renewal, beauty, harmony, and goodness."

PHIL NUERNBERGER, PH.D., author of *Strong and Fearless* and *Eternal Self*

❧

"John Harvey opens the doorway to nature and leads us through. *Nature's Pathways to Mindfulness* is a well-researched, thoughtful, and wonderfully written guidebook on how to get the most from nature—wherever we live. He explains that many of us think of nature as only that which is far away, remote, or in the deep woods where 'real' nature exists. That limiting view stops many from enjoying and benefiting from the wildness that is as close as a deck with a potted plant, a backyard, or a city park. Experiences in nature make us healthier and happier, and Harvey cites the research and draws from his own experiences to validate that conclusion. This is a must-read book for nature lovers, psychologists, therapists, and teachers."

ERIC WADE, author of *Upstream: In the Alaska Wilderness* and *Squirrelland: Imagination and the Alaska Red Squirrel*

"Like Nature herself, *Nature's Pathways to Mindfulness* is a soothing antidote to daily stress and anxiety. Filled with beautiful visuals, lyrical descriptions, and practical wisdom, it shares John Harvey's infectious love of wild places. By reminding us that nature reveals herself to those who sit and wait, this book crystallizes a vague and generalized fondness for the outdoors into something deeper, helping us to love it even more."

DAWN McINTYRE, author of *The Paper Pirate*

Nature's Pathways to Mindfulness

John Harvey

SHANTI ARTS PUBLISHING
BRUNSWICK, MAINE

Nature's Pathways to Mindfulness

Published by Shanti Arts Publishing

Designed by Shanti Arts Designs

Cover image: rural-explorer / unsplash.com

Shanti Arts LLC
193 Hillside Road
Brunswick, Maine 04011
shantiarts.com

Printed in the United States of America

ISBN: 978-1-962082-26-6 (softcover)
ISBN: 978-1-962082-27-3 (ebook)

Library of Congress Control Number: 2024944945

To my grandchildren: Olivia Harvey,
Lovis Harvey, and Aiden Harvey

Contents

EXPERIENCES IN NATURE MINDFULNESS

SIT SPOT GUIDANCE

Acknowledgments

Nature was my teacher, my inspiration, and my solace during the long, arduous, exciting, and mostly solitary process of developing the ideas for and writing this book. I am grateful for all that was given to me during my "times in nature."

I also appreciate this second opportunity to work with publisher Christine Cote. She has a unique gift to understand even better than I did what the message of this book was and to develop a vision for the best ways to refine, organize and present that vision. It is a remarkable experience to work with someone who has this gift.

I want to thank all of my "sit spot friends"—Jerry Swendsen, Michael Smith, Pat Sanders, Bill Johnson, and Ellington Bliss for agreeing to venture out with me, follow the guidelines I offered, and share their impressions. In many ways what they wrote and said provided more eloquent descriptions of nature mindfulness than I could come up with myself.

Even though researching and writing this book was a solitary process, there were several books that exerted a profound influence, books that I read and reread, understanding more each time. These books became my companions on the writing journey:

Jon Young's *What the Robin Knows* gave me the initial inspiration and practical guidance for conducting a sit spot session. It was my year of weekly sit spots that opened the door to nature mindfulness for me. Each time I checked back in and reread passages in this book, I learned more and appreciated more the many layers of meaning in his book.

The Nature Fix by Florence Williams woke me up to the scientific validation of the benefits of time in nature. Written in an engaging style and thoroughly grounded in science, this book was at hand throughout the process of writing this book. If I had my way, *The Nature Fix* would be required reading for high school students.

M. Amos Clifford's down to earth and comprehensive *Your Guide to Forest Bathing* helped me to understand that there may be certain universal and practical steps in the process of nature mindfulness.

Other books that became favorite companions included Jon Kabat-Zinn's *Mindfulness for Beginners*, *Ornitherapy for Your Mind, Body, and Soul* by Holly Merker, Richard Crossley, and Sophie Crossley, and *Rewilding* by Micah Mortali.

During the many hours I spent alone in my office, combing through the scientific research on the benefits of time in nature, I slowly came to feel like a member of a vibrant worldwide community. I read studies originating in Japan, Korea, Australia, Finland, the United Kingdom, the United States, and elsewhere. The amount of research occurring worldwide is truly impressive and clarified to me the importance and timeliness of the role of science in verifying, explaining, and facilitating the human-nature (re)connection.

Finally, I am grateful to you the reader for offering your time and interest. I hope that what I have shared brings interest, well-being, and joy to your life.

INTRODUCTION

A Nature Mystery

❧

O N A COLD, GRAY, WINDY MORNING IN FEBRUARY OF 2013, I embarked on a one-year commitment to go to the forest once a week, sit for an hour, and observe nature. My goals were straightforward—spend more time in nature, learn more about the environment around me, and challenge my capacity to meet a commitment. Fifty two weeks, six states, and two continents later I fulfilled this commitment.

At first the weekly obligation posed a challenge, but as the weeks went by, my project picked up momentum, and it became easier to carve out an hour a week. During the year I discovered much about the process and value of making and sticking to a commitment. During my hours of stillness, I (re)learned to more fully see, hear, smell, and feel. I began to look forward to my weekly sessions in the forest at my "sit spot" on a little peninsula along the shoreline of nearby Prompton Lake.

With my awakened senses I also learned a great deal about nature—the trees, birds, wind, and wildflowers. I witnessed the subtle, steady, and beautiful weekly progression of the seasons. I saw how the flora and fauna responded and adapted to ever-changing conditions.

I kept a journal of my weekly observations and reflections. Later I wrote them up, edited them, added photos, and shared my experiences in a book: *The Stillness of the Living Forest: A Year of Learning and Listening.*

My year in the forest was richly rewarding, and all of my initial goals were met. Yet at the end I was left with questions. I had noticed surprising and cumulative effects from my weekly sojourns in nature. I felt physically rejuvenated, emotionally restored, mentally reinvigorated, and even spiritually transformed.

I also found that I was more sensitive and responsive to nature— even incidental exposures to nature. The sound of house sparrows chirping as I walked across a supermarket parking lot caught my attention and instantly connected me with the positive feelings from my nature sitting experience. Similarly, the roadside flight of a red-tailed hawk, a vista of a verdant hillside forest, a glance at a sunrise, or the scent of pine needles all seemed to automatically and spontaneously bring forth feelings of joy, energy, empathy, and optimism. Something had changed within, changes that were locked in and residing just beneath the surface of my consciousness, ready to manifest given the slightest cue.

I had no ready explanation for these positive effects of being in nature. From my years of practice as a clinical psychologist, I knew about various methods for emotional and mental therapy and healing. As a management consultant, I taught personal stress management and understood its value. As a longstanding daily practitioner of mantra meditation and yoga asanas, I knew about personal techniques to promote wellness and self-development. Yet somehow, during my year of weekly one-hour sessions at my sit-spot, I stumbled upon mechanisms, experiences, or something that seemed more effective and more beneficial than all of the professional strategies and personal techniques I had tried and taught to others.

The mystery grew deeper and more important as I began to promote my book through lectures and book signing events. I found myself struggling to explain the full benefits and effects of my year in nature. I understood in a general folk-wisdom sense that being in nature is beneficial. I knew that taking a walk in a park can be relaxing and lift a person's mood. I knew the value of being on vacation at the beach, watching the waves and water, and viewing an ocean sunset.

But I never put these casual benefits associated with being in nature on the same level as evidence-based medical interventions such as psychotherapy, surgery, targeted medication, vaccines, antibiotics, and antidepressants. These seemed like real therapies, real medicine. Time in nature fell more into the category of a soft medicine intervention, one that would cause no harm and might lead to positive effects.

Still, the benefits I experienced seemed quite real. I began to feel the restlessness of a quest to better understand these benefits. The first hint on the direction my quest might take occurred one afternoon when I was wandering through a bookstore and came across *The Nature Fix* by Florence Williams. Within its pages I found a compelling review and synthesis of the scientific research on the benefits of time spent in nature. Her subtitle told the story: *Why Nature Makes Us Happier, Healthier and More Creative.*

Suddenly, I began to see the changes I experienced in a whole new light. Science verified and validated what I had experienced. Keeping an eye out for the latest findings on the positive effects of time in nature, I discovered a rapidly expanding and remarkably consistent body of research on the physical, emotional, and cognitive benefits.

For example, in 2022 Lam Thi Mai Huynh and her colleagues at the University of Tokyo explored the contributions of nature to human well-being in a systematic review of 301 peer-reviewed research articles from 62 countries. They found 227 unique pathways through which time spent in nature created beneficial effects. They sorted these pathways into 13 mechanisms that link time in nature with improvements in human well-being. These pathways included new learning, a greater sense of connection, improved mood, greater creativity, better mental health, an enhanced sense of identity, and improved physical health.

This and other research confirmed my experiences and heightened my appreciation for the value of time spent in nature. While the research consistently documented the physical, emotional, and cognitive benefits of a nature connection, there were also findings regarding what might be called higher-level benefits such as profound feelings of connection, improvements in self-knowledge, a sense of personal transformation and spiritual growth—results that dovetailed with what I had often read in the rich tradition of nature writing.

With this tantalizing scientific information in hand, it was, I realized, time for a sequel to *The Stillness of the Living Forest*, time to take an all-embracing journey through both contemporary scientific and traditional literary sources to understand how and why time in nature is so beneficial.

❦

This book is divided into three sections. The first is an exploration of existing scientific information on the benefits of time spent in nature and the processes and theories that explain these benefits. The second section is a recounting of a number of my experiences in nature conducted in various settings and organized around themes, such as nature healing, the seasons, positive attachment, nature in nearby places, and more. The third section provides step-by-step guidance on how to conduct a nature sitting experience to deepen your nature connection.

Let's begin where I started—trying to understand why time in nature so effectively enhances human well-being.

TIME IN NATURE

CHAPTER 1

Nature and Well-Being

T HE TENSION EASED OUT OF MY MUSCLES AS I GAZED UP AT the winter silhouettes of the trees, tracked the puffy white clouds drifting across a blue sky, listened to the wind whooshing through the branches, and felt the brisk February air touch my face.

The feelings of relaxation were a surprise. I had anticipated an effortful and tiring trek, lugging my gear down a narrow forest trail and forcing myself to sit still on a rickety camp chair for an hour in the cold. Instead, at the end of the hour I felt as relaxed as if I had had a full body massage and as energized as if I had just awakened from a power nap. I sensed that my heart rate and blood pressure had dropped as well.

Given these noticeable and positive effects from merely sitting in nature, I was especially interested in what the scientific research might reveal about the physical benefits of time spent in nature. I hoped to verify and understand my experiences.

Delving into the literature, I discovered compelling and consistent evidence of a wide range of physical benefits from time spent in nature. What follows is not a formal review of the literature but more a summary of the physical, emotional, and cognitive benefits that are known to accrue when people experience nature in its many forms. For more information on the science, refer to the chapter notes.

PHYSICAL HEALTH

Much of the groundbreaking research on the physical benefits of time in nature has been conducted in Japan by scientists studying the effects of *shinrin-yoku* ("forest bathing"), a practice during which participants are led on a leisurely, mindful walk through selected natural settings. Here are some of the findings from this and other research from around the world.

Spending time outdoors in nature can lead to:
  decreased systolic blood pressure;
  decreased diastolic blood pressure;
  decreased heart rate;
  decreased cortisol levels (a stress hormone);
  decreased muscular tension;
  slower, deeper, and more rhythmic respiration;
  increased heart rate variability;
  decreased blood flow to the prefrontal cortex;
  decreased sympathetic nervous system activation;
  increased parasympathetic nervous system activity;
  lower body mass index;
  reduced prevalence of disease;
  improved immune system function, including increased
      natural killer cells;
  increased functional activity of antiviral cells and higher
      amounts of intracellular anticancer proteins;
  reduced obesity;
  increased healing; and
  lower mortality rates.

Among all of these impressive results, the decrease in sympathetic nervous system activity may be particularly important. This nervous system is one branch of the autonomic nervous system (ANS) that regulates a number of crucial internal functions, including heart rate, blood pressure, cortisol levels, respiration, and digestion. The sympathetic branch of this system is in sympathy with and supports the so-called flight or fight response by essentially jacking up all of these physiological parameters in preparation for a massive mobilization to either flee danger or fight. The other branch of the ANS, the parasympathetic nervous system, mediates the so-called rest and digest response by slowing down all of these parameters.

The sympathetic nervous system is designed for immediate and short-duration emergency response with little concern for the judicious, long-term use of physiological resources. This system was perfectly suited to times when humans faced occasional and clear threats—a prowling saber-toothed tiger or an attack by an unfriendly tribe. The principle here is for the body to rise to the crisis and then shift back to the rest and digest mode.

In contemporary society, however, we face a constant and very real array of stressors that range from low to high intensity—job stress, crowding, traffic, media sensationalism, noise, pollution, and global conflicts—all of which cause us to turn on and then leave on the sympathetic flight or fight response. Many of our chronic diseases are thought to be caused or exacerbated by this constant and unrelenting activation of the sympathetic nervous system. Chronic overactivation of this stress response also constricts our attention, limits our creativity, and increases feelings of anxiety, irritability, and frustration.

One explanation for how and why time spent in nature is so good for our health is found in the Stress Reduction Theory originally advanced by psychologist Roger Ulrich in 1980 and subsequently refined and supported by extensive research. The idea is that time spent viewing, hearing, smelling, and even feeling the tactile sensations of nature immediately de-escalates the flight or fight response, allowing the rest and digest response to take over, and we then feel better and are healthier as a result.

Among the positive physical changes, the increase in heart rate variability is particularly interesting. When we are in a flight or fight response, our heart rate goes up and stays up. Our body becomes locked in a stress response mode. When we get out in nature and relax, our heart rate decreases, which allows a reset to a more dynamic and healthy balance between sympathetic and parasympathetic activation. We regain a natural responsiveness to the shifting demands of our environment, a finely tuned interplay between activation and recovery, an exquisite sensitivity to even small changes in our environment.

The decrease in blood flow to the prefrontal cortex probably means that mental scanning for danger and the consequent activating and maintaining the flight or fight response gets damped down as well. It is almost as if time in nature provides a mild sedative, a sedative without negative side effects or addictive potential other than wanting to get back out into the forest.

Researchers in Korea have found that the boost in immune system function seems to be especially activated by those wonderful fragrances we inhale when strolling through a forest filled with pine, spruce, cedar, or fir trees. These natural fragrances are called phytoncides, the natural oils that plants produce to protect themselves against pests.

Even a twenty-minute stroll through an evergreen forest inhaling these chemicals can give the immune system a boost that lasts up to thirty days. And research indicates that there may be other beneficial nature fragrances such as the smells of the forest floor, the earth, other plants, and even water.

Overall, the evidence is dramatically clear that spending time in nature benefits physical health.

EMOTIONAL BENEFITS

Another change I noticed during my weeks of sitting in the forest was that I simply felt happier. The sound of the wind and colors of the water and sky were soothing. Settling into stillness, I began to grow more responsive to moments of beauty such as a brightly colored blue jay perched on a maple branch, the mournful *ooo-eek* call of a female wood duck taking flight, the pastel palate of pink, orange, and yellow of a winter sunrise, or the touch of snowflakes on my face.

By the third week of my year I began to regard my hour in nature as one of the best hours of my week. The positive feelings seemed to carry over through the week. Consequently, I was curious to see if the research validated these experiences.

I came across a study that grabbed my attention and connected the dots about the emotional benefits of nature that had been floating around in my brain. The research was conducted in 2011 by environmental psychologists Elizabeth Nisbet and John Zielinski at the University of Trent in Ontario. I first read a mention of the study in *The Nature Fix*, by Florence Williams, and was so fascinated that I had to pore over the original study.

Here was the setup. College students were asked to either walk to the other side of campus through an underground tunnel or to walk along a picturesque nature trail beside a canal. The canal walkers (nature experiencers) rated their mood along with their sense of connection to nature both before and after the walk. They were told that they were participating in a study of personality and campus impressions and were given the slightly misleading instructions to "be observant" while they walked as they would be asked afterward about their impressions.

After just a seventeen-minute walk, the nature experiencers were—in the words of the authors—"much happier" than those who had taken the tunnel. Specifically, the subjects who had traipsed along the canal reported increased positive affect, greater feelings of relaxation, an increased sense of soft fascination, less negative affect, and stronger feelings of connection to nature.

I was stunned by these results. Just seventeen minutes walking along a canal on a pleasant autumn day lifted the subjects' overall emotional state and feelings of well-being. The immediate and powerful benefits of time in nature on emotions became abundantly clear to me and confirmed my longstanding experiences of feeling happier during and after my hourlong sitting sessions.

The subjects had not been given direct instructions to focus on the beauty of nature. When subjects were asked to forecast in advance how they would feel, they consistently underestimated the pleasurable impact of being in nature. So even without conscious awareness and effort, nature quickly and significantly improved the subjects' emotional states. I wondered how much more beneficial the results would have been if the subjects had been told to tune into their environment.

I subsequently kept an eye out for research on the effects of nature on emotional functioning and discovered two broad categories of findings. The first described reductions in negative feelings while the second demonstrated increases in positive feelings.

In terms of negative feelings, numerous studies have shown that anxiety, depression, worry, pessimism, and sadness all decrease when we get out in nature. Additionally, decreases have been documented in feelings of anger, hostility, aggression, fatigue, confusion, and tension, as well as in perceived stress, obsessive-compulsive thinking, and a sense of being rushed.

While these so-called negative emotions can be considered a natural and necessary part of living, they become counterproductive when they persist beyond a natural response to challenging events.

Persistent negative emotions limit our quality of life and adversely affect our health and social interactions.

Managing and reducing persistent negative emotions is the goal of self-help, psychotherapy, and medication-based psychiatry. Given the results described above, time in nature could complement and reinforce these therapies.

In terms of positive emotions, subjects reported a broad range of positive feelings after spending time in nature. These included greater feelings of happiness, calmness, and tranquility. Subjects also reported feeling refreshed, restored, and more comfortable. Other benefits included increased feelings of gratitude, optimism, empathy, compassion, resilience, vigor, and even a greater willingness to share feelings with others.

When immersed in nature viewing a sunset over the ocean, a sunrise vista from a mountaintop, a forest panorama, or a deer stepping across a dew-laden meadow, people often reported feelings of awe. These moments of awe brought positive feelings of joy, satisfaction, wonder, and a sense of connection to nature and to a greater whole.

The cultivation of such positive emotions is the foundation of what is known as positive psychology. This branch of psychology is based on the premise that cultivating positive emotions is a more efficient and natural way to improve and sustain mental health than trying to undo longstanding negative thoughts and feelings. Proponents of positive psychology note that feelings of gratitude, joy, and thankfulness are fundamental to optimal mental health.

Spending time in nature may then be one of the best ways we can promote and maintain our emotional well-being. One vast study with thousands of subjects showed that people who spent just two hours a week in nature reported increased feelings of satisfaction and well-being. A walk in the park, a moment to enjoy a view of distant hills, a hike through a verdant forest, or taking a minute to contemplate a wildflower might be seen as doses of positive psychotherapy. Such nature engagement is likely to pull you out of a grumpy mood, get you feeling happier, and help you leave the blues behind.

Conceptually, the positive emotional benefits of spending time in nature link up with what is known as the Biophilia Hypothesis, which suggests that humans have an innate attraction to, love of, and appreciation for nature. The term biophilia was originally coined by the humanistic psychoanalyst Eric Fromm, who defined it as the "passionate love of life and all that is alive." The definition was expanded by the renowned biologist Edward O. Wilson in his book titled *Biophilia,* in which he advanced the idea that humans have an innate, genetically-based tendency to focus on and affiliate with nature and other life forms.

The underlying idea is that through uncountable centuries of evolution, humans were sheltered by the trees of the forest, warmed by the sun, fed by the plants and animals that surrounded them, and sustained by the fresh waters of nearby springs. Consequently, when we are surrounded by nature, when we see, hear, feel, and smell those aspects of nature that have nurtured and protected us, we simply feel happy. We feel content, nurtured, protected, and safe. Nature is our true home.

A corollary of feeling connected to nature is the realization of the need to take care of the nature that takes care of us. Subjects who found joy, felt gratitude, and experienced awe while spending time in nature spontaneously developed what might be called a conservation ethic—a recognition of belonging to a community within nature, which then strengthened the desire to take care of the environment. In a world filled with concerns about climate change and environmental degradation, such a deeply held conservation ethic may be crucial to our health and the health of the planet. During my year in the forest, I too felt the emergence of a strong and heartfelt conservation ethic.

COGNITIVE BENEFITS

Once I understood that time in nature improved physical health and emotional well-being, I began to wonder if it might also improve mental skills or what are more formally called cognitive abilities. In other words, if we feel better physically and emotionally, do our brains work better too? I had a particular interest in this realm due to my many years of administering, scoring, and interpreting educational, psychological, and neuropsychological tests, all of which measure various aspects of cognitive performance.

I quickly discovered research confirming that time spent in nature does improve attention, memory, problem solving, executive function, and even boosts creativity. These cognitive benefits are fairly straightforward to measure and usually involve tests that look at the ability to maintain focus on a task (attention), to repeat back numbers forward or backward (short-term memory), or to recall and find target numbers or symbols in an array of targets (working memory). All of these tasks also require executive function or the ability to figure out how to best do the task and how to inhibit interference.

The common thread in these studies seemed to be the quality and duration of attention. When we can focus long and deeply and inhibit distractions, memory and other cognitive tasks are performed much better. Time in nature seems to improve attention, which is the key to improving a wide range of cognitive skills.

These findings resonate with Attention Restoration Theory (ART), a conceptual model developed by Stephen and Rachel Kaplan at the University of Michigan in the 1980s. As one researcher wrote, "ART is based on past research showing the separation of attention into two components: involuntary attention, where attention is captured by inherently intriguing or important stimuli; and voluntary or directed attention, where attention is directed by cognitive-control processes."

Voluntary or directed attention is also called top-down attention. It is the type of focus we need when taking a test, performing a work task, or writing a report. It involves activating learned and systematic ways of processing information, reasoning, and problem solving. Simultaneously and necessarily, we inhibit interference from distractions by actively blocking out radio, TV, kids playing, and people talking in the background.

Top-down processing is extremely useful for school and work and many everyday activities. It is the kind of cognitive processing that helps us get good grades, earn money, keep our house and yard in order, and receive recognition from others. Consequently, top-down processing gradually becomes our default mode.

The problem, however, is that top-down processing consumes a lot of energy because it takes considerable effort to focus on one thing and forcefully inhibit or limit our attention to everything else. After an hour or more of top-down processing, we become fatigued, feel stressed, and most importantly, the quality of our cognitive performance declines. Our focus is narrowed, and we increasingly fail to notice other interesting, important, and enjoyable things around us. A vicious cycle can begin. When our top-down attention flags, we often reach for a cup of coffee for a boost or push ourselves to focus harder, eventually leading to even more fatigue.

Involuntary attention—bottom-up processing or so-called fast thinking—is characterized by feeling more relaxed, having more open attention, noticing more things around us, and creatively seeing novel connections and associations. During bottom-up processing, we quickly and almost effortlessly notice patterns, connections, and relationships, although it may be in a tangential or non-linear way. Intuitive insights arise. Involuntary attention takes on the feel of a pleasant state of reverie.

Both top-down and bottom-up processing are useful and necessary. Ideally, we would switch back and forth between the two systems in response to environmental demands and challenges. The problem once again seems to come when we get locked into one type of processing and lose the ability to shift smoothly from one to the other.

The Kaplans discovered that spending time in nature is an optimal way to shift into involuntary attention or bottom-up processing. They found that there is something about nature—the open vistas, the colors, the sounds, the sensations—that presents an array of pleasing stimuli that provides just the right amount, the right degree, and the right kind of change and interest. Nature allows for what the Kaplans call "soft fascination," and that is the key to restoring involuntary attention. After an interval of refreshing and restorative involuntary attention, we can then shift back to effortful attention with renewed capacity; hence the improvements in memory, problem solving, and creativity.

I like to put important concepts like this into a personal framework to see if it fits with personal experience. Considering top-down versus bottom-up processing, I thought back to my first week in first grade. I grew up in what is now suburbia but back then was "the country." As kids we were turned out of the door after breakfast and allowed to roam through our yards and nearby fields and woods, making up games and adventures through the day.

At age six I started first grade in a rural two-room school— one teacher and four grades to a room. The old yellow brick school building had polished wooden floors, tall spacious windows, and was situated between two farm fields along the shoreline of Lake Michigan. I recall sitting at my desk during the first week of school,

---

gazing out the windows, checking out the clouds floating across a blue September sky, and looking curiously at the adjacent cabbage fields, thinking about the pattern and spacing of the heads of cabbage and wondering when and how it might be harvested.

I was in a classic and pleasant involuntary attention mode, openly noticing patterns and considering possibilities, a kind of musing. Suddenly, a voice shattered my reverie. My teacher trying to teach me and my classmates the letters of the alphabet said, "John! Look up at the board and pay attention."

This was a call to shift into top-down processing, to focus on the instruction, to inhibit attending to all the fun and interesting things going on outside. It was a call to direct my attention and effort to learning to read, calculate, and write. Truth be told, this was not an easy transition for me, and my grades through elementary and high school were inconsistent. After a stint in the military, I finally mastered effective and productive top-down processing, graduating with honors from the University of Wisconsin.

However, some years later I had a moment of insight into the cost of my acquired, dominant top-down processing. While on vacation I visited the building where I attended graduate school, stepped into the elevator, pushed the button for the third floor where my office had been located. As the door slid shut, I suddenly noticed profound physical changes. My heart rate jumped up, probably blood pressure too, muscles braced, breath sped up, and my focus narrowed. My body and mind remembered! This was a place for intense directed attention and top-down processing, processing that helped me academically and professionally. But, I had paid a price.

When I reflect back on certain experiences from my year of sitting in the forest, Attention Restoration Theory and the experience of bottom-up processing makes sense to me. I remember the first time I sat still, observed nature, and began to shift to a state of soft fascination. I began to see and hear so much more. I remember suddenly noticing the rich burgundy color of wild raspberry stems, hearing the distant calls of blue jays, and feeling microgusts of breeze touch my face.

The effects of soft fascination seemed cumulative, and slowly I gained a greater appreciation for the quality and value of involuntary attention. As the year progressed, I began to not only see and hear more, but I began to notice patterns and relationships in nature. I developed greater access to intuition by, for example, sensing danger before it happened, or turning to look at a tree or up in the sky and suddenly seeing a squirrel or a bird appear because my open and fast-thinking mind knew when and where to look.

As I think back on it now, perhaps one of our graduate classes should have included spending quality time in nature, taking a walk, writing up a reflection on a nature sitting experience, or participating in a weekend forest retreat. The research suggests that it would have improved our academic performance, set us up to be more productive in our careers, and helped us to maintain our health and well-being.

THOUGHTS

The science is real. Time in nature is good for us. Reviewing the research on the physical, emotional, and cognitive benefits confirmed what I had experienced and reinforced my belief in the value of getting out in nature.

These physical, emotional, and cognitive benefits are most likely intertwined as they interact positively and occur simultaneously. The three models explaining the benefits of time in nature—Stress Reduction Theory, Biophilia Hypothesis, and Attention Restoration Theory—offer different perspectives and different points of emphasis on the connections between nature and human well-being.

After reviewing the research I felt encouraged and inspired by the value of being in nature. Much of what I had noticed during my year of forest stillness had been validated and explained. But I had more questions. How much time in nature is needed? What are the best ways to be in nature? And there were other experiences from my year—transcendent moments, integrative events, and sublime feelings of connection—that the research hinted at but didn't measure. There were, I realized, more mysteries to explore. I decided to start by looking at how much time in nature is needed.

CHAPTER 2

How Much Time in Nature?

※

LOOK TO THE GREEN

A S THE HOSPITAL ELEVATOR DOOR SLID OPEN, MY GAZE FELL upon a large framed photograph across the hallway, a view of a forest stream flowing around a large rock. Boughs and branches of maples and ash reached over the stream, their sunlit leaves adorned in early autumn shades of gold and orange. I could almost hear the water splashing around the rock.

Looking at the photograph, I felt knots of tension release from my shoulders and spontaneously took a long, slow, deep breath. My experience was probably similar to others who stepped off the elevator, glanced at the photograph, and felt their cares lessen and their hopes rise as they went to visit a friend or family member.

I wondered how long my view of the photograph lasted. On my next visit I counted six seconds while the elevator door opened, I stepped out, and headed down the hallway. I concluded that the photo was not randomly placed. It and the others that decorated the hallway—a field of red tulips in bloom, a wooden bridge over a river, a mountain lake under a high blue sky—were most likely placed purposely to relax, soothe, and reduce the stress of visitors, patients, and staff.

Someone in the administration knew the research, knew that even a quick view of nature can produce beneficial effects on physiology, mood, and mind. This was smart policy as these effects would act to reduce healing time for patients; improve the quality of life, job satisfaction, performance, and productivity of employees; and make visitors like me more helpful and agreeable.

My experience with this photograph reminded me of something I learned years ago when conducting stress management sessions for residents of a senior living community. One of the participants, a soft-spoken gentleman from a village in Switzerland, related that he had worked in a small optics factory, performing tasks requiring sustained detailed attention. He said that his boss instructed him and his coworkers to take a break every hour, step outside, and "look to the green."

It was easy for me to imagine his view of a verdant mountain meadow dappled with multihued wildflowers and topped by steep snow-covered peaks, a view that would certainly relax me quickly and deeply. I subsequently took his advice to heart and often while working in my office would pause and walk to a window for a view of the trees or step outside to "look to the green."

Recently, this man's advice has been verified by research. In a study conducted in Australia, subjects were instructed to look at a green, grassy, rooftop garden dotted with flowers for forty seconds while comparison subjects looked at a bare concrete roof for the same amount of time. The subjects who took the brief green microbreak performed better afterward on a cognitive test. It seemed that even a forty-second look to the green rested and restored attention.

Additional research has indicated that looking to the blue—to a stream, river, pond, lake, ocean, or the sky—may be just as effective for quickly restoring well-being. Other research indicates that the sounds of nature—wind, waves, and birdsong—may have similar effects.

These scientifically validated effects of nature sounds make sense to me. I make it a point now to take brief breaks while working in my office. I step outside and tune in to the *cheerily, cheerup* song of a robin in the yard or to the sound of the breeze whispering through the leaves.

EACH DAY

In terms of longer intervals in nature, as noted in the previous chapter, Lorien Nesbitt and her colleagues in Canada found that just a seventeen-minute walk along a scenic canal-side nature trail led to greater feelings of happiness and nature relatedness. Exploring the concept of a daily dose further, Genevive Meredith and her colleagues at Cornell University tried to determine the "minimum time dose in nature" that would have a positive impact on the mental health of college students.

Meredith and her team reviewed the scientific literature and found over ten thousand references documenting the benefits of time in nature. They then selected 155 papers that qualified for a full reading and review. From these they chose fourteen articles that focused on college students, were peer reviewed, and used adequate scientific methodology. Their analysis of these papers revealed "that as little as ten to twenty minutes and up to fifty minutes of sitting or walking in a diverse array of natural settings has significant and positive impacts on key psychological and physiological markers."

The array of natural settings included viewing a wooded or other type of nature scene, sitting in a park, or walking through a forest. Comparison subjects either walked in urban settings or looked out a window at a city view. Physiologically, the results from the subjects who spent time in nature included decreased heart rate, blood pressure, and cortisol levels, and a decrease in overall sympathetic nervous system activation—the fight or flight response. Psychologically, the nature subjects showed a decrease in negative emotions such as tension, hostility, anger, anxiety, depression, somatization, fatigue, and confusion. On the positive side of the mood ledger, subjects reported increased feelings of vigor, happiness, refreshment, calmness, and comfort.

Based on these findings, the authors suggested that providing options for and encouraging college students to spend time in nature could be beneficial for their mental health and physical well-being, Also, encouraging time in nature may be a factor to consider in environmental design and public policy. They added that some colleges and universities have already instituted programs in nature therapy and park prescription programs. The authors recommended that future research address the question of how much time in nature is needed each week.

Per Week

The question of time per week was addressed in a study conducted in the United Kingdom by Matthew White, of the University of Exeter, and his colleagues. White and his team looked at the relationship between recreational nature contact and self-reported health and feelings of well-being. Data from almost twenty thousand subjects revealed that people who spent two hours a week in nature had a significantly greater likelihood of reporting good health and higher levels of well-being. The authors suggested that 120 minutes in nature per week may constitute an important threshold above which significant health and well-being benefits accrue.

The researchers carefully ruled out confounding variables such as socioeconomic status. They also determined that the 120-minute threshold applied equally to people living in both high and low greenspace areas. They noted other research indicating that these positive benefits aren't just due to increased activity or an exercise effect. And they found that the 120-minute threshold worked equally well for both healthy individuals and those battling illness and disability.

Their data also revealed that the positive benefits from spending time in nature increased only slightly after 120 minutes and in fact peaked between two and three hundred minutes a week with no further gains noted with more outdoor time. Spending two hours a week in nature might represent a sweet spot for positive effects.

White and his colleagues found that it didn't matter where people reached the 120-minute threshold. The benefits were the same for people who traveled a distance to nature areas and parks and those who ventured into nearby greenspaces. Furthermore, it didn't matter if subjects achieved their hours with longer weekend hikes or briefer and more frequent visits to local parks. Consequently, the authors suggested that it may be important to consider personal preferences in terms of how, when, and where to spend time in nature.

Per Month

How much time is needed per month then? Liisa Tyrväinen, a researcher in Finland, conducted a survey of over three thousand urban dwellers and found that the greatest improvements in feelings of restoration and positive mood occurred for individuals who spent more than five hours in nature each month.

Tyrväinen found additional support for the five-hour-a-month guideline in an experimental study in which subjects were either driven by van to city center, a groomed city park, or an urban forest. In each location the subjects were asked to sit for fifteen minutes and then stroll for thirty minutes. The subjects who spent time in the park or forest reported significantly greater feelings of restoration and vitality along with improved positive mood and decreased negative mood.

Blending the recommendations of White and Tyrväinen together, it seems that spending five to eight hours a month in nature leads to significant benefits. We can choose a city park, a nature trail, a forest preserve, or regional park with wilder woods, fields, lakes, and streams. We can divvy the time up into ten-to-twenty- or forty-to-fifty-minute chunks, or get the total on several longer hikes.

Tyrväinen also offered an intriguing hint that there may be even greater benefits from spending more time in nature. She sees five hours a month as a minimum to hold the negatives—depression, anxiety, stress, and burnout—at bay. But more hours could lead to more positive benefits. Florence Williams quotes Tyrväinen: "If you can go for ten hours, you will reach a new level of feeling better and better." Tyrväinen also noted that wilder might be better as subjects in the urban forest realized greater benefits than those in the urban parks.

THE THREE-DAY EFFECT

While the above research has established guidelines for our weekly and monthly doses of nature, there may be additional benefits from spending even longer and more intensive time in nature. David Strayer, an environmental psychologist at the University of Utah, has proposed what he calls the Three-Day Effect. Strayer, who loved hiking in the desert, consistently noticed that after three days of wilderness backpacking, he felt more relaxed, his thinking was clearer and problem-solving skills were sharper, and he noticed a boost in his creativity. He realized that he came up with some of his best ideas while camping out under a starlit desert sky. He observed similar results with his fellow three-day hikers.

Strayer tracked a distinct progression over the three days. The first day was about letting go of all of the impressions and mental momentum of urban civilized life. As day one transitioned to day two, he noticed a shift in awareness, an openness, and a tuning into the natural environment—the clouds floating across a blue sky, the dry smell of the desert air, and the sound of the wind through trees. And his sense of linear hourly time and calendar days and weeks faded away. By the third day, his senses, mind, and heart had shifted to a "new reality."

Strayer's Three-Day Effect made sense to me. I remember visits to my dad's hunting shack in the north woods of Wisconsin when I was grinding away in graduate school. The shack was located ten miles from the nearest town on a forty acre forest plot surrounded by thousands of acres of national forest. To get to the cabin I had to turn off a paved county highway, drive two miles down a gravel road, and finally head slowly for a mile down two ruts through the woods. The cabin had no electricity and only outdoor plumbing.

At first the quiet was unnerving. I could still hear the buzzing sounds of the city in my mind and feel tension from the pace of urban life. On the second day, these residual sounds and tension gradually faded away. By that afternoon, engulfed in the great quiet, I would often unexpectedly drift off into a long nap. By the third day my senses were fully awakened. Then I began to hear the distant calls of ravens, the wind whispering through the pine boughs, and the rhythmic chirping of the crickets. I began to see the brilliant and varied greens of forest and field and the changing shades of blue on the water of the lake. On the third day I felt simultaneously relaxed and energized, both calm and happy, and definitely clearer mentally.

These, of course, were my personal and subjective findings. As a scientist, Strayer wanted to find out exactly what was going on with the Three-Day Effect. He began to test groups of students that accompanied him on his three-day excursions. First he and then others looked at outcome measures and documented a stunning 20 to 50 percent increase in creativity after a three-day nature sojourn.

Then he began to look at process measures, trying to find out what might be occurring in the brain as subjects progressed into this new nature reality. Using a portable EEG to measure brain waves, he found significantly decreased activity in the frontal theta waves, which he interpreted as an easing of the top-down processing, directed voluntary attention system, the system that gets worn out from overuse. He also found decreased posterior alpha activity, another neural indicator of resting the directed attention system.

Strayer theorized that the "soft fascination" offered by extended exposure to nature rested the overworked directed attention system and allowed for a natural increase in healthy, open, clear, and creative attention. He also observed that these brain effects continued for a while for his students even after returning to face the stress of final exams.

GUIDELINES

Overall, the research reveals a continuum of options for spending beneficial time in nature, ranging from forty seconds to twenty minutes or more a day, to five hours a month, to the three-day immersion once a year. One of Strayer's former doctoral students, Rachel Hopman-Droste, organized these options into a nature pyramid to provide guidelines for spending time in nature, similar to the way the food pyramid guides dietary choices. The base of her pyramid presents the guideline of spending twenty to forty minutes in nature three to four times a week. The next level, consistent with Tyrväinen's research, would be to spend five or more hours a month in nature. And finally, the top of the pyramid is one of Strayer's three-day nature intensives. The pyramid offers an easy to remember formula of 20-5-3—20 minutes a day, 5 hours a month, and 3 days a year.

After looking at the research, I would modify her pyramid by adding a new base layer to include 60-second microbreaks—the quick looks to the green or blue, the brief tuning in to the songs of birds or the sounds of the wind. And I would also add an hourlong sit spot session into the monthly quotient. My formula would be 60-20-5-3, easy to remember and manageable to do—the Time in Nature Pyramid (p. 40).

To reiterate, this pyramid offers many options for obtaining the benefits of nature. On the first level, a glance out a window to view a tree in bloom, a distant forested hill, or clouds drifting across the sky can quickly and effectively enhance well-being. Even nature photographs may provide a beneficial lift. Stepping outside to listen to the wind or to birdsong for even a minute can be restorative.

The next level for garnering benefits is a daily twenty-to-forty-minute nature interaction—a walk in the park, a stroll on a nature trail or through a greenspace, or a pause to sit on a park bench. The data for these types of interactions is impressive. Many studies

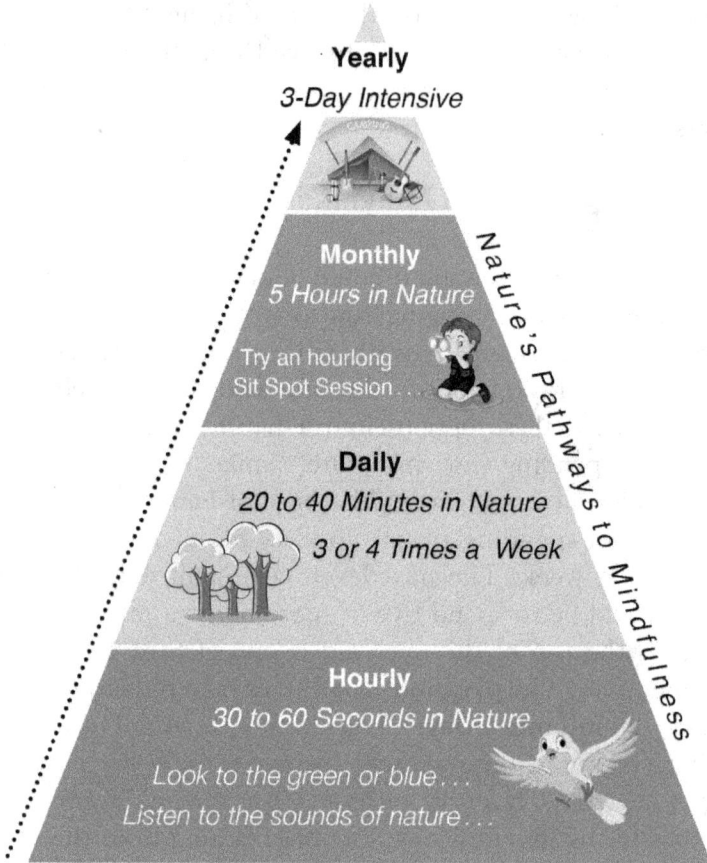

Time in Nature Pyramid — 60-20-5-3

have demonstrated significant physiological benefits—reduced stress response, improved mood, decreased negative emotions, and increased positive emotions—and improvements to cognitive abilities—better attention, memory, and problem-solving skills, as well as enhanced creativity.

Regularly achieving the nature interactions of the first two levels allows you to hit the sweet spot of five or more hours a month. For this monthly goal you can incorporate options of longer weekend hikes or paddles, and you can choose from a greater variety of venues such as city parks, nature reserves, adjacent forests, or nearby state or national parks. I would recommend that at least one of the five hours be an hourlong sit spot session—the nature activity that I found so beneficial.

Finally, there is the annual three-day intensive, perhaps a Strayer-style backpacking trip for those who feel able and up for it. For those less fit and adventurous, perhaps camping out or staying in a forest cabin or beach-side lodge are ways to secure the Three-Day Effect.

These options leave plenty of room to accommodate different preferences, different personality styles, varying living situations, and individual daily schedules. Each option may also contribute to well-being in different ways. For example, the quick looks to the green provide a quick health reset. The daily and weekly nature forays reduce negative effects of stress and begin to accumulate positive well-being. The monthly five hours in nature consolidates these gains. Finally, the annual three-day intensive can deepen the beneficial effects and create a new baseline of nature responsiveness.

There is also flexibility built into these guidelines. While it may be ideal to take a break every hour to look to the green, if you manage four or five microbreaks a day, you are improving your well-being. Similarly, being in nature every day for at least twenty minutes is optimal, but if you can get out three or four times a week, you are definitely enhancing your overall wellness. And when it comes to the five-plus hours a month, you can attain that goal in various time blocks and settings.

The Next Question

Learning about these various options felt like good progress on my quest to understand the benefits of time in nature. Then, a new question emerged. All of the research I reviewed consistently documented the physical, mood, and cognitive benefits of nature but did not directly address what might be called higher-level changes, including a clearer sense of meaning and purpose in life, greater feelings of fulfillment, and a profound and deep sense of connection to nature. It was these transformational changes—what might be called spiritual growth—that I needed to explore next.

CHAPTER 3

Higher Realms

GOING IN

JOHN MUIR, ONE OF MY NATURE HEROES, WROTE, "I WENT OUT for a walk, and finally concluded to stay out until sundown, for going out, I found, was really going in." This statement resonated with my year of forest stillness experiences. As the weeks proceeded, as I became more adept at settling in, letting go of daily concerns, and merging into the present moment, I too felt that I was "going in" to a deeper connection with nature and to a truer version of myself.

In the scientific research on the benefits of time spent in nature, I consistently read similar descriptions threaded into the results. Participants stated that being in nature helped them to gain personal insights and feel spiritually transformed—more integrated and more connected with a "true self." And there seemed to be benefits from time in nature that went beyond the physical, emotional, and cognitive. It was these more profound effects from nature connections that I wanted to understand. I decided to comb carefully through the research.

I discovered an interesting framework formulated by Gregory Bratman and his colleagues in a 2019 article on perspectives on nature and mental health. He wrote that psychological well-being not only includes the hedonic components of positive emotions—such as happiness and enjoyment—but also includes eudemonic components—such as a sense of purpose and meaning, feelings of fulfillment, a drive toward self-actualization that recognizes the importance of optimism, adaptive problem-solving skills, acquired resilience, wisdom, and the ability to maintain healthy relationships.

Similarly, in their 2022 extensive review of the research on nature and human well-being, Huynh and her colleagues identified two pathways that described similar benefits. The first they labeled Intuitive, which they defined as the "sensual experiences, human instincts, and feelings (often of a spiritual and religious nature) via interaction with nature." In their description of this pathway, they noted that many people experienced "something spiritual" when they interacted with nature. This sense of spirituality in turn brought faith and hope, instilled personal beliefs and values, and created a sense of empowerment.

They labeled the second pathway Transcendentive and defined it as the "benefits that lie beyond the physical realm, more often associated with religious or spiritual values via interactions with nature." They described the effects of this pathway as feelings of being connected to something greater and grander. They noted that for some people, being in a natural setting made them appreciate a sense of connection to "all things in the universe." Some describe this as nature-relatedness.

These comments led me to look back and reflect on my forest sitting experiences, especially those moments when the rhythm of my breath joined with the greater breath of the rising and falling wind or the waves lapping on the shoreline. In those moments the barriers and boundaries between my little individual self and the bigger realm of nature around me fell away. I felt increasingly connected to and part of the cycles and seasons that unfolded before me. These feelings of connection to nature were comforting, strengthening, and transcendent.

During these moments I became open to insights, to seeing parallels between processes occurring around me in *big* nature and in *little* me. When spring rolled around and the warblers and woodland songbirds returned, I noticed how each species unerringly found its own unique habitat niche—ovenbirds patrolled the leaf litter, common yellowthroats skulked through the shoreline shrubs, yellow warblers perched in the lower tree branches, and Baltimore orioles gleaned leaves high in the forest canopy. These observations led me to reflect on my niches in life as well as the niches of those that I knew and cared for, reflections followed by positive feelings of acceptance.

Sitting in complete stillness, I noticed movement and action all around me—gusts of wind, insects in flight, spiders on the hunt, cardinals singing, tree seeds and flowers dropping to the ground, squirrels on the move, leaves unfolding, and even roots beneath my feet reaching out for water and nutrients. Life forces were all around me, seen and invisible, heard and silent. Vitality permeated all of nature, and I sensed, felt, and appreciated this same vitality coursing through me.

Visiting week after week, I saw growth and change—a progression of wildflowers blooming, birds nesting and all too soon fledging. In response to lingering cold or torrential rains, I saw adaptability—plants and mammals and birds pushing the pause button and then resuming growth as soon as conditions were favorable. I saw the resilience of saplings growing around obstacles, finding a way around a fallen branch to reach for the sunlight. As a result, the concepts of growth, change, adaptability, and resilience all took on deeper meaning.

These transformative nature insights arose unbidden and unsought, spontaneously, at different times and in different ways. Cumulatively, these insights settled in my mind, heart, and soul. The experiences felt as enriching as studying philosophy, as inspiring as reading a profound passage of scripture, as uplifting as listening to and singing along with a beautiful hymn. Intuitive, transcendent, spiritual—all of these words seemed accurate descriptors.

MINDFULNESS

But as meaningful and transformational as these experiences were, they also made me uneasy. The trained scientist in me began to voice doubts and raise questions. So many of these effects were hard to measure. No sensors, wires, or blood tests could detect such personal and subjective results. I worried that I was drifting into a la-la-land of amorphous and dreamy claims about the benefits of being in nature.

Huynh and her colleagues found reports of many of the same things that I noticed and wrote that these more numinous contributions of nature pathways are "subjective and intangible," leading to different descriptions that in turn make systematic analysis difficult.

In other words, there are a range of benefits and experiences occurring during interactions with nature that are consistently reported and woven into nature literature, and while they resonate with my personal experience, they are hard to define and measure. These benefits are simultaneously real and important yet elusive and ephemeral.

I began to search for some concept, some overarching model that could both explain and legitimize these beneficial effects. The Stress Reduction Theory explained the physical benefits, the Biophilia Hypothesis accounted for the emotional benefits, and the Attention Restoration Theory explained the cognitive benefits. What could explain these transcendent, intuitive, transformational, and spiritual outcomes?

I started my search by examining the minute-by-minute process of sitting still in the forest. I thought back to my first session, recalling that it took me a while to settle in. At first my mind was filled with a running narrative about tasks I had to do at home and feelings that I had about recent events and interactions with others. It was as if my thoughts and feelings and preoccupations were creating my reality. In a sense, I was in the forest physically but not mentally and emotionally.

After twenty to forty minutes of sitting still, this chatter wound down. There came a tipping point, a moment when my awareness shifted into the present, when the narratives stilled, and I suddenly became open to and more aware of my surroundings. Looking at a blackberry cane that arched right in front of me, I suddenly saw the rich burgundy color, the stout sharp thorns, and the tightly packed leaf buds waiting to unfurl. Beyond these canes I saw complex patterns of wind-blown snow decorating the icy surface of the lake. I took in the view of the forest across the lake, a dense, layered, and textured array of maples, ash, pines, and hemlocks. I heard the cheerful springtime *clear, clear, clear* song of a tufted titmouse. Gusts of winter wind touched my face. I inhaled the invigorating fragrances of woods, snow, and fallen leaves.

My awareness shifted away from the world of everyday thoughts and feelings and toward a present-centered space where I began to truly perceive what was around me. It was a shift away from a narrative consciousness to a more experiential consciousness. With this shift came physical feelings of relaxation and vitality, an emotional shift to joy, awe, wonder, and contentment, and a clear, focused mind. In these moments of open sensory awareness, the shell of the little narrative-based, self-created me fell away, and I felt connected to the greater whole of nature around and within me.

Reflecting back on this first and subsequent weekly shifts in consciousness, it suddenly came to me—present-centeredness, open awareness, clarity, peacefulness, a sense of wholeness and integration, a connection to a truer self—these all sounded like mindfulness, in this case nature mindfulness.

John Kabat-Zinn, in his book *Mindfulness for Beginners,* offers the following definition: "Mindfulness is awareness, cultivated by paying attention in a sustained and particular way: on purpose, in the present moment, and non-judgmentally."

His definition fit my nature sitting experiences. The crucial element was a shift in awareness created by focusing attention minute after minute for a full hour. And the focus was done in a particular way, in this case, via a soft sensory focus on nature—watching, listening, feeling, and inhaling.

My hourlong sessions were done on purpose, intentionally, initially to learn about nature but increasingly for the happiness, the moments of awe, and the transformational insights. The key became slipping the bonds of preoccupation with past and future and immersing myself fully in the richness of the present moment. And part of being in the present was simply observing everything around me, letting go of the inner judging chatter and evaluation, and simply noticing.

Mindfulness seemed like the just right framework for understanding the benefits of time in nature. Mindfulness in the form of Mindfulness-Based Stress Reduction (MBSR) is a well-documented therapeutic and wellness-promoting intervention. Research has found that the regular practice of mindfulness reduces the physical markers of stress, decreases inflammation, boosts immune system function, and actually promotes beneficial structural changes in the brain. Mindfulness has been found to reduce the rumination, worries, and conflicts associated with depression and anxiety, and to increase the presence of positive emotions.

As a result, mindfulness has achieved wide public acceptance and is taught and practiced in medical settings, psychology clinics, businesses, schools, and prisons. Mindfulness has been incorporated into specific interventions such as cognitive behavioral therapy, pain management, and stress reduction.

The practice of mindfulness incorporates stress reduction. And since the regulation of attention is the essential element of mindfulness, it also incorporates Attention Restoration Therapy. But mindfulness also provides a ladder that allows one to ascend to the higher realms of transcendent, intuitive, and spiritual experiences.

ASCENDING

Mindfulness comes from a meditation tradition and is ultimately a method for personal growth and spiritual transformation. As Kabat-Zinn notes: "Mindfulness influences and potentially transforms the quality of our experience in the service of realizing the full range of our humanity and of our relationship to others and to the world."

Mindfulness is often described as having two elements: bare attention and clear comprehension. Bare attention is the open, accepting, present-centered focus. Clear comprehension is an awareness of things in relation to other things, an awareness that gradually and increasingly allows for the development of self-knowledge and wisdom.

There are different approaches to achieving a state of mindfulness. One is breath awareness, in which the practitioner simply observes the sensations and rhythm of the breath in an accepting, non-controlling manner. When the mind wanders, one notices non-judgmentally and returns the focus to the breath. Another approach is body scan meditation, where the participant simply notices body sensations happening in the present moment.

A third approach is sensory awareness: focusing one's attention on the surrounding sights, sounds, sensations, and smells in the present moment. It is this approach that is compatible with and a natural extension of spending time in nature. Nature settings, with their enjoyable, intriguing, and ever-changing stimuli, and the opportunity for "soft fascination," provide an ideal format for the sensory awareness approach to practicing mindfulness.

For more than forty years before I started my year of forest sitting sessions, I had engaged in a daily practice of mantra meditation. To my surprise I found that sitting still and focusing on the sensory stimuli offered by nature was a particularly effective and easy approach for achieving and deepening mindfulness. Nature mindfulness reinforced and deepened my practice of meditation.

But then I wondered about all of the positive feelings of happiness, joy, awe, and contentment. Wasn't mindfulness all about being non-reactive, about stepping back from the ups and downs of emotional reactions?

Reading further I discovered that these positive feelings are in fact part of a deep baseline state. When we use mindfulness to slip the constraints of reviewing and ruminating on memories and projecting and pondering the future, we gradually cease the process of creating an emotionally turbulent reality. What remains is a natural, subtle, quiet state of joy, contentment, and happiness. When we shut down the negative, the positives are uncovered. As William Kuyken wrote, "Joy is an intrinsic attitude of mind . . . that supports a capacity for appreciation, contentment, and gratitude."

In his book *Silence*, Thich Nhat Hanh explains this from the perspective of Buddhist psychology. He employs the analogy of a house where the living room is our everyday busy consciousness and the basement is our store consciousness, where seeds for joy and peace are stored as well as seeds for suffering. The practice of mindfulness waters and nourishes the seeds of joy, peace, and happiness so that they flourish and fill our consciousness. This offers an explanation of the profoundly positive experiences that arise during nature mindfulness.

Of course, at times during mindfulness practice, various seeds of suffering may emerge as well. But in a state of mindfulness we can watch, release, and gradually de-energize these seeds. It has been my experience that any suffering that does emerge does so under conditions of right timing and personal readiness.

Mindfulness gave me a model, a scientifically validated model to explain the deeper and more profound transcendentive and transformational effects of time in nature. The specific practice of sensory awareness offered insights into the minute-by-minute process of nature mindfulness.

But as so often happens on both literal and figurative journeys, reaching one destination opens the door to consider the next destination. Answering one question inevitably leads to new questions. Now I began to ponder: what are the best methods or techniques for interacting mindfully with nature?

CHAPTER 4

Mindful Time in Nature

T HE SCIENTIFIC STUDIES REVIEWED IN PREVIOUS CHAPTERS show that almost any type of interaction with nature enhances human well-being. This can be as little as a quick glance at greenery or water, a nature photograph, or a window view of a park. A walk through a city park or a hike along a nature trail also provides benefits.

All of these interactions involve exposure to nature, being outdoors, seeing the scenery, hearing nature sounds, feeling tactile sensations, and inhaling fragrances. The strength of these positive findings from exposure offers testimony to the power of the nature effect. But I wondered what might change when individuals engage with nature in a mindful manner.

Mindfulness means paying attention in a sustained and particular way—on purpose, in the present moment, and nonjudgmentally. Are there ways to engage with nature that incorporate these dimensions?

POWER TRAILS

In *The Nature Fix*, Florence Williams describes the work of Finnish environmental psychologist, Kalevi Korpela, who has designed mindfulness-inducing Power Trails that wind through a forest and require about thirty minutes to traverse. At selected spots, he places signs with instructions. Trail walkers are to pause, read, and follow the instructions, which are designed to systematically create a mindful and beneficial nature connection.

The first series of signs provide messages to encourage relaxation and observation of the environment; for example, walkers are told to look around and allow themselves to be enchanted by nature or to keep breathing peacefully. The next series of signs facilitate direct connection with nature; examples include finding a favorite place in the immediate area or choosing a specific nature detail to hold in memory. The final series of instructions promote reflection and insight; walkers are encouraged to look around for something that represents them or their current life situation, or to identify new thoughts that have arisen while being in nature.

The aim of the scenic trail and the crafted instructions is to enhance the value of time in nature by purposefully creating relaxation, improving mood, restoring attention, and inducing reflection. Korpela noted that such paths can easily be constructed in and near urban areas and be accessible for stressed city dwellers, making nature mindfulness more accessible.

ORNITHERAPY

In the book *Ornitherapy for Your Body, Mind, and Soul,* lead author Holly Merker provides an approach to purposeful engagement with nature built around bird watching. She explains how birds are interesting, charismatic, and most importantly, all around us. Observing birds can offer an array of possible connections to and interactions with nature. She recommends fifteen-to-twenty-minute sessions of bird watching that can take place out a window, in a backyard or park, or in a nature preserve. Anyone with any level of knowledge of birds can participate. The key elements are to bring awareness into the present, observe carefully, reflect on your observations, and notice the feelings and insights that arise. The book offers fifty-eight mindfulness-based explorations to guide bird watching and nature learning, and to facilitate transformational introspection. Examples of explorations are Finding Diversity, Seeing Color, We Are Connected, and Celebrating Roles.

In the We Are Connected exploration, participants watch birds in action and recognize the chains of life and ecological systems that connect and support birds. Participants can study a particular bird—like a common backyard robin—and see the dependent relationships in its life—its unique food and habitat needs, what it contributes to the environment, and how it adapts to changes. The goal is to see the robin in a matrix of connected and supportive relationships. From this foundation participants are guided to consider how their physical, emotional, and mental needs are met through relationships to their human and natural surroundings. And finally, participants are invited to consider responding to the question: Which relationship between yourself and something in nature are you most grateful for?

Interspaced among the fifty-eight explorations are guided meditations designed to help participants "slow down and become mindful of the present moment." The meditative skills of awareness and mindfulness are used to observe nature. For example, in the Soundscape Surroundings meditations, participants are guided to close their eyes, notice the sounds without and within, and use the continuing and deepening awareness of sounds to anchor themselves more and more into the present.

For each exploration, the authors provide a journal page for writing observations and insights, indicating that "Taking notes is key to looking closely at anything." Each of the journal pages begins with a writing prompt based on the personal memories and insights of the authors. They emphasize that such focused journaling helps to build attention and reinforce nature learning.

The authors point out that the mindfulness basis of Ornitherapy promotes well-being, self-awareness, and a deep, caring connection to nature. For lead author Merker, Ornitherapy has deep personal importance and relevance. She developed it as part of her efforts to overcome an aggressive form of breast cancer and restore her physical, emotional, and mental health. She writes, "Let birds be your guiding light toward a happier and healthier lifestyle for your mind, body, and soul."

FOREST BATHING

The best known mindfulness-based approach to engaging with nature is *shinrin-yoku,* translated as "forest bathing." This system was developed by Tomohide Akiyama in 1982 while he was serving as head of the Japanese Forestry Agency. He was looking to give a name to health-improving forest visits, a kind of branding to promote wellness-based ecotourism.

As M. Amos Clifford notes in his book *Your Guide to Forest Bathing*, *shinrin-yoku* combines both structure and flexibility. The structure makes forest bathing into a practice, a sequence of standardized steps to guide the experiences of participants all over the world. This structure has allowed researchers to take physiological measures before and after forest bathing. The research data obtained has been crucially important in scientifically documenting the benefits of mindful time in nature.

At the same time, flexibility is used to respond in a spontaneous way to the needs and readiness of the individual and to the unique condition of nature at the time and in the setting. This flexibility allows forest bathing to be a flow experience, where participants can immerse themselves in the restorative dimensions and soft fascination that nature offers.

Clifford outlines eight steps in forest bathing:

1. INTENTION

One usually dedicates two to four hours to a *shinrin-yoku* session, and each session should begin with a clear intention to devote time and attention to the specific purpose of being in the forest, in the present moment, and in tune with sensory input. Forming such an intention aligns with the *on purpose* aspect of mindfulness. Forming an intention separates forest bathing from going on a hike. It is as Clifford notes: all about being "here and not there"—being *here* in the present and not preoccupied with getting *there*. It's a time and opportunity to go within and set aside socializing and electronic media.

2. THE THRESHOLD OF CONNECTION

One enters into forest bathing by crossing a literal and metaphorical threshold. The goal is to leave behind typical everyday consciousness and step into the realm of openness to perceptions and experiences outside of daily life. Clifford recommends incorporating a real physical threshold—an arching branch or a stepping stone over a brook. At that spot, one pauses, gazes ahead at the forest path, shifts one's focus to body awareness, and speaks the intention internally or externally. Additional elements include specifying the amount of time you will be committing, and then opening your heart, expressing gratitude, asking for support, and requesting safe passage. Clifford describes this step as transitioning into a liminal state, an open, intuitive mode.

3. EMBODIED AWARENESS

After traversing the threshold, forest bathing then involves responding to a series of invitations, each of which is followed by a council. Invitations guide participants to take in nature and use the senses in a particular way. Councils are brief group meetings where a guide encourages participants to consider and then share what they have noticed. This reflecting and sharing is a way to more deeply notice and fix the experience in awareness. Invitations and councils are not mandatory but are elements of practice intended to deepen the experience.

The first invitation is called embodied awareness or pleasures of presence and is designed to fully engage sensory awareness in the present moment. The goal is to awaken a sense of body awareness by noticing your body standing on and being supported by the earth. One can sense gravity by picking up and holding a fist-sized stone, closing the eyes, and noticing the effort to hold the stone up. Then one moves the stone to the front and side to notice the actions and sensations of all the muscles. This is done for two to five minutes. Participants then set the stone down and are guided to notice the input coming into the other senses. This might start with noticing sensations of touch, such as the temperature of the air or the feel of the wind, humidity, or dryness in the air. Participants are guided to notice different tactile sensations on different parts of the body, and then for another two to five minutes, track how the sensations change and if any are enjoyable.

Next, for at least three minutes, participants are invited to listen to all the sounds they hear—birds singing, wind sighing, water flowing, or insects buzzing. Participants are encouraged to notice changes and interactions in these sounds and to observe any feelings of enjoyment that these sounds engender.

Then participants focus on the sense of taste for three minutes by breathing in through an open mouth and noticing any subtle taste sensations, textures, and pleasures. Switching to breathing through the nose, participants are then directed to notice any scents, smells, or fragrances. Perhaps the smells of leaves, pine needles, water, or snow are noticed again with the instruction to track changes, inter-actions, and enjoyments.

With the eyes still closed, participants are next invited to focus on the sensations of their body in space, to move slightly and notice how those sensations change. This knowing of the space around us is what Clifford calls body radar. Using body radar, participants move and scan until they find a direction that feels right. Then slowly opening their eyes, participants are invited to see their nature surroundings in a fresh way, seeing colors, objects, shapes, and patterns not noticed before. Participants are guided to gaze at their surroundings, using their imaginations to see meaning and patterns and to feel impressions.

Upon completion of this invitation comes the first council. If forest bathing as a group, participants can share their observations by using the template phrase: "I am noticing . . . " Responses can be single words or phrases, and choosing not to vocalize a response is fine too. Those who are forest bathing solo can speak their observations out loud, if they wish.

4. WALKING IN FOREST TIME

The next invitation is to walk slowly through the forest and simply noticing what is in motion. Clifford explains that in nature, even on a seemingly still day, there is motion—a touch of breeze, insects or birds flying, a stream flowing, leaves swaying, waves lapping, and clouds floating. Internally, there is motion as well—the movement of thoughts and feelings, many of which are of the past and future.

All of the movement in nature gives us something interesting to focus on, something to help bring our attention into the present. Then we can begin to bring our awareness to nature. The calm, soothing flow and motion of wind or water or of leaves and clouds can create a calm, soothing state within. Walking mindfully in forest time aligns us with the rhythms and patterns of nature.

Clifford notes that this process can be challenging. Things that we see or hear or feel can trigger memories, feelings, or thoughts, and soon we are pulled into the past or future. Such distractions are similar to what occurs when people meditate. Fortunately, all of the movement in nature provides an interesting and appealing realm of focus, making it easy to bring our attention back to the present.

This losing and then returning to mindful focus may happen several times during the fifteen minutes allotted to this invitation, especially for people beginning the practice of forest bathing or people who are feeling stressed. Fortunately, motion in nature provides an ideal palette for soft fascination. Every time on the trail, every time of day, in every season of the year, the motion will be different. At the end of this invitation participants again council to share what they have noticed.

5. INFINITE POSSIBILITIES

At this point in the forest walk, the guide selects an invitation that fits the circumstances in nature or the readiness and needs of the participants. Clifford notes: "Invitations are everywhere in the forest." Over time guides and individuals can become adept at sensing and responding to the invitations the forest is offering. In his book Clifford offers numerous examples of invitations organized around the elements of earth, water, fire, and air, and around the particular senses employed.

An example of an earth invitation is to get down on your hands and knees and carefully examine a small patch of forest floor, with your eyes, with the help of a magnifying glass, with your sense of touch, and your sense of smell. An air invitation might to be to lie down on your back and gaze at the clouds, using your vision to see colors and motion, and your imagination to see animate shapes and form. A water invitation suggests sitting by a small waterfall and taking in the sensations of the fine mist in the air, absorbing the vitality of the circulating negative ions, and listening to the changing sounds of the cascading water.

After fifteen minutes participants go to council to share what they have noticed and then move on to more invitations.

6. SIT SPOT

Toward the end of the forest walk, participants are invited to engage in a twenty-minute "sit spot." The directions are to find a spot that feels right and then simply sit still, engaging all of the senses and noticing what nature reveals. As Clifford notes this is a powerful practice in part because by the end of the walk participants are likely to be more tuned in to nature. The longer you sit the more you notice. Plants, animals, and birds make themselves known. Meaningful themes might emerge. Participants can simply sit or can jot down observations.

7.   TEA CEREMONY

At the conclusion of the walk, participants gather together while the guide prepares tea, possibly made from herbs gathered during the walk using water heated on a carry-in backpacking stove. Each guide or solo walker can come up with their own type of tea and their own version of the ceremony. The purpose of the tea ceremony is to provide a transition from a state of forest mindfulness back to everyday life; it's a social ritual to celebrate and honor the completion of the forest walk. Perhaps the taking in of tangible nutrition parallels the taking in of the more abstract but real sensory, psychological, and spiritual sustenance of the forest walk. Plus, the heightened awareness gained while forest bathing can add appreciation to the flavors of the tea and the nuances of supportive social interaction.

8.   THE THRESHOLD OF INCORPORATION

After the tea ceremony, participants cross back over the threshold, pausing, as Clifford writes, "to consider the gifts you have received on your walk." Participants can take a moment to consciously incorporate any gifts of knowledge, understanding, or connection as they rejoin everyday life.

There are many advantages to the forest bathing approach to engaging mindfully with nature. First, there is a definite structure, a clear sequence of steps to follow that deepen engagement with nature. The use of sensory awareness, the letting go of distractions, the persistent refocusing in the present all help participants merge into nature mindfulness.

Second, for individuals who are less familiar with and less comfortable in nature, forest bathing provides an experienced, trained, and certified guide to smooth, secure, and structure the experience. The guide chooses trails that are manageable, safe to traverse, and rich with interesting features of nature. Participants don't have to bushwhack through the wilderness. And traveling with a group can enhance feelings of safety and security.

Finally, the effectiveness of forest bathing to produce beneficial physical, psychological, and cognitive effects has been diligently documented again and again. Participants can trust that they are getting a real dose of restorative and healing nature.

SIT SPOT

Sit spot is the practice that I used to discover and engage in nature mindfulness during my year of forest stillness. I learned about the sit spot in Jon Young's book *What the Robin Knows: How Birds Reveal the Secrets of the Natural World*. I took his recommendations, applied and modified them over the course of my year.

The core concept is fairly simple. Find an appealing and interesting spot in nature, sit still for an hour, open your senses, notice everything around you, and jot down your observations every ten minutes in a notebook. (Detailed instructions on conducting a sit spot experience are provided in the third section of this book—Sit Spot Guidance.)

Young recommends finding a sit spot close to home and convenient to access so that you can go weekly or even daily. A good sit spot might be located at edge habitat where field and forest meet, or near water, such as a stream, pond, or lake. He also recommends going at different times of day and in different seasons to broaden, deepen, and enrich your nature observations.

Once at your sit spot you begin to train the senses to hear, see, feel, and smell more and more acutely and accurately. Young emphasizes that this is a process of uncovering latent capacities as opposed to building new skills. We all have the capacity for fuller awareness of the natural environment.

As noted in the subtitle of his book, Young placed considerable emphasis on learning to hear and understand bird songs, calls, and behavior. He explains that birds communicate much about the state of the immediate environment in real time and thus provide a gateway into the realm of a nature connection. Tuning into the language and behavior of birds also creates a connection to the entire nature context, to noticing all of the flora and fauna, recognizing unique aspects of habitat, and tuning into the impact of the weather and the flow of the seasons.

Young states that a nature sitting practice is very much a developmental process. In the beginning you may notice little and what you notice may seem overwhelming, even chaotic. But with time and frequent sessions, your natural capacities will help you to simultaneously sense more and to recognize patterns.

Young also presented the key concept of a forty-minute threshold, explaining that it often takes about that long for nature to settle down and re-establish a baseline after your intrusion. And it takes about that long for the average person to let go of the created reality of thoughts and feelings of past and future that they bring with them. After forty minutes, sitters are usually more engaged in the present, are beginning to truly see, hear, and feel the natural world around them, and are ready to merge into mindfulness.

At my sit spot I learned to keep things simple—a camp stool to get me up off the ground, maybe binoculars, a notebook on my lap, and a pencil in my hand. I observed through six ten-minute sensory awareness circles. For each of these intervals, I drew a circle in my notebook, put a dot in the middle that represented me and then noted the location around the circle of everything that I heard, saw, smelled, or felt.

This sensory awareness circle became a key part of my experience. It pulled my awareness into the present. Drawing a new circle and starting over every ten minutes was, as one of my sit spot friends explained, like hitting the refresh key on your computer; it helped to clear the screen, let go, refresh the view, and immerse yourself ever more deeply in the present.

With each ten-minute interval, my sensory abilities seemed to grow more acute. The circle of sounds expanded outward. I began to hear more subtle sounds and parsed out layers in complex sounds. I saw things near and far with greater clarity and in greater detail. The sensations of wind and temperature and humidity registered more accurately. I gradually detected the fragrances of the wild, the leaves composting on the forest floor, the smell of fresh water, and the aroma of pine needles. Also, across the ten-minute intervals, I tracked change and movement. The wind would rise and fall. Clouds would come and go. Fog and mist would rise and dissolve. A snow or rain shower might pass through the woods. Birds and mammals would appear and depart. I could sense the vital life force of nature all around me, a dynamic, always changing world providing an ideal context for soft fascination.

As my sensory acuity increased and I became more and more immersed in the present, a state of mindfulness spontaneously arose. I would often feel that unique combination of being both relaxed and invigorated. My mind became clearer. Happiness and a pantheon of positive emotions emerged. And when moments of unique beauty arose like an icy coating on the tree branches sparkling like diamonds in the first beams of sunlight, my heart was open to awe.

During a sit spot session, my perception of time changed. Even though I tracked ten-minute intervals, I would often transition away from linear time, away from the temporal structure of making this phone call at this time, arriving for this appointment at a set time, preparing dinner at a certain time, and so on. Paradoxically, time would simultaneously speed up and slow down. An hour sitting, which initially seemed like a daunting assignment, would fly by, leaving me wanting to stay longer. Yet I also felt immersed in vast slow time— cycles of nature, days, seasons, and years all orbiting around again and again, a kind of timeless time.

Moments of nature mindfulness seemed to provide insights, unbidden, each on its own schedule, and each seemingly attuned to my degree of readiness. It was these moments that touched on what Huynh and her colleagues called the transcendent and intuitive, what others have called the journey to knowing the true self, and what still others might call spiritual experiences.

Following Young's guidelines I often attempted to process my experiences by considering several questions: What did I observe? What did I learn? What do I need to learn? How did the experience change and/or help me? These questions can be answered through internal dialogue, by speaking out loud to yourself or journaling, or if other individuals did sit spot sessions at the same time, by sharing your observations with them. I chose to write a weekly journal.

One of the advantages of a sit spot practice is that it is very simple. You don't need a guide, although it may help to have someone assist you the first time or two. You can do a sitting experience in your yard, a city park, or nearby field or forest. You can do it whenever you want. And each person can modify it to their liking.

However, the sit spot approach to nature mindfulness may not be for everyone. People who are less comfortable and less experienced in nature my find it daunting, even anxiety provoking; the idea of sitting in nature alone may be intimidating to some, so finding a guide to help would make for a more positive experience.

A sit spot practice is also a very individual experience. For those who are more introverted, like me, the idea of having time alone is appealing, but not so for extroverts. Consequently, some may prefer the security and social aspects of a group format and may enjoy the process of sharing what they have noticed with others.

COMMON ELEMENTS

We've seen that there are many approaches to achieving purposeful and mindful engagement with nature, but the various approaches share a few common elements:

SLOWING DOWN

All approaches involve slowing down the process of being in nature. In forest bathing, participants might only cover a half mile in two to four hours. With a sit spot practice, one literally sits in the same place for an hour. On Power Trails, signs with psychological tasks create pauses to further one's engagement with nature. And in Ornitherapy, the emphasis is on taking time to observe bird life and surrounding nature more deeply.

INTENTION

Forming and mentally or verbally stating the intention to devote time to being in nature is the first step in forest bathing. Similarly, before heading to my spot in the forest, I mentally formed the intention to sit for a full hour, dedicating time to be in and engage with nature. Participants in Ornitherapy are asked to intentionally devote at least fifteen minutes to watching birds.

Intention is making a decision to budget time and attention to engage with nature and to experiencing mindfulness. Forming an intention activates behavior and may create a readiness for new experiences and new learning.

Intention may also be developmental. The depth and strength of my commitment developed over the course of the year. In the beginning it was difficult to carve out the time slot, and it was challenging to sit for an entire hour. As the months proceeded, it became easier, and I looked forward to my weekly hour in the woods.

TRANSITION

I named the ten-minute walk to my sit spot the zero interval. It was a time to tune into nature, try to sense the unique configuration of conditions, and to feel the mood of the moment externally and internally.

As in forest bathing, I crossed a threshold when I stepped across a seep—a watercress-laden trickle of spring water flowing down a hillside. There I would pause and reflect gratefully on my departure from my everyday world and my entry into what became the fascinating world of nature.

The fact that I spontaneously stumbled upon the notion of a threshold similar to the threshold step in forest bathing makes me think that such a clearly demarcated transition may be an integral aspect of mindfully interacting with the natural world. The physical act of crossing a threshold opens the mind and heart to new perceptions and insights.

PRESENT MOMENT

Another commonality is an emphasis on being in the present moment. The idea is to shift from typical consciousness structured by concerns and preoccupations of the past and future to concentrate on the now. It is in the now where deep engagement with nature is possible.

INVITATIONS

Invitations seem to be a key part of mindfulness-based nature interactions. Along the power trails, signs offer invitations to engage with nature; in ornitherapy, explorations are provided to guide nature interactions; and in forest bathing, a wide range and variety of awareness-invitations are offered.

During sit spot sessions, I often noticed that something in nature would offer an awareness invitation. These invitations seemed to arise spontaneously in response to or in synchrony with the unique conditions of nature and perhaps my in-the-moment readiness. The arrival of a yellow warbler with its sweet song might trigger contemplation of timing, persistence, astounding migratory skills, and the bird's innate ability to find its niche in life. The first lilting *sweetie-pie* spring song of a chickadee on a cold February morning might trigger an awareness of coming change and signs of hope in times of darkness. The generosity of the trees to feed insects, birds, and animals, the generosity of each layer of nature to support other layers would evoke feelings of sharing gifts I had and promoting a sense of relatedness to and desire to care for nature.

The invitation to become aware of movement in nature is found in forest bathing and ornitherapy and arose spontaneously for me. On a hot, still summer day when I presumed that nothing was going on, I noticed a single blade of grass swaying slightly in a breeze too subtle for me to feel. Watching the grass move, I then became aware of myriad motion around me—insects, birds, clouds, water, roots, leaves were all in dynamic movement. I realized then that nature is always in motion, a realization that remains with me and has permanently changed my perception of my surroundings.

Incorporation

After my hour was up, I usually felt refreshed on many levels. I labeled my return through the woods the plus 1 interval, a walk back over the seep, down the trail to the parking lot and to my car. It felt natural to move slowly, to look again with refreshed vision at the world around me and to reflect on all that was different internally and externally. This seems similar to the conscious incorporation of change in forest bathing.

Processing

Both ornitherapy and forest bathing include activities for processing the experiences of nature engagement through journaling, sharing in a council, or speaking out loud. This processing adds depth and meaning by providing an opportunity to consider, contemplate, and find the right words to describe one's experiences and insights.

My typical way of processing my experiences and addressing the four questions noted above was to write a weekly story as well as a blog post. Sometimes it took a day or two of reflecting to truly understand

and appreciate what I had experienced. When I conducted shared sit spot sessions, I enjoyed a back-and-forth discussion, noticing both overlapping and individually unique experiences.

CLOSING

Similar to the tea ceremony in forest bathing, I felt a need for some type of closing ceremony. For me this often ended up being a quiet celebratory breakfast after I returned from a sunrise sitting session. It was perhaps a kind of anchoring of all the mental and spiritual nutrition that I had received with tangible food and drink.

CUMULATIVE EFFECTS

All of these approaches are designed to be repeated, thereby creating cumulative effects. The nature connection experienced in the first sitting session enhances the second one. Becoming more aware of, more comfortable with, and more knowledgeable about the sounds, sights, and sensations of nature in one session prepares one for deeper experiences in the next. There is a kind of layering that occurs from one session to the next.

Gradually, repeated intervals of nature mindfulness create changes that seem to stick. I label this the ratchet effect. Once you click to a certain level of nature awareness, it stays with you. I noticed that during my year of forest stillness, I developed sensitivity, always noticing bird songs and calls, hearing the sounds of the wind, and seeing views of greens and blues. It was as if I had downloaded or perhaps more accurately activated a nature app that remained on in the background of my mind, continually registering nature inputs.

But the best was still to come. These registered nature inputs then accessed an accumulated reserve of well-being residing just under the surface of my daily consciousness and brought forth relaxation, happiness, health, and feelings of nature connection.

SENSORY AWARENESS

Sensory awareness is another shared element in all of the mindfulness-based approaches to nature engagement. Deeply seeing, hearing, feeling, tasting, and smelling all aspects of nature are key elements in forest bathing, a sit spot practice, ornitherapy, and on power trails. Sensory awareness is also a foundational technique in mindfulness meditation. It is the process of deepening sensory awareness that facilitates bringing one into the present and creating openness for the insights and moments of nature relatedness that facilitate personal growth and transformation.

When practicing sensory awareness, we make choices with our attention that lead to mindfulness and to the many benefits of a nature connection. Was there, I wondered, something unique, something inherently facilitative about sensory awareness in nature?

CHAPTER 5

Sensory Awareness—
Gateways to Nature Mindfulness

❧

HEARING

T HE SHIFT OCCURRED EARLY ON A BEAUTIFUL SPRING MORNING in May. Above me a full canopy of new minty-green leaves blanketed the branches and tree tops. Around me the woodland shrubs—honeysuckle, red osier dogwood, and wild blueberry—were laden with new green growth. The ferns, grasses, jewelweed, and garlic mustard stood tall upon the forest floor.

The sunrise birdsong chorus was in full swing—warblers, catbirds, robins, and crows—fifteen or more different species singing and calling. But surrounded by the dense foliage, I could see very little. I was forced to shift to hearing as my primary sensory modality. I began to scan the soundscape a full 360 degrees around me.

Later, as the sun rose and breeze picked up, I heard more— wind-blown wavelets splashing onto the shoreline, leaves sighing in the wind. In the distance a stream trickled down a hillside. An animal moved through the woods ahead, maybe a deer or a fox. Something splashed out on the lake. More and more sounds to take in.

My hearing grew more acute. I began to identify the different sounds, to locate sources near and far, and track movement. I parsed out the different birdsongs—the *sweet, sweet, sweet, a little more sweet* of a yellow warbler, the *witchety, witchety, witchety* of a common yellowthroat, and the insistent *teecha, teecha, teecha* of an ovenbird.

I tuned in to patterns of sound—the waves of wind approaching and rising and whispering through the leaves, then falling and fading into the distance. I heard the ever-changing trickling of the distant brook. I noticed subtle differences in the splashes of the waves against the shoreline rocks—soft, soft, soft, loud, loud, soft, soft.

Immersed in this soundscape I found myself pulled more and more into the present moment. The birdsong chorus was pleasing to my ears—musical, almost symphonic, inspiring, uplifting, and enchanting. The sounds of the wind, brook, and waves were soothing, calming, and relaxing. I felt a deepening sense of connection to nature, a resonance with the soundscape as I noticed the sound of my breath and the beat of my heart joining in.

Ever since that day, hearing has become a primary sensory mode when out in nature. And no wonder. I was fortunate enough on that morning to have experienced what Florence Williams calls the "trifecta of salubrious listening," namely, wind, water, and birdsong.

It may be that humans are particularly tuned into this trifecta, an attribute that evolved over centuries that allowed early humans to accurately and quickly detect both dangers and opportunities in the environment. For example, birdsong usually indicates a safe environment and one where humans might find food. When the song stops, danger may be nearby. According to Jon Young, the information provided by birdsongs and calls can provide an ongoing and highly accurate report of what is going on in nature. Listening to and understanding bird language opens a door to connecting with nature. The morning birdsong chorus never fails to offer a sense of reawakening, renewal, and a fresh start.

Young explains four different kinds of bird vocalizations, each of which provides valuable information. The most familiar vocalizations are the springtime territorial birdsongs, like the sprightly *cheerily, cheer up, cheerily, cheer up* of the American robin that is heard in yards all over from early spring until July. These songs are a way for a male bird to claim a territory and attract a mate. Thus there is evolutionary pressure for the songs to become more enchanting and attractive to other birds.

Spring birdsongs are perceived as lovely by humans. The notes, frequencies, ranges, and patterns are pleasing to the human brain, and listening to them creates relaxation and lifts the mood. There is abundant research validating the positive influence of listening to birdsongs.

Birds also emit flock or contact calls, often soft, quiet chirps that allow flock members to stay in touch as they feed in thick foliage. Examples are the *tseet, tseet, tseet* of dark-eyed juncos and the *chink, chink* of white-throated sparrows. Hearing and appreciating these contact calls is a bit of an acquired taste, but once recognized, these are some of the sweetest bird vocalizations. Contact calls indicate birds in a social group feeding or traveling peacefully, providing more evidence of a safe and possibly food-producing environment.

Alarm calls are another informative category of bird vocalizations. Often sounding similar to contact calls, the alarm calls are louder and more urgent. For example the *tink, tink, tink* contact call of cardinals turns into a loud and insistent *TINK, TINK, TINK!* Other birds such as wrens and titmice call and scold. Alarm calls that typically indicate the presence of a bird- or egg-eating predator, such as a hawk, cat, weasel, or snake, are recognized by all birds and constitute a call to disperse and hide.

The ultimate point of listening to bird language is that it offers a rich source of information on the state of the environment. Singing and contact-calling birds signal a peaceful and safe environment, which for our ancestors was valuable, crucial, even life-saving and life-sustaining information. Sometime during the course of evolution, it seems that this positive information grew to be aesthetically pleasing; in other words, a safe and productive soundscape became beautiful music to our ears.

Listening to bird language is a way to engage mindfully in nature. As Young writes, by listening to the language of birds "we can come to our senses, quiet our (everyday) mind and (re)establish a sacred, healing, and transformational connection to nature."

❧

What about the second member of the soundscape trifecta, the wind? During my year of nature sitting sessions, I learned that the wind was *everything* as it blew both sounds and fragrances my way. I learned to face into the wind to hear what was around me and what was coming my way. I sniffed the air and inhaled the fragrance of pines and ferns and water, and after a time I could distinguish the smell of high or low humidity or of a pending rainstorm.

I learned to listen to the gusts, which I discovered last for only about ten to twenty seconds. I detected waves of wind rising and ebbing, a backdrop to the nature soundscape. Gentle breezes and quiet gusts told of safe and comfortable conditions. The rising and falling, sighing and whooshing of the leaves, the whispering of the pine boughs, and even the clacking of branches in winter—all beautiful, all soothing, all transporting, all mindfulness inducing.

For our ancestors, the wind was another vital source of information. Over eons humans learned to feel, sniff, and listen to the wind and found favorable conditions aesthetically pleasing. A breeze was a blessing, a headwind a challenge. Strong gusts and stiff breezes warned of conditions that needed to be monitored and adapted to with extra layers of clothing, more alertness to animals approaching, and more attention to dangers of storms and falling branches. Once again, survival instincts, nature perception, and aesthetic appreciation became intertwined.

While sitting still in nature and listening to the soundscape trifecta, I began to notice the interplay of silence and sound. The intervals of restful silence sensitized me to hear more and more from further and further away. Silence is the canvas on which the sounds of nature are painted. Canvas and paint, silence and sounds—both are needed.

It was with hearing the sounds of nature that I clearly noticed the ratchet effect. A part of my perception, like a smartphone app, is now constantly on, always primed to hear surrounding nature sounds. Even when engaged in such mundane tasks as taking the recycling out to the garage or walking across a parking lot, I register the sounds of the wind and the songs of birds. These nature sounds then trigger, in a positive sense, a flash of joy and a restorative reconnection to nature. I have developed an auditory sensitivity that I can't turn off even if I wanted to. Of course I don't want to and am grateful for the shift in my hearing.

SEEING

One early morning in May, the view across Prompton Lake in the early sunlight was breathtaking—an expanse of blue water, a defined rocky shoreline set off by green-leafed willows merging into a hillside of maple and ash trees decked out in rounded robes of new yellow-tinted, spring-green leaves rising to a band of dark-green hemlocks and pine topped by a vast blue sky dappled with fluffy white clouds.

It was a vista now embedded in memory, one that when recalled immediately draws forth a multi-level response—slower, deeper breathing, a letting go of thoughts and worries, a spreading sense of happiness, and rekindled feelings of awe and inspiration.

Was it, I asked myself, just a pretty view or were there distinct elements in this lake-forest-sky scene that created such a profound response? Once again it turned out that I had stumbled into a collection of scientifically appealing visual elements, elements that signaled safety and food—survival cues turned into aesthetic pleasure. The key ingredients I learned were color, shape, vitality, texture, vistas, and patterns.

In terms of colors, science suggests that blues, greens, and purples are naturally appealing to humans. Shapes, such as the rounded contours of the trees are also pleasing as humans prefer rounded contours to jagged shapes. My view was filled with greens, a variety of rounded shapes, and topped by blue.

The health of the forest seems to be another appealing aspect. Humans like to see a vigorous, vibrant, growing forest where there are likely to be abundant plants, fruits, nuts, and seeds to harvest and animals to hunt. A verdant forest also provides a safe hiding place from predators, natural shelter from the elements, and materials to make a home. The forest I viewed certainly looked healthy.

A relatively open vista is another inherently appealing dimension. My view across the lake was open enough for me to clearly see any flora or fauna that could provide food (thrive) and to see any danger (survive). My spot in the woods allowed me to see without being seen.

Certain visual patterns in nature have also been found to be intrinsically appealing and stirring. My view of the forest across the lake was filled with what are called fractals, patterns that repeat at increasingly finer magnifications. An example of a fractal pattern is a tree bough, to branches, to smaller branches, to twigs, to leaves, to the veins in the leaves—a pattern repeating at ever finer gradations.

Nature vistas are filled with fractals. Flowers, ferns, grasses, and mosses offer them up. Rocks, dunes, raindrops, swirling rivers, shorelines, waves, and clouds provide more fractals. The forest I viewed, that at first seemed like chaos, in fact had an underlying mathematical pattern, an order.

Importantly, fractals, particularly those that have just the right degree of complexity—low to medium seems ideal—have been found to be dramatically and instantly appealing to the human eye and can produce immediate soothing effects. Researchers measuring brain waves of people viewing nature scenes filled with fractals have documented a 60 percent decrease in the stress response accompanied by feelings of pleasure and satisfaction. Viewing nature fractals has even been found to accelerate post-surgical healing.

The beauty of fractals is that the more you look the more you see, which is what makes them perfect for inducing mindfulness. In summer the branches, twigs, and leaves provide flow and complexity, while in winter a tree silhouette offers visual fascination.

Research on brain activity while viewing fractals found some expected areas of activation, including visual processing and visual-spatial memory areas. What was unexpected was activation of the parahippocampus, an area responsible for regulating emotions, and an area that is engaged while listening to music. It may be that fractals are like visual symphonies.

Our relationship with fractals may be even deeper and more complex. It seems that when visually scanning, our eyes fall into a pattern of saccades—jumpy movements. This pattern involves scanning first for big elements in the scene and then making repeated smaller and smaller passes to pick up on more and more details. This is essentially a fractal pattern and is an efficient search strategy.

Our connection with fractals runs even deeper. The branching in our lungs and our circulatory system, and even the web of neurons in our brain are fractals. Thus when we immerse ourselves in viewing fractals, it is not like some mechanical camera viewing something external. It is more like fractals viewing fractals using a fractal-scanning pattern.

Sitting still in nature, settling in, and really seeing may best be described as an experience of resonance with nature, where subject and object merge, where the feelings of connection and oneness make perfect sense. It is a state where the pulses and frequencies of light and sound synchronize with the beat of our heart and the rhythm or our breath.

This state of outer and inner fractal resonance supports nature mindfulness. Our brain settles into an open flow state, moving from narrow directed attention to flexible nondirected attention. We become more open to divergent, creative, associative processing, to seeing patterns and divining meaning within those patterns.

I recall a sitting session when after forty minutes a wind-blown twig dropped down on a huge rock in front of me. My attention was directed to the rock where for the first time I noticed a vibrant and complete world of life—mosses, lichens, grasses, spiders, flies, and even a wildflower. It was a micro self-sustaining, self-perpetuating, moisture-and-forest-debris-collecting community—a finer-grained version of the forest in which I sat. Heartbeat, breathing, thoughts, and emotions synchronized as I gazed at all of the life on the rock. It was a moment of fractal immersion, another click of a sensory ratchet, creating a sensitivity to seeing fractals, to seeing and responding to scales of life large and small all around me.

SMELL

I sat at my sit spot on a frigid winter morning huddled against the cold and the wind. Two hundred yards upwind on the frozen lake, an ice fisherman fired up his gas-powered auger to drill a new hole. In the brief, only secondslong interval while I was processing my annoyance at the startlingly loud and disruptive sound of the augur, my nostrils were suddenly flooded by the pungent smell of combusted gasoline.

I was stunned by how quickly the strong chemical smells traveled across the open lake and how fully I experienced it. It was like an olfactory slap in the face, quite unpleasant, but it fully alerted me to the impact of smells and awakened my sensitivity to the fragrances around me. As the odor of the combusted gasoline dissipated, I purposefully sniffed the air and began to detect other scents—a faint smell of snow and a freshness in the northwest wind, a wind that blew cold and clear down from the forests of Canada.

After that I began to add an olfactory scan to my sit spot sensory awareness circle. Most of what I noticed through the year would fall into the category of woody/resinous smells, which includes earthy, mushroomy smells. Sometimes when the wind was from the right direction, I would inhale the aromas of white pine needles and pine resin. Rain and snow and mist seemed to enhance these smells.

Sometimes in spring and summer I inhaled sweet fragrances. In particular I remember a day when I was enveloped in the thickly perfumed air of Russian olive blossoms. Other days I noticed an almost minty fragrance as I walked through and brushed up against ferns. Sometimes after a string of rainy days I picked up on an earthy smell of last year's leaf litter composting.

These olfactory impressions were typically not in the foreground of my awareness but floating in the background and contributing to overall feelings of well-being and comfort in the forest. I subsequently discovered that there were good reasons for my positive reactions. The sense of smell is uniquely wired to be immediately informative, emotionally laden, linked to memory, and cognitively complex. Smells powerfully attract and warn us, utilizing memory and emotions. Think here of your reactions to the smell of vegetables or burgers on the grill, to the enticing fragrance of a floral perfume, or the disgusting odor of rotten food.

My olfactory reactions are supported by the emerging research on phytoncides, the volatile oils emitted by trees and plants. As described in the previous sections on the health benefits of time in nature, some of these phytoncides, such as those emitted by pines and cedars, cause an immediate boost in immune system function. Researchers in Korea have found that inhaling these chemicals during just a twenty-minute stroll through an evergreen forest can give the immune system a boost that lasts up to thirty days. And research is indicating that other forest and field fragrances may be beneficial, such as the smells of the forest floor, the earth, other plants, and even water.

Although we cede the award for best noses to our pet beagles and golden retrievers, we humans have a pretty good sense of smell too. And it seems that the fragrances of nature are not only noticed but can contribute immediately and powerfully to our mental, emotional, and physical well-being, and in turn they help to ease us into a state of nature mindfulness.

For many of us, the task in nature is to reawaken and to then consciously notice the olfactory inputs of forest and field. The ratchet effects are that whenever I head out for a hike, a brief stroll through a green space, or a quick turn around my yard, I spontaneously inhale a long sniff and smell the goodness. And whenever I walk through a pine or cedar forest, I take extra sniffs and derive extra pleasure and probably health benefits as well.

Touch

Our skin is our largest sensory organ, and it is continually sending tactile inputs to the brain. On bitter cold mornings when I was out sitting, my skin sent complaints as I stepped out of my warm car and trudged through the frigid woods to my sit spot. But usually after twenty minutes or so, I began to acclimate to the cold. The discomfort slowly faded away as my skin adjusted. And then there came a tipping point after which I began to feel comfortable, to feel embraced by the air. As I adapted to the cold, the tactile sensations became some of my most memorable sit spot sensations. A particular favorite was when the first rays of morning sunshine touched my neck and shoulders. The warming effect from the first rays of the sun was a profound experience, one that lifted me out of my little personal self and joined me to eons of human experience as people welcomed the first warmth of the day.

Over the months that I sat still during my hourlong sessions, I noticed more and more tactile sensations. After months of winter cold, I welcomed the touch of the warm mild air of spring and summer on my skin and the lightness of wearing a T-shirt instead of heavy layers of shirt, sweater, and coat. I noticed humidity as well, the degree of moisture in the air. Sometimes mist, fog, rain, or melting snowflakes brought moisture to skin. And I found that my skin was particularly sensitive to the wind, to the entire continuum from gentle summer puffs to fresh fall breezes to winter gusts. I became more of a toucher through the year, sometimes placing my hand on the smooth trunk of a beech tree as I walked by or running my fingers through a cluster of honeysuckle leaves.

From the perspective of mindfulness, my sense of touch, my active noticing of the myriad and ever-changing tactile sensations not only made me feel settled and comfortable but also brought me into the present moment. To this day, when I go outside to work in the yard or take a walk, I notice that point when I feel acclimated, when I feel more comfortable outside than inside.

Taste

That cold morning when big fat snowflakes drifted slowly down, I admit that I stuck out my tongue to catch a few. They tasted like delicate wafers of water, like a nature communion offering. Once in a while, I plucked a stem of grass and stuck it between my teeth, an old-fashioned country toothpick with the bonus of an herby, grassy taste. And if I did bring along a thermos of tea and sip a cup, I noticed how good it tasted in the solitude and fresh air.

In forest bathing the sense of taste is beautifully emphasized during the concluding tea ceremony when leaves from a forest plant are steeped in hot water, producing a natural herb tea to be savored while reflecting on the nature sojourn. In this case the sense of taste offers another literal and figurative means by which to connect with nature in the present.

Sensory Awareness, Mindfulness, and a Question

I well recall those moments from my forest stillness year when I would be distracted, and I would take a deep breath, re-establish even breathing, and re-engage in sensory awareness. I remember thinking that practicing sensory awareness in nature was easier and almost more productive than the formal meditation I had been practicing for years.

I now understand that this makes sense as science has shown that it is in our nature to pay attention to nature. It is easy, softly fascinating, and engaging to notice the ever-expanding, ever-more subtle sensory inputs surrounding us. The longer we sit, the more we notice, the more our experience deepens, the more we merge into the present moment and then into nature mindfulness.

Sensory awareness in nature helps us shift from top-down, directed attention, to open, non-directed, flow-state attention, to full mindfulness where we touch base with inner joy, release locked-in suffering, gain insights, and experience a connection to something greater than our self. In mindfulness we also rest and restore our physical health.

All that I learned about the five senses explained much about the quality and depth of my year of sit spot experiences. However, during the course of the year, I began to notice some additional sensory experiences—strong feelings about the location of a sit spot, turning to look before something appeared, sensing the mood of the lake and forest, or easily finding my way down a trail in the dark. I began to wonder if there were more than five senses, more ways to experience nature, additional sensory pathways that might deepen mindfulness.

CHAPTER 6

Beyond the Five

I TURNED AND GLANCED UP AT AN OPENING IN THE THICK FOREST canopy. Seconds later a bald eagle flew across the gap in the leaves. I saw its bright white head and tail feathers shining in the morning sunlight. I heard its powerful wingbeats.

Why had I suddenly turned and looked at the opening right before the eagle appeared? Such prescient glances began to happen more often. Unbidden, unprompted, I would turn, look, and then a yellow warbler, a chipmunk, or junco would appear. It felt as if I was developing some type of sixth sense.

And there were other experiences. When I tried to sense the mood of the forest, I was surprised at how quickly and easily it happened. Stepping from my car, I would pause, open my senses and mind, and quickly discern the mood of nature at that moment in that place. Descriptors such as abundance, satisfaction, growth, fulfillment, change, tension, and even melancholy came to mind. Then while on my way to or when I was at my sit spot, I would see something to substantiate the mood I had detected. Later I would detect changes and shifts in the mood and state of nature. I felt as if I was acquiring or uncovering yet another sense. Reflecting on these experiences, I decided that I needed to explore beyond the typical five senses and find out if there were additional sensory channels supporting and deepening nature mindfulness.

Proprioception and Interoception

The first additional sense I came across was proprioception or kinesthesia, defined as the body's ability to sense its location and movement in space, an ability that allows us to walk without consciously thinking about it. Utilizing input from eyes and ears and joints and muscles, proprioception helps us to know where all of our body parts are relative to each other and relative to gravity, a kind of ongoing autopilot view of how we are moving through three-dimensional space.

Slow walking through the woods past trees, through branches, and over roots and fallen logs activates our sense of proprioception. During a sitting session, closing our eyes and sensing our position in the natural world of shapes and forms also utilizes this sense. Nature mindfulness probably makes us more aware of our position in space, and that awareness in turn is one more input to bring us more intensively into the present moment.

I noticed proprioception coming into play early one morning when I needed to go to my sit spot before sunrise in order to help out a friend later. I stepped onto the West Shore Trail and followed it unerringly in the dark, my feet feeling and knowing the way, and my body knowingly weaving through and by branches and boughs.

Another additional sense is interoception—the awareness of internal states. Examples would be awareness of breath, heartbeat, muscles, digestion, and the need for elimination. It includes our sense of whether we are cold or warm, hungry or thirsty. Accurate ongoing interoception and appropriate responsive action or inaction is a crucial element of well-being. Some research indicates that a lack of, blocked, or inaccurate interoception may contribute to the onset and persistence of mental health disorders such as depression, anxiety, post-traumatic stress disorder (PTSD), and obsessive-compulsive disorder (OCD).

In a typical state of directed attention, we may suppress our awareness of inner states. When sitting or walking slowly in nature and accessing open, non-directed attention, we become more aware. In a state of mindfulness, we are able to notice these inputs in an open and peaceful way and respond as needed.

In the forest we are surrounded by examples of flora and fauna simply registering and responding to internal states and needs. The mammals and birds all live simply—eating when hungry, resting when tired, eliminating when needed, and drinking when thirsty. Affected by the influence of these examples and with the increased awareness fostered by nature mindfulness, I felt increasingly aware of internal inputs and increasingly free and direct in my responding. After a morning sitting session, I felt hungry, and I ate—direct, simple, and satisfying.

Four More Senses

In addition to the above two senses, both of which have been well explored and researched by science, there may be, as Amos Clifford notes in his guide to forest bathing, four additional senses that come into play. These are subtle senses, harder to document and define, and possibly existing in that borderland between sensing and perceiving, between noticing and creating.

The first of these and the one closest to known science is mirror sensing. The human brain possesses so-called mirror neurons that allow us to fall in resonance with others, to move and gesture, to respond and emote in tandem with others. This can be seen when two friends or even two strangers establish conversational rapport and echo or mirror each other's gestures and voice tones.

Mirror neurons are crucial for social integration and the development of empathy. Some have theorized that deficits in the functioning of these neurons are one of the causes of autism—the inability to sense, know, and respond to the minds of others.

In the forest, mirror sensing may, as Clifford suggests, allow us to feel the mood or unique energy of the forest on any given day and during any hour. This seemed to be a sensitivity that I developed during my year of forest stillness. While approaching my sit spot, I learned to be open to the unique state of nature in the moment—quiet, turbulent, soothing, restful, restless, unsettled, poignant, and joyful were all moods that I came to sense.

Mirror neurons may also help us to absorb positive forest archetypes in an almost psychotherapeutic or personal growth sense, a process known to many indigenous cultures. Think here of taking in the wisdom of the owl, the strength of a bear, the speed of a deer, the smarts of a fox, or the vision of an eagle.

Sitting and observing nature, I found myself often noticing, feeling encouraged by, and absorbing the life trajectories of the animals and plants around me. I felt energized by the time-sensitive opportunism of the ducks—lingering in the fall until the ice formed and then reappearing in the spring as soon as there was open water. I felt wellsprings of resilience whenever I saw wildflowers spiking through layers of leaf litter to bloom or saw a tree severed by lightning that sprouted a new trunk to continue its skyward growth.

Body radar is another possible sensory pathway. Clifford defines body radar as responsiveness to something in the forest calling or beckoning us. It is a sensitivity to a gestalt of conditions beyond normal selective attention—an intuitive call to perhaps sit in this specific place, follow this particular path, walk along this stream, or pause beneath this grand old maple. It may be a way to sense what is known as the spirit of a place.

Body radar may be more readily available than we imagine. Early in my forest stillness year I heard a clear call from within to move my sit spot to a location thirty yards toward the tip of a peninsula. I heeded the call, and fifteen minutes later, a large black bear stood on the very spot of my first location.

I also noticed that after several months, I developed the ability to quickly see a good sit spot without going through a slow mental checklist. I have noticed the same sensibility rapidly develop in people that I have taken on sitting sessions as they subsequently are able to find ideal sit spots on their own.

A controversial notion but one that most people who spend extensive time outdoors grow to acknowledge is that nature has sentience—a certain type of intelligence. The research on how networks of trees communicate and share resources supports this notion. Clifford labels this imaginal sensing and defines it as our way of tuning into this sentience. Letting go of our materialistic and reductionistic skepticism, we can open our imagination to hear the messages of the trees and the animals. He explains that in a state of deep connection to nature, some of the insights, the flashes of understanding, the moments of awe, and the emotional epiphanies come from without not solely from within.

During my year of stillness, I befriended the big black cherry tree under which I sat on so many mornings during my hourlong sitting sessions. I tracked the tree's changes and moods from winter to spring, through summer and into fall. I came to feel this tree's benevolence. Similarly, the seep, over which I slowly stepped on the way to my sit spot, seemed, with its murmuring across the rocks and its evergreen cress, to speak to me of life and abundance.

Finally, Clifford describes a felt sense of the present moment or what he also calls the heart sense. This is probably that moment when all of the sensory input flows together and joins to create a total experience of that moment in nature. It is an integrative, emotional experience to be felt in the heart and not explained through words in the mind. It is infused with that subtle joy we experience during full moments of nature mindfulness.

As Clifford writes, "The ability to dwell without analysis in the felt sense of the present moment now strikes me as a large part of what I have long sought through spiritual practice."

For me, the heartfelt sense of awe and the feelings of joy that I have experienced during moments of nature connection have, as a ratchet effect, remained in my heart where they can be activated by a glimpse of a green hillside, the sound of the wind through the leaves, or the fragrance of spring time lilacs.

❧

After thoroughly exploring the many pathways of the senses, I felt as if I had a good understanding of how the systematic practice of sensory awareness in nature establishes nature mindfulness and deepens a nature connection.

Let's move on now and explore a variety of nature sitting experiences that illuminate different moments of mindfulness, different moments of awe, and different instances of nature-inspired insights. Let's begin by looking at the contributions of nature mindfulness to the process of healing.

EXPERIENCES IN
NATURE MINDFULNESS

CHAPTER 7

Nature Healing

W HEN I THINK ABOUT THE ROLE OF NATURE IN HEALING, the image that comes to mind is a row of tall green trees seen through a hospital window. In a 1984 study, Roger Ulrich analyzed the medical records of patients recovering from gall bladder surgery. Twenty-three patients looked out at a row of trees while twenty-three matched patients viewed a brick wall.

The patients "with windows looking out on a nature scene" had shorter hospital stays, required less pain medication, had fewer post-operative complications, and received fewer negative evaluative comments from the nurses caring for them. These restorative effects of a view of nature are impressive benefits from a remarkably simple intervention.

Ulrich believed that it was the stress reduction effects of nature that supported the healing process. Reducing the energy committed to the flight or fight response allowed the natural rest and digest processes to take place.

Holly Merker, in the book *Ornitherapy for Your Body, Mind, and Soul,* describes how observing birds as a way to connect with nature helped her to recover from an aggressive form of breast cancer. She recounts a spring day when she watched a tiny, brilliantly colored cerulean warbler singing energetically and guarding the nest where its mate sat. As she contemplated the challenges of long distance migration and the trials of nesting that this little bird faced, she felt the weight of her concerns lighten and her determination grow. If this little bird could manage its challenges, then she could manage her challenges as well.

In their book *Your Brain on Nature,* Eva Selhub and Alan Logan, two physicians, write about the healing power of nature, known for centuries by the Latin term *vis medicatrix naturae.* They offer the idea that this term is best defined "as a healing response written into our DNA." They note that the quality of our interaction with nature may be important for activating this response. To optimally activate healing, they write that "mindful immersion in and contact with" the natural world is required.

In this chapter I present three sit spot stories that address mindful time in nature and healing. The first, **A Healing View**, describes my efforts to enlist the healing powers of nature before and after neck surgery. In the second, **The Rewilding of Hankins Pond,** I explore how quickly and dynamically nature can heal itself when given a chance and note that this spontaneous restoration provides a model to inspire human healing. The third, **Sister in the Sunrise,** tells how I discovered a surprising way in which nature can address emotional issues, heal grief, and foster the development of positive coping skills.

A HEALING VIEW

As the day designated for my surgery loomed steadily closer, I began to experience anxious moments complete with graphic images of disfigurement, disability, or death. After all, this operation would require a precise incision across the front of my neck. In calmer moments I tried to push these images aside and direct my attention to practical issues, to taking care of everything that needed to be done beforehand.

One morning, ten days before the surgery, my mind jumped past the operation to the recovery process. I pictured myself immersed in a scene filled with the plant and animal life surrounding a nearby beaver pond. I imagined myself drawing healing energy from the scene.

I realized, with a sense of relief, that I could bring this image to mind at any time. But then, with a trace of unease, I thought that I might not have the full story on the healing potentials of nature around the beaver pond. I realized that I needed to find a way to squeeze in a sitting session before my surgery.

APPROACH

Usually when planning a sitting session, I look ahead at the forecast for a clear, sunny morning so I can enjoy the full sunrise experience. But with the time pressures of preoperative lab tests, appointments, a COVID-19 test, and the rush to wrap up work and home tasks, only one morning was available, and the forecast called for thick clouds.

I awoke at 5:15 a.m. Minutes later, in the faint first light of dawn, I walked across my backyard, through a stand of slender ash trees, and on to the mowed path that led down a long hill toward the beaver pond. Glancing up at the cloudy sky, I was surprised to see color—delicate swirls of pink tinged with bands of orange and yellow. I remembered what I had learned during my year of sitting at Prompton Lake. Every sunrise creates a light and color show; some are dramatic and fill the sky with broad bands of bright colors, and some, as it was this day, are subtle and delicate with fleeting swatches of pink and slender ribbons of orange and yellow.

MORNING MIST

A layer of gray mist floated above the valley surrounding the unnamed stream that fed the beaver pond. The mist shrouded the trees, drifted over the marsh, obscured a distant hayfield, and seemed to stretch foggy fingers up toward the low gray clouds. There was no wind. The still, moist air created a cathedral-like quiet. Every sound registered clearly, every tone resonated and lingered. I took a slow, deep breath, settled comfortably into my camp stool and began to scan the circle of sound around me.

To my left a swamp sparrow trilled a musical *chinga-chinga-chinga*, slowly, melodiously, a sacred bell sound. Another swamp sparrow to the right joined in, a faster trill, a second ringing bell calling supplicants to prayer.

I heard more songs: the lilting *maids-maids-put-on-the-tea-kettle-let-tle* aria of a song sparrow, the chatter of a house wren, the distant *caw* of a crow, the harsh *chek* of a red-winged blackbird in flight, and the soft, overlapping hymn-like *cooo, coo, coo* duet of two mourning doves.

Sky Dancers

Soft lilting chatter sounded above me. Glancing up I spotted a barn swallow in flight. Training my binoculars on the bird, I saw its buff-colored breast, rufous throat, blue-black back, trademark forked tail, and the best feature of all, its long, slender, streamlined, swept-back, flight-ready wings.

More chatter filled the air. A flock of twenty or more barn swallows surrounded me. Perhaps because I was sitting still or perhaps because I was partially camouflaged by the mist, they ignored my presence and flew within feet of me. I watched them flap and glide and lift and dip and turn and swirl. One reason for these deft maneuvers was to snatch flying insects, but there also seemed to be social dimensions—the soft chattering back and forth; the swirling up next to each other, almost touching wings, and then peeling away. The swallows looked like a troupe of sky dancers—dancers born with stunning flight skills, skills honed by hours of flying, and now performing in the morning mist.

Seed Heads

Field grasses grew directly in front of me at the apogee of summer growth, displaying a diversity of stems, leaves, and seed heads. I counted seven different types of grasses and decided to sketch them to better observe their unique qualities.

To my left grew a short, stiff-stemmed grass with thick, tubular, brown seed heads. Next to it, a thin grass with narrow, pale-green leaves topped with slender pale seed heads flecked with tiny strands of yellow pollen. Next, a medium-height, thick-stemmed grass with short alternating leaves and a loose, brown seed head that reminded me of a stalk of wheat. Then a grass with a droopy stalk, and next to it the tallest grass, at least five feet high, topped with a loose spray of tan seed heads. Then a thick-stemmed grass with long angular leaves and a blocky head; and finally, a shorter plant with a spray of slender swaying stems. All of this diversity was packed into about two square feet of earth, all of it sown by nature.

Gazing at the patch of grasses, seeing the diversity of forms, the expression of every possible height, shape, and color, I felt as if I was looking straight at adaptive intelligence.

Reset

I reflected that these grasses—just like humans—need calcium for health, development, and structural strength—bones in humans and the gravity-defying cell walls in plants. And it was calcium levels that were the crux of my medical issue. My parathyroid glands, four little grain-of-rice-sized glands located around the thyroid, are tasked with secreting a hormone to regulate the amount of calcium in the bloodstream. One or more of my glands were enlarged and overactive and as a result drawing too much calcium from my bones. There were no overt symptoms with this problem, but it is generally an insidious progression that can lead to weak bones, hip fractures, and possibly kidney stones. And calcium is so crucial to cellular metabolism that any irregularity can also compromise mood, memory, and energy. The standard treatment is surgery to remove the offending parathyroid glands.

As I thought about the surgery, about slipping beneath the fog of anesthesia, about "going under the knife," I lost interest in my sit spot session. Feelings of annoyance and impatience took over. Why had my body betrayed me? What was I doing here? When would this stupid sit spot hour be over? What was the point?

In fact there wasn't even a beaver pond there anymore. The beavers had left, died out, been trapped, or shot in the spring. April downpours had destroyed their untended dams. All that remained was a shrinking, mud-edged crescent of water to the left, and a shallow widening of the stream to the right.

Then I caught myself. These thoughts were powered by anxiety, doubt, and discouragement, and distracted me from awareness. One never knows when these subterranean voices might emerge to raise roadblocks and devise detours. Fortunately, I had a few ideas on how to handle this insurrection.

First, I recalled some words of reassurance. A friend of mine, a veteran of many surgeries, said, "If they are letting you go home the same day, it's not that big of a deal. You'll be fine." Second, I pushed the internal reset button, brought my attention back to sensory awareness, back to the present moment. Above me I again saw the swallows pirouetting. In the distance I heard the flute-like, downward-spiraling *vrdi-vreed-vreed-vreer-vreer* song of a veery. A robin tutted, a swamp sparrow trilled, a woodpecker drummed, and a cardinal whistled its clarion, *birdy-birdy-birdy-birdy*. A breath of breeze caressed my face.

WELL-BEING

The sun lifted higher into the cloudy sky, the mist vanished, and the sky grew bright. The breeze grew steadier and swayed the grasses in front of me. Over eons the grasses had learned to bend and flow with the breeze. These two, the wind and the grasses, were old friends. They knew how to dance together. They even made music together. I heard the soft *wishhhhh* of the breeze blowing through the stems and leaves.

I inhaled the dry fragrance of the grasses, the fresh scent of nearby flowing water, and the heady, rich, fertile smell of full summer growth that emanated from the sun-warmed soil. Clusters of bright red berries festooned a nearby honeysuckle bush. A catbird mewed. I felt embraced by a sense of well-being.

THE VIEW

A mourning dove took off from a large willow tree across the pond and flew over me. I watched its streamlined body, heard its wings flap, and admired its steady, straight, purposeful flight. A fluffy white insect hovered like a helicopter in front of me and then darted off toward a Russian olive tree bedecked with clusters of burgundy berries. A common yellowthroat sang its slow, enchanting *witchety-witchety-witchey* song.

I looked through the grasses to the vibrant green new shoots on the mudflats; to the filled-in, leafed-in, rounded shapes of the bushes; to a stand of tall, densely leafed maples beyond the pond; to a gently sloping, green hayfield dotted with purple milkweed flowers and white yarrow blooms; to a line of tall trees at the edge of a green forest—successive layers of growing green beneath a vast blue sky.

I felt my vision shift to vignette mode, the periphery blurring, the stepwise matrix of verdant growth from grasses to bushes to trees to field to forest pulsating with life, a view that pulled me into a peaceful state. This was a healing view.

SIX DAYS LATER

The nurse belted my torso and arms to the operating table. The anesthesia technician asked me to take a few deep breaths of oxygen from a mask and said, "I'm going to start the anesthesia now. I want you to think of a nice scene in nature."

"I've got that covered," I said with a smile.

During the week after the surgery, as my neck healed, my strength returned, and my body recovered, I walked down to the beaver pond at sunset to listen to the birds sing, to see the color show in the evening sky, and to take in a healing view.

THE REWILDING OF HANKINS POND

In 2013 the Pennsylvania Fish and Boat Commission determined that the 170-year-old, hand-built stone dam at Hankins Pond posed a "high hazard" for flooding. If it were to give way in a heavy rain, there was substantial risk for downstream property damage, even loss of life. Once the determination was made, the old stone slabs that held back the ninety acres of impounded water were lifted and the pond was drained.

Since then Hankins Pond has been in a state of limbo. The Fish and Boat Commission looked into options to rebuild the dam. Concerned citizens organized, circulated a petition, and lobbied for restoration. The state ultimately decided that the hazard was too high, the cost too great, and the only solution was to rip a 150-foot-wide chunk out of the old dam to permanently reduce the hazard. The county in turn filed an injunction to stop the demolition, and in 2019 eventually negotiated an agreement to take over the site, fix the dam, and restore the pond. But when the COVID-19 pandemic hit, the project was put on hold.

During this eight-year squabble, ever-opportunistic, ever-resilient, ever-healing nature took full advantage of the state of human-created limbo. A wetland arose where a pond once stood. Grasses and reeds grew. Rains came, water levels rose and fell. Mudflats appeared and disappeared. Swatches of open water emerged and evaporated. Beavers assisted by constructing a low dam that raised the water level a few inches.

REWILDING

Hankins Pond sits in a natural bowl surrounded by hills and woods. Several unnamed streams and a number of natural springs flow into this bowl. The area most likely was a wetland before the Delaware and Hudson Canal Company built the dam in the early 1850s to store water needed to maintain depth in the canals that carried barges of anthracite coal from Pennsylvania to the Hudson River and then to New York City.

When the old dam was breached in 2013, the wetland returned. No humans oversaw or managed this transition, an example of what might be called accidental rewilding.

Here is a description of rewilding that I found online: "Rewilding is a progressive approach to conservation. It's about letting nature take care of itself, enabling natural processes to shape land and sea, repair damaged ecosystems and restore degraded landscapes. Through rewilding, wildlife's natural rhythms create wilder, more biodiverse habitats."

For the birds and mammals, the rewilding of Hankins Pond did not go unnoticed. Birds, it seems, constantly seek "just right" habitat. Every year a greater variety of ducks began to land, rest, feed, and breed in the hidden reaches of this new wetland. Sandpipers and snipes came to patrol the mudflats and feed on the abundant invertebrates. Coots, grebes, gallinules, and bitterns swam or step-slithered through the dense cattails and bulrushes. Red-winged blackbirds and tree swallows appeared in abundance to swoop and circle over the rich wetland, prospering and proliferating in a perfect habitat.

Where the birds gather, bird watchers follow. Hankins Pond became an eBirding hotspot with 170 species recorded. Nature watchers strolled along the old road that runs along one side and came to sit—a bench has been installed by the Friends of Hankins Pond—and to look and listen.

MORNING SONGS

The first rays of morning sunshine pierced the dark, green woods at the upper end of Hankins Pond. Haunting rising and falling *kek-kek-kek* calls carried through the swirling strands of gray mist that floated over the pond. I stepped onto dew-laden grass, slipped on my binocular harness, shouldered my camp stool, spotting scope, and backpack, and began a slow, transition-into-nature walk down the old road that runs along the edge of the pond.

Reaching my destination—a little peninsula that sticks out into the wetland—I set up my camp stool beneath a red maple, a location that offered a good view across the marsh. I settled in, quieted my mind, and began to listen to the sounds around me.

I heard the sweet bell-like trill of a swamp sparrow and the lilting aria of a song sparrow. A red-winged blackbird, its orange shoulder bars gleaming in the morning sunlight, perched on a cattail in front of me swayed back and forth and sang a bright *konkaree-konkaree*.

And then the weird, wild sounds started, the ascending and descending, crazed, laughter-like call of a pied-billed grebe—*kuk-kuk-cow-cow-cow-cowp-cowp-cowp*. Another grebe answered. Next, the complaining, whining *kek-kek-kek* call of a common gallinule was answered by two others from across the wetland. A coot joined in with a grating, guttural *kuk-kuk-kuk-kuk*.

These marsh birds are not to be heard on a typical lake or in a park. They need a large undisturbed wetland to feed and breed, to feel safe and secure. I scanned the marsh with my binoculars and scope but couldn't spot any of them. They were well hidden among the grasses and reeds.

The Sun Rises

The sun inched above the green wooded hills that surround the pond. For a few moments the sunlight transformed the mist from gray strands to luminous gold threads. Then, as the temperature rose, the mist vanished. Around the marsh frogs called, green frogs with their tuneless banjo *twang* and bullfrogs with their deep, base *hrrrrmp*—wetland background music.

I heard a rooster crow. There is a farm just across the highway from the dam, a reminder of how wild and domestic can exist in close proximity. I heard splashes and wings flap out on the wetland, scanned but saw nothing. A hint of motion in the grasses in front of me, binoculars up, a brilliantly colored male wood duck swam slowly by, pausing and preening before swimming on. A drake mallard flew over the far end of the pond, set its wings, glided down, and splashed on the water amidst tall green grasses.

From the upper end of the pond, a *coo-coo-coo* call. I listened carefully and tried to echolocate the bird. Quiet. Then it called again—*coo-coo-coo*. More silence. Was it a black-billed cuckoo or a least bittern? Then the bird called steadily. The tone and the location in the grasses at the edge of the pond confirmed that it was a least bittern; an uncommon, hidden, solitary marsh bird had found a home at Hankins Pond.

Three bigger birds flew across the marsh with slow steady flaps.

What were they? Binoculars up, I caught a glimpse of them in flight and watched as they landed in the bare branches of a tall dead tree. I identified them as green herons, another unusual sighting, as they are uncommon and usually solitary. Could this be a family, two young birds reared in the quiet and plenty of the wetland, learning how to live independently with the instruction of their mother?

I looked down and noticed bands of vegetation. In front of me at the edge of the high ground, red osier dogwood bushes yielded to tall goldenrod plants with russet-tinged top leaves. At water's edge pale-blue wild irises transitioned to slender, tubular moisture-loving grasses. On a newly emerged black-brown mudflat, tendrils of sprouting grass looked like green stubble. Past a patch of open water grew true marsh plants—tall, pale-green, thick-stemmed cattails and slender, dark-green bulrushes. Each plant grew precisely in its preferred habitat as if arranged by an invisible and highly informed hand.

Behind me I heard the woodland songbirds—the energetic *teecha-teecha-teecha* of an ovenbird; the rich melodious *pidoo-pidoo* of a Baltimore oriole; the haunting, ethereal, descending *vrdi-vrreed-vrreed-vreer-vreer* of a veery; and the flute-like *ee-o-lay* of a wood thrush.

PRESENT AND FUTURE

My gaze drifted back to russet-tipped goldenrod leaves. This plant was, I discovered, a wrinkleleaf goldenrod, a flowering perennial that favors wet soils, a wildflower that in late summer and early fall provides a rich supply of sweet nectar and abundant pollen to more than a hundred species of butterflies and moths, and that in winter yields plentiful seeds for juncos, sparrows, and finches.

Something about this plant growing in a perfect location in this wild wetland, providing for the insects and birds, and in turn being propagated by those same insects and birds seemed to draw me closer to a deep pulse of life, a pulse that instantly induced a shift toward mind/body wellness and a connection to that matrix of life.

Perhaps Hankins Pond will remain in limbo. Or maybe this wetland will be designated as a nature preserve. I pictured a guided nature path, a boardwalk out into the marsh, and an observation tower where all could come to see, listen, and connect with the complex and ever-changing beauty of a wild wetland, a place where all could appreciate the healing gift of wildness that nature bestows.

SISTER IN THE SUNRISE

The boardwalk, a tenth of a mile long, crossed over a wide, scrubby salt marsh, providing a transition from the paved parking lot to a four-mile-long stretch of undeveloped barrier island beach. The day I visited, the marsh, a beautiful natural habitat, was home to clapper rails that greeted the day with *tek-tek-tek* calls. A mockingbird, another early riser, saluted the dawn with harsh *tchack-tchack* calls.

Reaching the end of the boardwalk, I saw bands of orange and yellow inching above the eastern horizon. With a sense of relief, I realized I would make it to the beach in time for sunrise.

Down the steps, onto the beach, toward the surf I walked, passing by a flock of sanderlings—small, gray, ubiquitous sandpipers. They had been roosting for the night high on the beach, crouched down on the sand or resting on one leg. In the dim light, seemingly still half-asleep, the sanderlings barely responded as I walked by. Early morning beach buddies I thought.

I set up my chair near the shoreline, glanced down at the sand, and saw a scattering of tiny sanderling footprints At first glance the footprints seemed random, but as I studied them I realized that in the moment of their making, each step of the sanderlings had been purposeful—a search for food, shelter, a mate, or for a purpose known only to them.

On Time

A brightening band of orange pushed above the ocean topped by a yellow arc crowned by a puff of pink. Right on time, the life-giver, the symbol of hope and renewal, the bright yellow orb of the sun inched above the horizon.

I watched the sun continue its steady ascent, saw it change from a tiny ball to a large glowing orb topped by a bright, golden, mushroom-shaped cloud. Beams of light shot across the water toward the beach, illuminated the crests of the waves, and cast a glow upon the sand.

When the first beams of sunlight touched my chest, I immediately felt a shift in my breathing—open, smooth, full, satisfying, uplifting, and welcoming inspirations. Few things are better than being present for the sunrise.

SHELLS

I settled in, emptied my mind as best as I could, and directed my attention to the sights and sounds around me. Watching the crests of the waves form and fall, I heard the sounds of the waves thump and splash onto the shore. I inhaled the fresh salt air. The colors of the blue-gray water and the tan sand came to life in the brightening sunlight.

In front of me lay a patch of partially ground up sea shells, the bigger fragments catching and reflecting the sunlight. I studied the shells and discerned a variety of colors—white, beige, tan, brown, orange, gray. I saw the remnants of shapes—cones, fans, and tubes. I watched the waves pounding ashore, pile into the shells, and push them around. I was witnessing the grinding of shells into sand. Looking around I saw more finely ground shells to one side and fine, pure sand to the other side.

It was the great grinding of innumerable, uncountable seashells into fine sand. I felt small and insignificant in the face of this process. I could have felt diminished, could have felt that I too was a fragile chunk of minerals being ground to sand by the waves of time and circumstance, but instead I felt a sense of relief, felt joined to greater processes of life.

MOMENTS

Looking down the beach, I noticed patches of mirror-like wet sand forming as the waves receded. The shiny, wet areas seemed to be growing larger. The tide was ebbing, the water pulling back from the beach.

I recalled that the human body is 60 percent water. Is it possible that I too could feel the pull of the ebbing tide?

I always liked looking at the effects of the tide—the surge of high water inundating the salt marshes at high tide and the bird-attracting mudflats at low tide. Gazing at the receding surf, I felt a sense of connection with the rhythm of the tide.

A line of pelicans flew by, skimming just above the water, large and ungainly, almost comical-looking birds when perched, but graceful and powerful in flight, coordinated and efficient. The lead bird took on the wind, flapped and glided; the others followed in perfect unity, the delicate communication of the flock running on autopilot.

Fully absorbed in the view of the pelicans winging over the pale-blue water, watching their sharp silhouettes against a blueing sky, I experienced a moment of equanimity, a feeling of peace

SOUNDS

I listened to the waves, a soft hissing as the water rolled up on the sand. Further out where the waves first broke, a variety of sounds—*kerthump, poosh, fussshhh, paashhh.* The sounds overlapped and mingled. No pattern. Closer in, the waves offered endless variations of softer sounds—*kerpoosh, kershh, swooshhh.*

These were entrancing sounds. I had always thought about and listened to the collective sound of the surf, but now I heard complex, random, soothing, ever-varying notes and tones.

THE FELLOWSHIP OF THE SURF

There were others on the beach to view the sunrise. Two young men arrived just after I set up. They looked more like partying types, but there they were, dressed in hoodies, shorts, and baseball caps, quietly taking in the sunrise.

An older woman dressed in a yellow rain parka walked by. A young woman jogged by. Two fishermen wheeled a wagon jammed with fishing gear down the beach. A few people waved, smiled, or said hi as they walked by, but most seemed absorbed in their own thoughts.

It was toward the end of my hour when I heard a woman's conversational voice right next to me. "Oh, that's a good idea to bring a journal to the beach."

With a bit of reluctance, I pulled myself out of my focused state and explained that I was writing up my impressions from an hour sitting and watching the sunrise.

The woman continued, "I come out to the beach every morning and take a walk at sunrise."

I responded that that seemed like a great way to start the day. She elaborated that she lived in downtown St. Augustine and drove out to walk this stretch of beach, her favorite.

I was hoping that our conversation might wind down so I could enjoy the last few minutes of my sit spot hour, but it seemed like we were becoming conversational friends.

She said, "My younger sister died suddenly two years ago. She was the picture of fitness and health. When I come out here and walk the beach, I feel like I am with her."

I know enough from my years of clinical practice to understand the depths of grief and the difficulty of coping with loss. I felt myself slipping into therapist mode and accordingly offered comments of condolence, support, and what I hoped were words of encouragement.

And then, things got a little weird. She said, "My sister appears as a circle of light, a bright green circle of light above the ocean near the rising sun."

She paused and continued, "Her circle of light matches what's going on. If I've been to yoga, she is moving around as if she is doing stretches. If I'm in a quiet mood, she holds steady in the sky."

She pulled out her cell phone and showed me two photos. In each a small, green circle of light floated over the ocean near the sun. My western, scientific mind kicked into gear. I figured the circles were some kind of reflection or photographic artifact. I tried to hide my skepticism and murmured that I was glad that she had this connection with her sister and that it must give her a great deal of comfort.

At that moment a dolphin broke the surface of the water. The woman said, "Oh, if there is one dolphin there must be a school of them. I better get walking."

With that she said good-bye and headed down the beach. Just then another dolphin breached. She turned back toward me, pointed, and waved.

I dismissed the incident, putting it in the category of some of the strange ways people cope with loss. A week later when I was back home I looked through the series of pictures I had snapped of the sunrise that morning. Picture by picture I saw the steady sequence of the sun growing from a tiny ball to a large glowing orb. In the pictures—the sun, ocean, and sky.

But I stopped when I got to the last photo. There, next to the sun was a small, luminous, bright green circle, exactly as it had been in the photos the woman had showed me. Was it possible that her sister had paid me a visit too?

I was surprised and humbled. I realized there may be dimensions of healing in nature far beyond anything that was ever covered in my professional psychology training, my continuing education, or even in the scientific literature.

I felt thankful for the visit from this woman; grateful that she expanded my view of the healing potentials of nature.

CHAPTER 8

Returns

E ACH SIT SPOT SESSION I'VE CONDUCTED IS LOCKED INTO MY episodic memory like a video clip complete with sounds, sights, smells, and tactile sensations. The sensory memories in turn are linked to positive emotions—awe, joy, and gratitude—and accompanied by interludes of discovery and moments of insight. It is no wonder that I like returning to previous sit spot locations.

Those times when I practiced silence, sat still, and merged into mindfulness forged a sense of connection to nature. There, the superficial, the acquired, and the turbulent trappings of everyday life faded away. There, the self-understanding and increased access to inner depths of being seemed to open up space for unfolding my little share of human potential.

Given these experiences, I have an emotional attachment to each of these locations. Not the negative kind of attachment that leads to dependence, but a positive bond, a relationship that fosters growth and learning and encourages knowledge of self. It is an attachment to the places, times, and experiences that have mentored my growth and development.

These feelings of attachment fit with the biophilia model for explaining the benefits of time in nature. According to this perspective, since humans evolved in nature, we have a biologically based connection to nature and a love for nature that provided our ancestors with safety, shelter, and food. This connection is so deep that it now extends to "aesthetic, intellectual, cognitive, and even spiritual meaning and satisfaction." Accordingly, there is a desire to return to nature to resynchronize and regain physical, emotional, and mental equanimity.

When I have had the opportunity to return for a sitting session at one of my favorite locations, it has usually been an intriguing blend of same and different. Basic elements such as the location and the terrain remained the same, but other elements changed. A different season or a different time of day introduced shifts in the angles and intensity of light; in the sounds of wind, waves, and birdsong; in the animals present; in the growth phase of the plants and trees; and even in the fragrances of earth and water. That which remained the same deepened my appreciation of the spot. That which changed opened up new perspectives, new views, and new learning, all of which deepened my bond to the place.

The first return trip described in this section—**A Return to My Home Sit Spot**—is about what I refer to as my home sit spot located on a little peninsula along the shoreline of Prompton Lake. This is the spot I went to once a week during my year of nature observations described in *The Stillness of the Living Forest*. It is the place where I first passed the forty-minute threshold, where I learned to practice sensory awareness, first sampled forest mindfulness, and eventually formed a deep nature connection. I try to return at least once a year to check things out on the little peninsula. This particular return was for me a blend of revisiting the known and experiencing the new, of witnessing the changes created by ever-resilient, ever-responsive nature.

The second selection—**A Return to the Rachel Carson Preserve**—describes a return to one of my favorite sit spots—a beautiful preserve near Beaufort, North Carolina. My first visit there took place at the halfway point of my Forest Stillness year. At the beginning, that session didn't seem promising as it was squeezed in between social obligations and conducted on a cloudy, rainy, blustery morning. It turned out, however, to be a watershed experience.

I sat and watched the tide ebb and witnessed a distinct phase in the daily rhythm of a tidal marsh. I saw the shorebirds gathering to feed on the emerging mudflats and watched the terns and pelicans arrive right on time to hunt the shallowing waters. It was a scene that tuned me in to deep life rhythms of the tide. Ever since that day I look forward to returning to the preserve once a year for another view of the seaside nature that Rachel Carson loved, studied, and did her best to protect.

The third selection, **The Promise**, is about a sit spot in the forest that I returned to in the spring after having visited a few months before on a cold midwinter day, and I saw nature fulfill its promise of rebirth.

A RETURN TO MY HOME SIT SPOT

Before sunrise on a cold, gray morning in early December I pulled into the parking lot at Prompton Lake. Easing the car door open, I heard loud insistent cawing, looked up, and spotted six crows circling around a tall leafless maple tree. They landed in the skeletal branches, flapped back into the air, then landed again. When I stepped out of the car, the crows suddenly fell silent.

Quite a greeting, I thought as I shouldered my gear and prepared to walk through the woods to my home sit spot along the shoreline of Prompton Lake. Then a thought came to mind. The crows were scolding me for being away too long. When they saw that I was heading to my sit spot, they calmed down.

What a ridiculous idea! An idea, I reasoned, that was probably more a projection of my own guilt, my own feelings of omission for not visiting that site in the woods that had so rejuvenated me during the weekly visits of my Forest Stillness year. Or was it ridiculous? Maybe nature does speak to us in various voices.

Stepping onto the West Shore Trail, I felt motor memory take over as my feet guided me along the trail and through the woods. After stone-stepping across the softly flowing seep, my feet knew exactly where to turn off the trail and knew the way through the woods to the little peninsula. I walked past a huge rock dusted with snow, then by a long-ago discarded tire, a discordant image that I remembered well. The tire was sunk a little deeper in the ground and covered with more layers of leaf litter, but still there. Sadly, I realized that it takes a very long time for a tire to decompose.

A RETURN TO THE PROCESS

I set up my camp stool under the familiar big black cherry tree; sat down; pulled out my notebook; drew a circle for my first ten-minute observation interval; and began to look, listen, and jot down my impressions.

My vision jumped from tree to tree, out to the lake, and down to the ground. My hearing chased every sound—the distant whoosh of traffic along US Route 6, the roar of a pickup truck heading north on Creek Road, and the sigh of a jetliner flying high above. All of these human-made sounds annoyed me. Could I ever find a place free from the sounds of traffic, free from noise caused by humans?

I heard a few birds too—the distant honking of Canada geese, a blue jay calling a tinny *keedoo-keedoo*, a red-bellied woodpecker uttering a staccato *chur-chur-chur*. I scanned the woods but couldn't catch a glimpse of any birds, which felt disappointing and frustrating.

Then I remembered the steps to take when conducting a sit spot, the systematic steps of sensory awareness. I took three deep breaths, relaxed my shoulders, and pictured myself at the center of a circle of sights, sounds, and sensations. I began to listen, look, and feel, to simply be in the moment.

Gradually, I reentered that familiar state of forest mindfulness that I had discovered during my year of weekly visits. Nature around me began to seem coherent. I noticed the decorative white icing of snow topping the fallen trees that lay across the forest floor, the verdant greens of the mosses growing at the base of the trees, and the colonies of green and blue lichen that grew upon the tree trunks. Glancing up, I saw the symmetrical-patterned swirls of gray-black tree branches, pleasing fractals against a pale-blue sky.

The birdsongs began to slowly blend into a winter morning chorus— the back and forth *jay-jay-jay* of blue jays; the soft *click-click-click* of a flock of foraging dark-eyed juncos; and the distant, hoarse, far-carrying *cr-r-ruck-cr-r-ruck* of a raven. Nearby, I heard the faint *drip-drip-drip* of melting snow falling from an angled branch of the black cherry tree.

I thought there was no wind, but when I looked down I saw a single brown blade of grass sway ever so gently back and forth. Then I felt a faint breeze touch my cheek, felt the full and invigorating freshness of forest air caressing my skin. I inhaled the fragrance of earth and composting leaves and snow and lake.

THE THREE

On this gray morning I wasn't expecting to see a colorful sunrise, but decided to check. Turning around to the southeast, I was surprised to see a splash of bright gold surrounded by an aura of pale-yellow.

I remembered then—the sunrise always provides a color show, sometimes spectacular and multicolored, and sometimes, like today, subtle with hues of gold and yellow on a gray-blue canvas.

Looking at the woods ahead of me, I saw the first beams of sunlight illuminate the tops of the nearby trees. I felt the first rays of sunlight and sun warmth touch my neck and shoulders. I felt the daily gift of renewal fill my heart.

I looked over the lake and spotted a seagull in flight—slender, graceful, long angled wings steadily and effortlessly stroking the air. It was a ring-billed gull, and it looked like it could fly forever. Glancing to the shoreline, I noticed bright red clusters of common winterberry—splashes of color on a gray morning.

Opened by these views of beauty, I thought about the three Platonic properties of being—the good, the beautiful, and the true. I reflected that the true could be considered the realm of the intellect, of science and philosophy, a realm realized through rigorous search. The good was the realm of the conscience, of the mind and heart that requires a constant and arduous struggle to find the right path amidst the constantly shifting demands and circumstances of life.

The beautiful was the realm of the senses and the heart. In this moment, surrounded as I was by the beauty of nature, it seemed the most accessible of the three. And I thought that perhaps the inspiration offered by the beauty of nature might energize and encourage the pursuit of the good and true.

FORTY-MINUTE MAGIC

Watching the minutes tick by, I remembered Jon Young's admonition in his book *What the Robin Knows* that it usually takes forty minutes of sitting still for the birds and mammals to settle down, for the sitter to calm down and blend in, and for the sitter to really begin to see.

Did I still have to pay this forty-minute price before nature might reveal any gifts? I checked my watch. Forty minutes had elapsed.

I heard distant squeaks and chirps drawing closer. Scanning the woods I spotted a little band of five chickadees flitting through the forest. Other than the two seagulls, these were the first birds I saw. The little gray, black, and white birds came closer, fluttered in, perched on nearby branches, chattered back and forth, noticed me, and spread the news of my presence with cheerful *chick-a-dee-dee* calls.

Looking ahead into the woods, I saw an impressively large bird flying through the trees, dipping up and down—a pileated woodpecker. Two crows flew overhead so low that I could hear their wing beats. The loud, clear, descending *kee-yer, kee-yer, kee-yer* of a red-shouldered hawk carried through the morning air.

Then, I was surprised to hear a raspy *quack, quack, quack* from the lake behind me—a hen mallard. I turned, spotted a patch of open water near the far shoreline, and scanned with my binoculars. No mallard, but I did spot a solitary female common merganser, crested rufous head and long orange saw bill, carving a V across the still cold water. The ducks, resilient and adaptable, lingered on the lake as long as there was open water.

I turned and gazed back into the woods. Something small and tan was moving. A leaf drifting down? No, it was moving up and down and back and forth. I stared steadily and then was stunned to realize it was a moth. I followed its flight and watched it land on the tan and brown leaf litter where it immediately blended in.

This was, I learned later, a winter moth, a species that emerges in November and December. Seconds later another moth took flight, flapped delicately through the woods, and landed on a patch of snow.

The forty-minute wait had been worthwhile. I could see, hear, and feel that the winter woods were alive with surprises and lessons, secrets revealed, and gifts for the mind and heart.

CHANGES

My hour was up. I stood, stretched, and then strolled around to explore the peninsula. I discovered a white pine seedling, just inches tall, tan growth bud atop a spray of delicate long green needles. Thirty feet away I found a hemlock sapling, almost two feet tall, a swirl of dense, dark-green, short-needled branches.

Both of these little trees were new to the peninsula. They represented the natural process of forest succession—the gradual return of the pines and hemlocks that had in precolonial times blanketed this portion of Pennsylvania. No one had planted these trees but they were there, the seeds spread by the wind, birds, squirrels, and chipmunks.

I noticed a patch of green at my feet—tiny plants that looked like petite Christmas trees. They were flat-branched tree clubmoss, more commonly known as princess pine, plants that were overharvested in the past to use for holiday decorations and are now legally protected. This plant of the shady mature forest had also returned.

Nearby I discovered a row of light-green, lacy-leafed plants, fan clubmoss, also known as ground cedar as the foliage looks very much like familiar cedar boughs. This is another plant that finds its way into returning forests and over time creates larges patches of green that are pleasing to the eye in winter.

I saw an ash tree that looked as if it had a collar of green around the base of the trunk. I walked closer and studied the dense fern-like tendrils. A quick check with my *Picture This* app informed me that I was gazing at delicate fern moss, aptly described as "delicate moss that resembles an assortment of tiny ferns." I read further that birds use it for nesting material and small animals use if for protective cover. This fern moss is said to symbolize fascination, sincerity, and magic.

Five new plants were growing on the little peninsula, plants that were part of a process of natural progression and succession. No human hand had sown these plants. They all found their timely way to this "just-right" setting, to the conditions they required.

I headed back through the woods, walking alongside an old stone wall, a moss-covered remnant that had once bordered a farm field. Visions of a hot breakfast of coffee, omelette, and toast came to mind for I had become chilled during my hour of sitting still. I reflected on the five new plants I had seen. Something about the appearance or perhaps the reappearance of these plants infused me with a sense of hope, a feeling I carried with me as I stepped back along the trail.

A RETURN TO THE RACHEL CARSON RESERVE

Four hundred miles to the north, hurricane Zeta churned out to sea. In Beaufort, North Carolina, the remnants of Zeta's outer wall blew fifty-miles-per-hour wind gusts down the narrow channel of Taylor's Creek. With this wind and the additional pull of a strong tidal current, I wasn't sure if it would be safe to paddle my kayak across the creek to the landing for the Carrot Island Boardwalk in the Rachel Carson Reserve, my destination for a sit spot session.

The reserve, with its salt marshes, tidal flats, vast beds of sea grass, maritime shrub thickets, and herd of feral horses, was one of my favorite sitting locations, and I very much wanted to return. I first visited the reserve during my year of sitting described in my book *The Stillness of the Living Forest: A Year of Listening and Learning.* On that occasion I witnessed the beauty of abundant life as the tide dropped, mudflats emerged, shorebirds flew in to feed—all of it revealing the nurturing cycle of tidal ebb and flow.

I supposed that I had developed a kind of psychological connection or attachment to this reserve. The stark beauty of the salt marshes; the reassuring, life-sustaining rhythm of the tides; and the life story of Rachel Carson, who loved, learned and wrote about this maritime world, touched my heart. This was an environment that had nourished and sustained her vision of humans feeling connected to and caring for the natural world.

So Close, So Far

With a scrape against the angled concrete of the boat ramp, I launched my kayak into the waves and wind. With extra strokes and some sideways paddling, I worked my way across the channel and safely reached the sandy landing. Jumping out of my kayak, I dragged it well above the high tide line and secured it to a piling with a bungee cord. I had no desire to be stranded on this island in these conditions.

Heading across Carrot Island, I followed a narrow sandy trail that ran next to and beneath the boardwalk. With each step I left behind the sounds of civilization that carried from across the creek— the buzz of traffic, the bleating of backup horns, the whirring of the big cranes at the marina. I slowly entered a nature soundscape, wind whooshing through red cedar boughs, gulls crying, waves crashing on a distant shoreline.

Alongside the trail the dark-green boughs of red cedars were covered with blueish berries that when crushed between my fingers exuded a fresh, spicy, juniper fragrance. Higher up on the sand dunes, stunted, shiny-leafed live oaks leaned into the sea breeze. Next to the trail, stems of butter-yellow goldenrod blooms and flowers of orange-yellow seaside asters provided spots of bright color. Near my feet hundreds of tiny ghost crabs scuttled across the sand, seeking shelter amidst sea grass stems.

I reached the marsh side of the island and sat down on a boat cushion on the sand beneath the observation deck where I was mostly out of the wind. With the sun warming my face I pulled out my notebook and began to write down all that I saw, heard, and felt during each ten-minute interval of my planned hourlong sitting session.

In front of me stretched a panorama of shrinking tidal pools, jagged black oyster beds, shiny wet mudflats, and vast swaths of tan and olive-green sea cordgrass. Beyond the sea grass stretched a zone of open, wave-flecked water edged far in the distance by the thin green line of Shackleford Banks, the slender barrier island that faced the North Atlantic Ocean. I inhaled the fresh salt smell of ocean air.

I was probably no more than a quarter of a mile from civilization but felt like I was in a completely wild and natural area. How wise it had been to protect this area from development, to preserve it in its natural state. What a fitting tribute to Rachel Carson!

A Murmuration

I began to feel as if I was sitting in an aviary. Three cormorants—sleek-bodied, long-billed, semisubmerged—swam smoothly in front of me. Scattered around the tidal pools, a half-dozen great egrets stood on long black legs in the shallows, snow-white plumage fluttering in the breeze, long spear-like bills poised to strike. To my right, on a widening mudflat, a pair of exotic-appearing, black-headed, orange-billed oystercatchers poked slowly through upturned shells.

A trio of white-and-gray laughing gulls flapped lazily overhead, calling *kiiwa, kiiwaa*. A blue heron took off with a loud hoarse squawk, long wings flapping, long legs trailing. Two willets flew by, flashing long, slender, dark-and-white-patterned wings, calling a clear ringing *kyaah-yah, kyaah-yah*.

Far over the open water I saw a long gray shape moving. Puzzled, I brought up my binoculars and focused on a vast flock of sandpipers, too far away to identify. I watched the flock grow in size, hundreds, no, a thousand or more birds, a cloud of birds. As I watched, the sandpipers organized themselves into a long slender column that began to move over the water. The front of the column dipped down, the rest followed. The front rose, the rest followed. Soon the column undulated across the water like a long, thick, loose caterpillar, rising and falling, crawling through the air—a murmuration of sandpipers. Spellbound I watched the rising and falling column of birds, the unspoken, fluid, ever-changing, precise coordination of myriad wings and bodies through space and time. How did they manage it? What was the purpose? Gradually, they faded from sight.

WILD

Binoculars still in hand I scanned the mudflats and the tidal pools to my left. Suddenly, my view was obscured by a tawny-brown shape. Pulling down my binoculars, I saw a feral horse, a stallion, standing about thirty yards away, head down, peacefully grazing on sea grass.

I was surprised and pleased. Last night I had overheard a woman at a restaurant saying how she had searched long and hard for a view of the wild horses, but without success. It was, I thought, a good reminder of the value of sitting still in nature, a reminder of how nature reveals herself to those who sit and wait.

The horse, seemingly oblivious to my presence, continued to graze. Surely he was aware, could smell and see me, but the opportunity to munch on a stand of thick grass available at low tide was most likely more important. He edged slowly forward. I studied his form—lustrous, rich-brown coat; sharp pointy ears up; long tail occasionally swishing back and forth. He looked robust and healthy.

As the horse stepped slowly forward, a white-plumaged egret waded slowly toward him. Soon the two living beings neared each other, each with its own manner of movement, its own deliberate style of feeding. The feral horse and the white egret were sharing space, coexisting, part of a greater harmony.

COMMUNITIES

Two terns flew by—white plumage, black eye patch, trim bodies, slender streamlined wings. They flew lazily yet alertly while scanning the tidal pool below. Suddenly, one folded its wings, dropped like a rock, splashed into the water, and emerged with a small shiny fish that it quickly swallowed. The second bird flapped a few feet further, dove down, but came up with an empty bill. The terns took flight and resumed their hunting patrol over the tidal ponds.

Out in front of me on a mudflat, three laughing gulls stood facing into the wind as if arranged by an artist, the birds choosing exactly the same angle of least resistance into the wind. There was something patient, timeless, soothing, and peaceful about their posture.

More shorebirds flew in and landed on the mudflat to my right. I was looking into the sun, so it was hard to identify them. Through my binoculars I saw brightly illuminated silhouettes—some small, some medium-sized, some larger, some with short bills, some with longer bills, some bills upcurved, some downcurved. Flocks of each kind flew in, landed, and began to busily move around and feed on the fertile mudflats, each finding its own feeding niche.

The stallion browsing nearby let out a loud *neeeigh*. A few minutes later, as if in response to his call, a line of horses emerged along the shoreline to my left. There were nine of them—of different sizes, some smaller and younger, each with a unique shade of brown and tan. They moved in a loose synchrony, maintaining proximity, feeding, walking along the shoreline, a community in motion, timeless, well-honed movement.

THE LONG SPEARS

In front of me at water's edge I tracked a little blue heron treading slowly through the shallow water, neck forward, head down, long, strong bill poised to strike. This was a handsome bird with striking slate-blue plumage and one I would not see at home in the Pocono Highlands of Pennsylvania. It slashed its bill down and came up with a small, tan, spiny-looking fish, held it, dropped it, speared it again, dropped it again. After a few more snatches and drops it finally left the spiny critter and moved forward. Not every catch turns into a meal.

The moment of absolute low tide arrived, and I noticed that six egrets were now wading aggressively through the shallow tidal pool in front of me. One speared down and came up with a silvery, wiggling fish. A trio of gulls moved in to steal it, but the egret held them off with a threatening wave of its bill. The other egrets were now slashing the water their long, sharp-pointed yellow bills, sometimes coming up with a fish, sometimes empty. The egrets seemed to know, to feel the moment of low tide, the time when the pool was at its shallowest, when the hunting was at its best.

The horses also seemed attuned to the moment of low tide. A contingent began to walk through the shallow water out to a distant bed of sea cordgrass, a bed that would be submerged at high tide but was now exposed and ready to be munched upon. I watched them walk slowly and purposefully out to the bed of sea grass, one leading, the others following, on time, yet part of a timeless pattern.

SHIMMERING

The late October sun settled a little lower in the sky, casting a shimmering light on the wavy wind-blown water, across the shiny black mudflats, and over the vast beds of sea grass. Strands of thick white clouds floated across the deep-blue sky. The stallion continued to feed contentedly nearby.

I noticed a tall, solitary shorebird walking through the grasses along the edge of the water in front of me. Binoculars up, I noted the field marks—brownish body, long downcurved orange bill, long orange legs. I thought white ibis, but the brown body threw me. I quickly checked my *iBird Pro* app and scanned the photos of the white ibis. This was a juvenile with brown plumage.

I was pleased. An ibis was another bird I wouldn't see at home. I also enjoyed figuring out that it was a juvenile. There is something about naming a bird, naming any part of nature. It's like learning someone's name; suddenly the relationship is deepened, the connection enhanced. With the knowledge of its name in mind, I watched the young ibis walk and feed, perfectly expressing the unique adaptations of its species.

LINGERING

My hour was up. Several more horses joined the stallion, and all of the horses were crowding in toward the observation deck. It felt like time to leave. I gathered up my gear, walked back till I found a low spot on the boardwalk, climbed up, and then came back to the observation deck.

I wasn't quite ready to leave but was past the need for systematic observation. I stood there taking in the scene—the rhythm of the tide; the movement of the feral horses, some near, some out feeding in the shallows; the calls of the gulls and willets; the whoosh of the wind through the branches. I felt the richness and abundance of life all around me. In the distance I saw the black-and-white tower of Cape Lookout Lighthouse.

I lingered and lost track of time. Even now as I write this sentence, I feel a longing to return to the Rachel Carson Reserve.

THE PROMISE

I had a promise to keep, one that I made while doing a sitting session on a windy, bitterly cold January afternoon. Surrounded by brown and gray, dead and dormant winter trees, I felt a need to see the symmetry of the seasons. I promised to return to the spot during the first week of June when the forest would be reborn, filled with new life, and resonating with spring birdsongs.

The instant I made the promise I knew I had stepped onto a slippery slope. Fail to fulfill a promise and there are consequences—a disappointment in self, an erosion of self-esteem. And to fulfill this promise I would once again have to battle my perennial twin nemeses of inertia and procrastination.

Late on the night of June 6, time, always a limited resource, was slipping away. The window of opportunity to honor my promise was almost gone. A check of the forecast revealed favorable conditions for the morning—sunny, clear, and cool. I went to sleep holding the intention to get up early and get back to the forest.

What part of the mind is it that links up with intention and brings help to fulfill commitments? My first help came in the form of spontaneously waking up at 4:30 a.m. A glance out the window revealed the faint illumination of first light beginning to spread above the horizon.

The second helper was sensory acuity. I heard a robin pierce the nighttime silence with a few tentative notes and then launch into a loud, clear, *cheer-a-lee, cheer-up, cheer-a-lee, cheer-up.* Seconds later a cardinal joined in with a whistled *purdy, purdy, purdy.* In the background a tufted titmouse softly called *here, here, here.* A gust of wind whooshed softly through the leaves. It was sit spot day and my senses were now activated.

The third helper was a cup of hot black coffee that I sipped while lacing up my boots. On sit spot mornings I could use the extra alertness that coffee always provides.

The Approach

It was over a mile to my spot in the forest, and I was glad to take an early morning walk—a simple and rich pleasure, an opportunity to transition into the world of nature. As the sun rose and cast a yellow glow on the landscape, I followed a path through a grove of newly leafed out ash trees and down a long hill surrounded by fields of tall growing grasses, wildflowers, and full foliaged bushes. I came to the edge of an old beaver pond, paused, scanned, and spotted a great blue heron standing on tall stilt legs along the far shore, preening itself with its long bill. I heard the musical *chinga, chinga, chinga* trill of a swamp sparrow, the enchanting *witchety, witchety, witchety* song of a common yellowthroat, and the harsh *chek, chek, chek* calls of a red-winged blackbird in flight.

I continued down a grassy path and then on to a little used gravel road. Arriving at the second-growth forest near my sit spot, I was surprised to see that everything looked different. The leaves were out, the weeds and grasses tall, and the shrubs thick with foliage. I wondered if I could find the spot again. Peering into the woods, I recognized a stand of tall hemlocks. I bushwhacked through a patch of blackberry brambles, located the old stone wall, found a gap, stepped through, and felt a sense of relief when I saw an old friend— Big Bob, the tall, thick maple I had named back in January.

Transitions

Setting up my camp stool in exactly the same place as last January, I sat down, pulled out my notebook, drew my first sensory awareness circle, and began to make notes. I had to shift gears to silent sitting mode. Even though I had felt immersed in nature while walking through fields and woods, I still had been moving, still hearing the sound of my footsteps, still talking to myself about directions—activities that keep mind and body busy. I took a few deep breaths and settled into silence.

I began to hear the rich soundscape around me. An eastern wood pewee whistled a plaintive *pee-awee, pee-awee.* A veery sang its ethereal, flute-like, downward spiraling *vrdi, vreed, vreed, vreer, vreer.* An ovenbird chattered its energetic *tee-cha, tee-cha, tee-cha* song. A wood thrush fluted a resonant, haunting *eee-o-lay* song. These were forest-dwelling birds whose songs share clear, resonant tones—tones that carry far in the forest.

When I was here in January, these birds were wintering down south around the Caribbean and into Central and South America. Now, after an epic journey, they had returned to this second-growth forest, to the habitat they preferred to mate, nest, breed, and feed.

I heard other sounds that had been missing in January—leaves whooshing softly in a gust of wind. Looking up I saw a thick canopy of minty-green, newly unfurled leaves, clusters swaying, rippling, and dancing in the wind.

A flash of light near the stone wall caught my eye—the gossamer strands of a spider web illuminated by the angled rays of the sun. I knew that this, like so many moments of beauty in nature, was a fleeting phenomenon requiring the just-right coating of morning dew and the just-right angle of the sun. I gazed appreciatively at the shimmering web. When I looked away and then looked back, conditions had shifted and the web vanished from view.

Hanging in Space

I hadn't seen a single bird yet but still felt surrounded by avian presence. It was, I realized, much more bird listening than bird watching. As I sat my hearing seemed to grow more acute, to reach further and further out into the woods. In the distance I heard another forest dweller—a black-throated green warbler, singing its buzzy *zoooo-zeee-zu-zu-zeet.*

A few year-round resident birds joined the morning chorus—crows cawing and a white-breasted nuthatch singing a nasal, single-pitched *whi-whi-whi-whi-whi-whi.* I wondered if these same birds had been here with me back in January.

A veery called a sharp *veer, veer, veer.* I echolocated it to a maple tree about forty yards away. A few minutes later it changed its call to *yeet, yeet, yeet.* After a few minutes another change occurred, this time to *dzup, dzup, dzup,* and then a minute later to a short, hoarse trill. One veery, variable calls. No bird guides list all of these alternative calls. I felt the delight of another nature lesson learned, a good reminder of the value of putting in "dirt time."

The angled sunlight illuminated insects fluttering through the air. I fixed my gaze in one direction for a count of ten seconds and tallied eleven insects in flight—a plethora of insect life, a fully laden table for the wood warblers and spiders. Not surprisingly, in a gap between two bushes, I spotted a spider moving on an invisible web, looking like it was moving in open space.

As I watched the spider move slowly to the left and then back to the right, I felt a sense of connection. Weren't we all like this little spider? Didn't we all have to leave the security of branch and twig and venture out into open space to find our way?

FROM THE HEART

A cloud covered the sun. The forest appeared gray and dim. The northwest wind gusted. I braced against the chill of the 54-degree air. It reminded me of January. Then the cloud floated away. Sunshine returned, warmed my face, and illuminated the forest. I relaxed into the warmth and light of spring.

A wild blackberry cane growing next to me was covered with green, serrated, arrowhead-shaped leaves and festooned with clusters of five-petaled, snow-white blossoms. The leaves were a full, rich dark-green, and in the angled sunlight I could see a fine, pale, down covering on the top of each leaf. Below the blackberry bushes grew lacy pale-green fronds of hay-scented ferns. Beneath the ferns lay last year's layers of brown and tan tree leaves, slowly breaking apart, gradually composting into the soil.

An ovenbird chattered loudly nearby. Another pewee sang its mournful song. In the distance a yellow-billed cuckoo sang a loud *cloo, cloo, cloo*. A pair of blue jays called *jay, jay, jay*. A woodpecker drilled on a hollow limb, a resonant *tat-tat-tat-tat*.

I heard the sound of my pencil tracing letters and forming words across the paper of my notebook. I was reminded of what my friend said when I took him out to a sit spot: Writing words around his sensory awareness circle brought him back to first grade when he first learned to write, when he first learned to express his inner world on paper. Sitting still and writing words to describe his observations recreated that powerful sense of discovery, that feeling of opening a door to a new world of awareness and expression. He said that as he listened, looked, and wrote, he could feel the flow of ideas from heart to mind to fingers to paper.

Fragrances

The wind blew steadily, now swishing, stirring, and whooshing the upper canopy of leaves in soft, soothing, susurrating sounds. At midcanopy the leaves swayed only a little and near the ground hardly at all. Last year's layers of brown and tan leaves covered the ground. The movement of their decomposition, of their steady return to the earth was too slow for me to detect. Only if I dug my finger down into the leaf litter would I be able to see and feel the progression from dry leaf to loam to forest soil.

I inhaled a fresh woodsy fragrance. I asked myself what exactly it smelled like. The only thing that came to mind was the fragrance of freshly washed sheets drying in breezy sunshine. But I knew that I was inhaling much more complex smells—the smells of fungi, ferns, leaves, dirt, and the volatile oils of growing trees. My nose was not sensitive enough to discern these specific fragrances, but I recognized the deep sense of well-being that these nature fragrances created. I could guess at the immediate and subliminal pathways the fragrances traveled in my brain. I could imagine the multiple areas in my cortex, nervous system, and immune system that were lighting up.

Progeny

It was good to be sitting next to Big Bob, the name I had given to the tall sugar maple growing right next to the stone wall. I liked his opportunism. He had sprouted just inside the wall thus getting a jump on the reforestation of this former pasture and now was probably over a hundred years old, approaching old growth status. If left alone he might grow for another two to three hundred years.

I liked the many signs of his resilience—the scar on his trunk from a wind-ripped limb, a stub from a storm-amputated branch, and the gaps and scattered dead branches in his canopy. Now he was burgeoning skyward into another season of growth, spreading another full green canopy into a clear blue June sky.

Because the leaves were out, I could see a wedge of young sugar maples growing downwind from Bob. The wedge was wider near Bob and then gradually tapered to a point some fifty yards downwind. These were his offspring.

Bob was actually a he/she. Starting around forty years old he/she produced drooping clusters of yellow-green flowers in the spring. Some of the flowers were male (pistillate) and some female (staminate). She/he relied on the blustery spring winds to spread the generous yellowish pollen from the boy flowers to the girl flowers. Every year clusters of fruit formed, V-shaped nutlets with a seed in the middle and with delicate wings spread at a 60-degree angle. In mid to late summer, Bob/Bobbi released the nutlets, which then helicoptered down to the ground. Those seed cases and seeds that weren't gobbled up by birds, squirrels, and chipmunks gradually decomposed, and in the warmth and moisture of the next spring, sprouted.

The leaves of the young maples were low and directly visible. I studied a single leaf, noticed its rich green color, its five delicate pointed lobes—a familiar form, the symbol of Canada, the emblem of maple syrup and maple candy.

The view of the green leaf backlit by soft, angled morning sunshine with its almost perfect form took my breath away. It seemed more beauty in form and color than was needed. But I had learned that nature was generous with beauty, spreading more than enough around, perhaps a catalyst for species evolution and individual growth.

WHO'S IN CHARGE?

A catbird flew into a young maple, chattered its jumbled mimicry song that ended with a string of plaintive *mew, mew, mew* calls. Two ovenbirds sang, one in front, one to the left. Two pewees sang, one behind me, one in the distance. A flicker flapped in, landed at the top of a dead tree, and launched into a loud, repetitive *kwik-kwik-kwik-kwik-kwik* song. The birds, I realized, were constantly on the move—calling, singing, searching for food, shifting, some patrolling their breeding territory, constant, purposeful, life-sustaining, life-advancing activity.

From the stand of hemlock trees across the stone wall, I heard a familiar *chick-a-dee-dee*. As I scanned the green boughs searching for a chickadee, I noticed that the hemlocks were in growth mode, each branch and twig end covered with a light-green tip. The equation for evergreen growth with green tips and branch divisions on every twig must be exponential.

Little saplings grew all around me. What were they? I snapped a picture of a leaf with my *Picture This* app and discovered that I was looking at sweet birch (*Betula lenta*), also known as black birch or cherry birch perhaps due to its mahogany-colored bark. The cluster of birch saplings must have been from a parent tree upwind.

Glancing around I noticed a cherry tree with a trunk that grew vertically and then angled horizontally for about five feet before continuing skyward. Right next to it grew two trees intertwined, an ash and a maple locked in an embrace, both striving for the light with their limbs, both seeking nourishment with overlapping roots spread across the forest floor, both determined to fulfill their mission of growth.

The whole forest seemed filled with vital growth force even though there were obvious signs of years, even centuries, of human impact. The old moss- and lichen-covered stone wall had been painstakingly built by the first settlers. The lingering traces of former fields and pastures told of years of agricultural use. And there was more recent evidence of human impact—harvested trees with pale stumps drying with growth rings exposed, and piles of confetti-like debris left by the chainsaws.

Objectively, based on this evidence, humans ruled this realm. But subjectively, I didn't feel that at all. The woods pulsed with life force. The signs of human impact seemed trivial, superficial, and as insignificant as drops of water off a duck's back.

My hour was up. I had fulfilled my promise by returning to the forest during the first week of June. The forest seemed to be fulfilling an even deeper promise, one that I felt, but one for which I could not find the right words. The best I could do was to describe it as the promise of perennial adaptability, resilience, and beauty.

CHAPTER 9

The Seasons

F OR MANY YEARS I LIVED WITH THE IDEA OF FOUR DISTINCT seasons—winter, spring, summer, and fall. This idea was ingrained during grade school when every September we cut out maple and oak leaves from brown, yellow, and orange construction paper and taped them to the windows of our classroom. In winter we traced and trimmed snowflakes and in spring pasted yellow daffodil flowers onto green stems. No art projects were needed for summer as my friends and I were free to run and play outside in yards, fields, and woods.

Content with these four seasons, I enjoyed and celebrated their coming and going. But during my decades of full-time work, I gradually lost touch with the seasons. The peak of the fall colors seemed to arrive during the middle of the work week. By the time the weekend rolled around and I could get out to enjoy the spectacle, rain fell, leaves dropped, and the colors were gone. Or the white fluffy snow that fell on Tuesday turned to gray slush or a layer of ice by the time I was free on Saturday. And the first warm day of spring found me looking longingly from my office window.

One of the reasons for committing to my year of weekly nature observations was to reconnect with and re-experience the seasons. I started my year in winter, and at first it just seemed like winter—cold, snowy, and windy. But as the weeks passed and my senses sharpened, as spring approached, and as more moments of mindfulness arose, I began to notice changes from week to week. I saw the progression from the first greening of the ferns, to the first tentative tree leaves, to a fully green canopy. I saw the colors of the leaves progress from a delicate yellow-green to a rich forest-green.

I noticed weekly changes in the bird life as well. As soon as the ice melted, the geese, mallards, and mergansers showed up on the lake to rest and feed and continue their journey north. By early April the first songbirds, robins, and red-winged blackbirds arrived, and I heard their territorial songs at sunrise. Every week new migrants appeared and new songs filled the air.

I watched the wildflowers progress from April wood anemones and trilliums, to June daisies and black-eyed Susans, and late summer purple asters, goldenrods, white bonesets, and dusty-pink Joe Pye weeds. I saw the coats of deer change from winter brown-gray to summer tan and in the fall back to brown-gray.

As I witnessed these weekly changes in the flora and fauna, my concept of the four seasons blurred and then faded away entirely. I began to think of multiple springs progressing from hints of spring to early-early spring, early spring, early mid-spring, mid-spring, full spring, and on and on. Each of the four seasons seemed similarly filled with constant gradations of change.

I also began to notice overlap between and interpenetration of the seasons. There were hints of spring as early as January when the male chickadees first voiced their sweetie pie calls. I saw hints of full summer in the opening willow leaves of April, hints of fall in the brown going-to-seed grasses of July, and hints of winter in the first frosts of October. Each week had its own story of the seasons, of change. Each week became a teachable moment, a lesson about the cycles and seasons of nature.

At first this learning was mostly nature-based content, but as time passed the lessons came to be imbued with insights. I observed how each plant and tree sped into and through its unique time slot to sprout, grow, blossom, bear fruit, and spread seeds. I saw the same with birds building nests, laying eggs, and hatching, and then I heard the feeding calls of the hungry juveniles and saw the busy parents caring for their young. Everything in nature moved quickly.

I saw how each living thing had its season, and I reflected with poignancy how the same certainly applies to humans. Sensing my own mortality, my first reactions were fear of death and sadness for the impending loss of the pleasures of life. But gradually, as I watched the story of each week unfold, my reactions began to shift. It seemed valuable to puncture the human delusion of unlimited time.

I began to realize that observing the seasons had the potential to promote a mindful nature connection. Micah Mortali explained in his book *Rewilding* that when we see the change of seasons, we are confronted with the reality of impermanence, a realization that can create uneasiness, feelings of loss, even sadness. But this discomfort, this unmooring from our normal perception can also nudge us to a more observational and mindful state. As Mortali writes, "It is in surrendering and opening to this essential impermanence of nature that we can begin to live in harmony with our world, taking each moment as a gift and giving thanks for the moments we have, as precious and miraculous as they are."

The following sit spot stories provide snapshots of little seasons within the big seasons, capture the richness and constancy of change, and offer opportunities for mindful reflection.

In the first selection below, **Fragrance Week**, I describe my discovery of what has become one of my favorite weeks in spring, It occurs at the end of May when the Russian olive and honeysuckle blossoms fill the air with fragrance, a fragrance laden with the promise of ripe berries. And while fragrance was the primary impression of the week, there were many other birds, plants, and insects actively engaged in their spring cycle of life. Now I anticipate fragrance week each year when it rolls around.

The second selection, **Midsummer**, tells the story of what I experienced in early July when the season of warmth and growth reached a peak and seemed as if it might go on forever. But amidst the fullness of summer, the signs of the speeding season and the coming dramatic changes of fall were there to be seen.

Through the events recounted in the third selection, **October Sunrise**, I learned that even as leaves fell, the temperature dropped, and most birds were flying south, some birds, in this case mallards, were busy courting, pairing off, and preparing for next spring's breeding season.

Winter Winds, the fourth selection, is about my decision to study the wind on a cold, gray December day in what at first glance looked like a lifeless forest. I learned that the winter woods are filled with life, the promise of renewal, and expressions of adaptability and resilience.

FRAGRANCE WEEK

The idea to conduct a sit spot session on a warm spring evening came to mind during dinner. Quickly finishing the dishes, I grabbed my binoculars and camp chair, cut across the yard, angled through a stand of tall, slender ashes and maples that had recently leafed out, and headed down the path to a beaver pond.

I found myself walking slowly, not due to a conscious decision but more likely as a response to the time of day, the lower angle of the sun, the softer illumination, the longer shadows, the sense that daylight was slowly sliding into night.

From a bush by the side of the trail, a bird sang loud, clear phrases. I discerned a pattern—two bell-like whistles, two chattery twitters, two clear high to low tones. It was the song of a brown thrasher, a spectacular mimic whose repertoire might include a thousand different song snippets.

Ahead on the path I noticed two brown lumps in the freshly mown grass. A quick look through my binoculars revealed two rabbits peacefully munching grass. A rustling in the bushes, twigs snapping, and a deer in its light-tan summer coat appeared, standing still and gazing at me with large, soft, brown eyes. The deer slipped silently away. I continued my walk.

A whiff of fragrance grabbed my attention. The fragrance grew in intensity. I felt like I was walking by a department store perfume counter. But these fragrances were cleaner and clearer, stronger and more compelling than any commercial perfumes. Looking around I saw that I was entering a vale of blossoms—Russian olive trees and honeysuckle bushes blooming in profusion along both sides of the trail.

I stopped to study the blossoms. The Russian olive trees were covered with petite, creamy-white flowers. The honeysuckles were blanketed with delicate tubular flowers—some soft-white, others light-pink. I inhaled the fragrance of each—a spicy, clove-like sweetness from the Russian olives and a sultry, melon-sweet aroma from the honeysuckles.

Savoring these fragrances, I continued on and arrived at the beaver pond, one in a series of ponds stretching upstream, hidden wild ponds mere minutes away from paved streets, neat houses, freshly mowed yards, and a busy state highway. The still surface of the pond reflected the far shoreline, a mirror image of trees, shrubs, reeds, and grasses. I set up my chair, sat down, and began to take notes on all that I saw and heard.

Familiar birdsongs sounded around me—the *sweet, sweet, sweet, I'm-so-sweet* of a yellow warbler; the rhythmic rolling *witchety, witchety, witchey* of a yellowthroat; the plaintive mew of a catbird; and the chatty aria of a song sparrow. It was late May. The birds were established on their breeding territory, guarding their turf with song.

Canada geese honked softly from an upstream pond. A beaver swam by, tracing a silent V in the water. Five deer grazed peacefully in a lush, green, hillside hayfield beyond the pond. The melancholy *coo, coo, coo* of a mourning dove floated down from a tall drooping willow across the pond. A cloud of insects swirled in front of me. A bull frog croaked intermittently.

Birds flew around the pond. Grackles, big and black with shiny, iridescent purple heads, singing a harsh *kh-shee* song. Red-winged blackbirds, the males flashing their brilliant orange wing bars, looping over the pond, perching on reeds, and singing a clear *konk-la-ree*. I heard a harsh squawk, looked up, and saw a great blue heron in flight, long wings flapping rhythmically, long head and beak protruding forward, long legs extended back like landing gear.

On an impulse I picked up my binoculars, scanned the top branches of the willow and spotted a bright orange and black Baltimore oriole perched on an uppermost twig. Soon its melodious piping *pidoo, tewdi, tewdi yeew* song joined the evening chorus. I loved these moments when it seemed as if intuition guided my gaze, told me where to look, and then rewarded me with a glimpse of beauty.

A beaver swam by dragging a ten-foot-long sapling with a cluster of green leaves at the top. Figuring this was an opportunity to study beaver behavior up close, I locked on with my binoculars and watched as it swam steadily, branch held firmly in its teeth, on course, undeterred by obstacles, toward its lodge, an impressive dome of branches, twigs, and mud.

Dark-brown and as big as a small chocolate Lab, the beaver climbed out of the water, dragging the branch in its teeth. Deftly lifting the branch up to the top of the lodge, it made a few quick and decisive adjustments with the placement, released it, turned, climbed down the side of the lodge, slipped into the water, and swam off to find another branch. The beaver looked like a decisive engineer at work, no need to double check the placement, just unerring and natural precision, and then dutifully on to the next task.

A puff of wind wafted the fragrance of the honeysuckles and Russian olives into my nostrils. I felt enveloped by and bathed in sweet fragrance. I inhaled deeply and savored the perfumed air. There had been no rain for five days, no downpours to dampen the flowers, just sunshine to open the blossoms fully. This might be the best week of spring, maybe even the best day of the year to smell the fragrance of these spring blossoms.

I reflected that these fragrances, so pleasing to me, were, in fact, part of a busy, time-urgent process. The sweet aromas were designed to attract pollinators—bees, butterflies, beetles, moths, ants, and even birds. I gazed at the nearest honeysuckle and saw that it was loaded with bees crawling over the flowers, spreading pollen, facilitating fertilization. In a few weeks this bush would be coated with tiny green berries, fruits that would ripen to a rich red in the summer sun.

Forty minutes had passed and I could feel my mind and senses and nervous system settling into nature. I began to discern songs that I hadn't noticed before—a swamp sparrow's reedy trill, a redstart's staccato burst, and the raspy *bee-buzz, bee-buzz* of a blue-winged warbler.

Three birds fluttered around the top branches of the big willow across the pond. A look through the binoculars revealed a trio of cedar waxwings perching on branch tips, sallying out, snatching insects, perching, snatching, and feasting on the bugs. A volley of musical twitters sounded above me—a pair of tree swallows swooping, dodging, weaving, and grabbing the mosquitoes that swarmed above the pond. A fluttering of wings ahead was an eastern kingbird perched on a snag that rose above the pond; it darted out, plucked bugs out of the air, settled back, darted and plucked again, feeding with ruthless efficiency.

The sun slipped below the horizon and daylight faded to last light. A draft of cool air drifted downhill, the first hint of the approaching night chill. The frogs, somehow knowing exactly when the sun set, began to tune up for their nighttime chorus of croaks and calls. Crickets started their steady chirping. Mosquitoes hummed around me.

My hour was up, yet I lingered. A part of me wanted to stay, pitch a tent, crawl into a cozy sleeping bag, watch the final strands of daylight fade, and listen to the soothing chorus of springtime night sounds. How welcome it would be to cast away the tasks and obligations that awaited me just a short walk away at home and immerse myself in nocturnal solitude.

Then it occurred to me that perhaps I could do both—come to this wild beaver pond for rest and rejuvenation and return home restored and refreshed. On a different day, at a different time, I could return for a different experience. But today I was glad that I had learned about fragrance week, a week that captured the essence of spring, a week I would look forward to in coming years.

MIDSUMMER

Wet, dew-covered grass muffled the sound of my footsteps as I strode down the wide, mowed path toward the old beaver pond. Small, young, brown rabbits, plentiful this summer, nibbled on the green grass and scampered away at my approach.

Ahead I saw the rounded form of trees rising above the early morning mist. There was something evocative about the shapes of the trees in full summer growth, something compelling about the form of branch upon branch, leaf upon leaf, rich rounded contours repeating again and again and again. I felt an uplifting, inspiring sense of beauty and at the same time a settled feeling flowing from shoulders to feet to earth.

Alongside the path, the midsummer wildflowers were in full bloom—flat, white, dainty umbrellas of Queen Anne's lace; bright white clusters of lacy-leafed yarrow; white and yellow daisies; yellow and brown black-eyed Susans. I also spotted dusty-rose milkweed clusters atop tall stems that I knew from childhood would, if broken, exude a creamy white sap. Lower down in this mid-July nature bouquet grew sprigs of white and yellow daisy fleabane, and lower yet, little yellow bells of birdfoot trefoil.

I arrived at the pond at 5:37 a.m., two minutes before sunrise. I set up my camp chair, settled in, pulled out my notebook, and began the process of looking and listening, of allowing sensory awareness to guide my experience.

Thick morning mist floated along the valley, enveloping me in a world of gray. It would be a while before the sun would ascend high enough and become bright enough to dissolve the mist and reveal the full palette of summer colors.

Two years ago the pond had been large and deep and a good

home for a family of beavers. But a two-day deluge wrought by the remnants of a hurricane ruptured the dam and drained the pond. Now, a little unnamed creek wove through a meadow of grasses and weeds that flourished upon mudflats where water had once stood.

The summer morning bird chorus was in full swing. I heard the songs and calls overlapping, rising and falling, coming and going. I listened intently to discern the different songs, to find out who was in the neighborhood and what they were up to. First, I focused on the familiar songs—the cooing of mourning doves, the sing-song of a robin, the whistles of a cardinal, the aria of a song sparrow, the cries of blue jays, the cawing of crows, the *chack, chack* of red-winged blackbirds, the *witchety, witchety, witchety* of a yellowthroat, and a veery's ethereal, downward spiraling, flute-like *vreer, vreer, vreer* song.

I willed my ears to hear into and beyond these familiar songs. Soon, I detected the wheezy, burry *RITZbew* of a willow flycatcher. Ah, flycatchers, I thought, a family of seldom seen solitary birds best identified by their calls. And this male flycatcher was right in his favored element—low, brushy vegetation in a wet area where he could perch on a branch, dart out, and snatch insects from the air.

Then I heard a musical bell-like trill, the song of a swamp sparrow, another bird that likes to live in marshes and near ponds. Nearby, a second swamp sparrow trilled, this time with a loud, clear, distinct pair of introductory notes before launching into its trill. Individual variation on a standard theme was one of the reasons that time spent sitting outside and listening is so important and so rewarding.

A small bird flew out of the mist and landed on a bare branch of a long-ago fallen dead tree. Binoculars up, focus adjusted, and I had a clear view of my swamp sparrow friend. It was a male with a rufous crown, wings, and tail; olive-shaded face and neck; compact, triangular, seed-crunching beak; and a bluish-gray breast. He hopped along the branch, stopped, reared back his head, and belted out his *chime-chime-trill* version of the swamp sparrow song.

I recalled one of the lecturers in the spring field ornithology course I took at the Cornell Lab of Ornithology saying that once he saw a bird singing its song, it was locked in his memory forever. I understood this now as I watched the swamp sparrow rear back like a tiny opera singer and belt out his musical trill again and again.

The sparrow edged to the tip of a branch close to tall stalks of field grass topped with heads of brown seeds that looked like wheat ready for the harvest. The bird stretched forward and deftly plucked seeds from the ripe grass. I knew sparrows ate seeds, but here was one showing me how they did it. Transfixed, I watched as it reached out and ate more seeds, hopped to another branch near more ripe stems, and ate more seeds. Nature provided the right food at the right time.

The slowly rising sun pierced the mist, illuminated my surroundings, and revealed the colors around me. Gazing ahead at the grasses and weeds, I saw shades of green—blue-green, light-green, dark-green, forest-green, yellow-green, and plain old Crayola-green. I noticed grasses of different heights and shapes with different leaves and tops—lacy plumes, small compact plumes, large seed heads, and small seed heads. Most of the grasses were green, but a few had reached maturity and turned brown.

Looking into the angled sunlight, I saw a veritable zoo of insects flying through the air, insects of all sizes and shapes—big, small, brown, white, tan, hovering, darting, flying, and even a few mosquitoes and deer flies flying around my arms and neck, looking for a spot to land to take a bite. The uncountable insects brought the insect hunters—the spiders. Everywhere I looked, I saw white webs coated in morning dew—thick webs; long, slender, strand webs; patterned webs; partial webs; low webs.

The riotous chorus of early morning overlapping birdsongs faded slowly away and was replaced by a sequence of separate songs. I heard a few new songs—the electric static buzz of a kingbird; the squawk of a great blue heron; the high pitched barely audible *sreeeee, sreeeee* of cedar waxwings; the rapid fire *kekekeke* of a kingfisher; and one of my summer favorites, the lilting musical *per-chik-o-ree* of goldfinches in flight.

The birds seemed to be flying more, on the move as daylight and sun warmth arrived. A pair of wood ducks flew above the stream with steady, strong wing strokes. A trio of jet-black crows flapped lazily across a light-blue sky. Robins flew steadily, purposefully, directly from tree to tree. A tiny house wren darted into a bush. A pair of goldfinches lifted and dipped through the air. And then there were the ballerinas of the sky—a quintet of barn swallows, cinnamon-throated, blue-black shoulders, long forked tail, and swept-back slender wings. I watched them swoop and swirl, dodge and dart, lift and drop, and pivot on a penny as if they owned the air, as if they were designed to defy gravity

A glance at my watch revealed that my designated observation hour was up. I was stunned. It had been the fastest sit spot hour ever. And although I was hungry and yearning for a hot cup of coffee, I wasn't ready to head home yet. I slowly packed up, shouldered my gear, and headed down a narrow path that ran alongside the creek, through scrub brush, under fragrant white pines, and alongside stands of poplar. It was barely 7 o'clock, but the air was already warm, humid, and heavy—perfect summer weather for plants to grow. I began to sweat in my long-sleeved shirt.

Spider web strands stretched across the path. I broke through them like a runner crossing a finish line. Then I realized I had walked down this same path last night at sundown. The spiders had worked overnight to restring their webs.

I spotted a tall wild blueberry bush offering a few ripe berries. I picked three, popped them in my mouth and chewed slowly. The taste wasn't fruit forward and sugary like store-bought berries, but light, refreshing, tart-sweet, a taste that lingered in my mouth. Further along I spied the first ripe blackberries of the year, plucked two, and ate them while visions of homemade blackberry jam spread on toast on a snowy winter morning came to mind.

Then I found a wild raspberry bush loaded with ripe red fruit. It had been a good summer for raspberries, the right amount and right sequence of sun and rain. I searched out the deepest red berries, reached in, grabbed gently, and when the berry pulled easily away from the stem, I knew it was just-right ripe. The taste was pure essence of raspberry—light, bright sweetness with a deep, rich flavor.

A robin flew out of the back side of the raspberry patch. Nearby, on the trail, stood a pile of fresh bear scat peppered with red fruit fragments and light-brown berry seeds. It seemed I might have to share this bounty of wild berries.

Fortified by my snack, I continued down the path. Coming around a turn I was surprised to see two wildflowers of late summer already in bloom—a spray of butter-yellow goldenrod and several clusters of dusty-pink Joe Pye weed. On this hot, sunny morning when it was easy to imagine that summer would go on forever, here were tangible signs that the season was rushing forward. Soon, the goldenrods—harbingers of autumn—would cover the fields with a blanket of golden-yellow.

OCTOBER SUNRISE

One morning in late October, after a night of heavy rain and strong wind had stripped the leaves away and left the branches gray and bare, the trees assumed a November look. It was no longer possible to think that the warm days of October might go on forever.

Walking across my yard in the dim, gray, predawn light, I saw the gray-black skeletal silhouettes of ash and maple trees—silent forest sentinels that would have to wait until next May for a new cloak of leaves to sway and dance and rustle in the wind.

The sound of my footsteps was muffled by a layer of rain-soaked leaves. I was heading to the beaver pond for an early morning, hourlong sit spot session with no agenda or theme in mind. I just wanted to sit still, observe fully, and see what I might learn.

SUBTLE SURPRISE

Nighttime silence still surrounded me as I stepped onto the wide, mowed, downhill path that led to the beaver pond. From a nearby bush I heard a faint, hesitant *tink, tink, tink*. Seconds later came an answering *tink, tink*. I checked my watch—6:45—more than a half hour until sunrise. It seemed too early and too dark for the birds to sing.

The *tink, tink, tink* calls grew louder, clearer, more emphatic and confident. It was a male and female cardinal waking up, starting their day, calling back and forth, staying in touch as they began to forage for food.

And then, as if the cardinals had broadcast an avian reveille, more songs and calls shattered the nighttime quiet. A robin called *tut, tut, tut*, a catbird mewed, and blue jays cried *jay, jay, jay*. Nearby I heard soft, faint *tseet, tseet, tseet* calls. Sparrows, I thought. And then the lovely, unmistakable song of a white-throated sparrow—a clear, whistled *old Tom Peabody, Peabody, Peabody* filled the morning air.

I was surprised. This song was normally sung in the spring on breeding territory. Maybe it was a young bird practicing. A few minutes later I heard another springtime song—a song sparrow singing a sprightly *maids, maids put on your tea kettle-lettle-lettle*. I felt as if I was hearing a spring chorus in the middle of October.

Arriving at the edge of the beaver pond, I set up my camp stool and settled in, hoping to hear more of this surprising morning chorus. But no more spring songs sounded, just regular calls from birds on the move shifting into their morning routine.

What had this fleeting spring songfest been all about? The only explanation that came to mind was that the birds must be hard-wired to respond to the break of day with song. To me these songs sounded like a celebration, seemed like a gift of musical beauty, felt like a spiritual reminder of the miracle of life starting another day.

At that moment I was glad I had woken up early in the dark and was out in nature to hear this fleeting chorus. At the same time I wondered why I wasn't up at daybreak every day. Getting up with the birds is healthy and natural.

Mallards on the Make

Slowly and gradually the light grew brighter. Gray clouds scuttled southward. A crow cawed. A red-bellied woodpecker called a clear, resonant *queeah, queeah, queeah.* A dusky-brown song sparrow fluttered in front of me, perched on a stem of grass, and then flew on. A female wood duck called a plaintive, ascending *oo-eek, oo-eek.* A beaver swam across the pond—brown nose, eyes and ears breaking the surface, carving a V across the still water. I heard splashes on the far side of the pond—ducks landing, I thought. Then I heard quacks, nasal *veep, veep* calls, and throaty chuckles.

Scanning the far edge of the pond with my binoculars, I spotted four mallards swimming, two drakes with luminous-green heads and two chestnut-brown hens. The drakes were chasing each other, heads down in the water, charging and countercharging, and at the same time chasing one of the hens. I was surprised. I thought courtship behavior occurred in the spring.

For ten full minutes I watched the ducks chase and dive and heard them quack and flap and splash. Because I was sitting still, the ducks were unaware of my presence, and I was able to see them in their natural state. Suddenly, the four mallards jumped up from the water, took flight amidst a chorus of quacking, and seconds later splashed down on the next beaver pond upstream to continue their courtship drama.

I read later that mallards pair up in October and November. What I saw were two drakes, plumage at an iridescent peak, blood stream loaded with testosterone, bobbing, weaving, and showing off to attract a female while battling each other. If it went well for a drake and he was found attractive by a female, she would nod her head several times and follow him as he swam off. The pair would migrate south and remain together through the winter. In spring they would fly north to a breeding ground selected by the female where they would engage in mating rituals, after which the female would build a nest and raise the ducklings.

I also read that in the spring, things get complicated for mallards. The drakes are on the prowl for extrarelational mating opportunities, and unpaired males will go after any hen they can find—sometimes in rough fashion. The hens in turn may spread their genetic options by having eggs fertilized by different drakes; they also seem to have an internal mechanism to deflect sperm from unwanted males. Pretty complex and pretty different from geese that mate for life, but the system seems to be working for mallards as they are widespread and their population is stable.

A Key

The light of the approaching day grew brighter. Swatches of pink and rose appeared in the sky. I saw all the colors in the landscape around me—green grasses, tan reeds, and brown, faded goldenrod flowers. A white-breasted nuthatch sang a cheerful *ank, ank, ank.* Another robin tutted. Behind me I heard the flutter of wings. Glancing up, I saw two blue jays flying overhead followed by a flock of twenty-five robins.

I loved those moments when I happened to look up and see birds in flight. Although the view lasted only a few seconds, it told a story—in this case, the story of robins flocking together for winter, some flocks migrating south and some remaining in northern woods.

People ask me if deep knowledge of birds is necessary for good nature observation. No, not really. A person could be into insects, wildflowers, trees, or shrubs and be similarly pulled into the pulse of life. But birds are plentiful, moving, and exquisitely responsive to climate, habitat, time of day, and seasons of the year. Their behavior tells the story of surrounding nature. Birdsongs and calls add layers to the story. Knowing birds is like having a key to open the door to a nature connection.

CHANGES

A breeze arose, puffs from the northwest. I felt a chill on my cheek. Ahead of me, slender grass stems swayed with each breath of wind. The breeze carried the smells of water, grass, and pine boughs to my nostrils.

I watched as the sky colors changed from pink to fiery orange and yellow and then to pale-blue. The rising sun, a tiny yellow ball, peeked through the bare branches across the pond. Once the sun finally lifted above the horizon, it seemed to grow quickly in size and ascend rapidly. A minute later I felt the first rays of sun warmth touch my cheek, one of my very favorite sensations.

RETURN

My hour was up. I wandered over to take a look at the beaver dam in part to marvel at its construction and to extend some sense of gratitude to the beavers for creating a life-supporting habitat. I spotted a low path through the brush, a little tunnel, grasses pressed down by beaver bellies as they busily made trip after trip, carrying freshly cut branches for their dam, and twigs and shoots of willow and alder for their winter food.

Walking back up the trail toward my house, I could see the curving, irregular line of my earlier footsteps in the wet grass. The sunlight, behind me now, cast a luminous light upon the lingering orange, yellow, red, and brown leaves.

Soon I arrived in my backyard and saw my house ahead looking cozy and inviting in the morning light. I was chilled after sitting still for an hour in the cool morning air. The idea of sitting by a fireplace and sipping a cup of hot coffee sounded very appealing. It was good to be out in nature, and it was good to return home on a chilly fall morning.

WINTER WINDS

My first immersion in waves of wind occurred during the second week of my yearlong Forest Stillness commitment. Thinking back, it might have been the first time in my life that I simply sat, listened to, and felt the wind.

Now, six years later, the memory of that day came to mind and brought with it an intense longing to relive the experience. Why was the longing so intense? Maybe because it was the beginning of December, and I wanted to enjoy the arriving winter. Maybe I had some sense that there was more to learn about the wind. Or maybe I wanted to gauge if I had changed in ways that would allow for a deeper understanding of the mysteries of the winter wind.

I began to monitor the forecast on my weather app for a day with strong winds. A week went by. Nothing. I wondered if I was going to have to give up on this idea.

Then, a winter storm in the forecast—two low-pressure fronts bearing down bringing sleet and freezing rain, and ending with snow. Such fronts were almost always followed by high pressure, clear skies, tight isobars, and a strong northwest wind—the perfect scenario for my purpose.

Monday night as the snow fell the forecast called for strong winds by morning. Anticipating the conditions, I set my alarm for 5:30 a.m. But when I woke up the air was calm and still. Disappointed, I rolled over and went back to sleep.

Then, later that morning, while running the snow blower I saw plumes of blown snow take flight and saw the branches above me sway. The hoped-for wind had arrived.

DRIVING

Driving through the countryside on my way to Prompton Lake, I saw trees swaying and bending in the wind, swirls of wind-blown snow race across open fields, and the tall, white windmills atop the Moosic Mountain churning.

I pulled into the boat ramp parking lot, stepped out of the car, and heard the wind roaring through the trees. Across the lake I detected the harsh *carruck, carruck* call of a raven, a wild call, a suitable greeting to the wintry scene around me.

Stepping cautiously across the snow-packed parking lot, I found the entrance to the West Shore Trail and headed into the woods through a grove of tall, slender ash trees where I had to duck under the heavily snow-laden branches. I walked slowly over the seep, a thin sheet of spring water nourishing a patch of bright-green cress growing amidst a white world of snow. Turning off the trail, I angled through the woods out to the tip of the peninsula, to my home sit spot beneath the big black cherry tree.

LISTENING

I pushed the legs of my camp stool down into the snow, sat down, and faced into the strong northwest wind, drew my first sensory awareness circle, and began to look, listen, feel, and make notes of all that I observed.

The wind roared through the trees, the branches swayed, cold gusts stung my face—all the same sensations I had noticed six years ago. It was, I thought, the true and eternal winter experience.

Then, a *tseee, tseee, tseee* sounded behind me. Turning, I scanned the shoreline shrubs searching for movement. Again, *tseee, tseee, tseee*. I looked, saw nothing, and then heard nothing.

Sometimes, that's the way it went. I would hear a bird call briefly but couldn't spot the bird. This time I recognized the call. It was a golden-crowned kinglet, a tiny gray and olive bird with delicate accents of yellow on its wings and a jaunty yellow crown—a winter warrior that used its short, strong bill to glean hibernating insects and caterpillars from the bare bark and branches. I felt a sense of gratitude for the presence of another creature coping with the winter cold and wind.

THE SURF

Waves of wind blew across the lake and through the branches of the trees. These waves started far upwind with a soft sigh, rose to a loud whooshing as they bore down, reached a crescendo roar above me, and then slowly faded away. I timed the cycle of the wind waves as they crested above me—one lasted twenty-three seconds, the next only fifteen.

Sometimes the wind subsided above me, but to my left I still heard gusts sighing and whooshing through the trees. To my right, across the lake where the forest was thick and continuous, where thousands of branches stuck up into the wind, the wind waves sighed, whooshed, and roared.

The sounds were created by the wind moving the branches back and forth, creating vibrations in the air, longitudinal pressure waves that traveled to and vibrated my ear drums. The stronger the gusts blew, the faster the vibrations, the louder the sound, and the higher the pitch. The invisible wind revealed its presence by playing the branches as if they were musical instruments.

Closing my eyes, the wind waves sounded like distant ocean surf landing on a sandy beach, a steady rhythm of rising and falling, whooshing and roaring.

A car drove down nearby Creek Road. The wind swallowed the sound. A jetliner flew overheard. The wind swallowed the sound. Gusts blew by my ear creating a loud crinkly sound.

All I could hear was wind—a kind of hearing and not hearing. Then, a lull in the wind, a quiet moment. I heard one lilting *per-chik-o-ree* call of a goldfinch before the wind roared and drowned out all the other sounds.

SEEING

Twenty minutes of sitting still. My vision was gradually opening up, growing more acute. I began to see more around me.

I studied three slender, gray birches, the bark pale-white in the sunlight, the branches a dark, delicate filigree against a cobalt-blue sky. To my left I spotted a small beech sapling still holding its brown leaves—as beeches do. On a long horizontal branch, the dry, brown beech leaves shimmed and fluttered like tiny streamers in each gust of wind.

I looked up at the tree tops where the branches of each tree seemed to have their own space and stirred silently in that space. During the strongest gusts, the branches moved out of their space and began to touch and clack and click. When the wind ebbed the branches withdrew back into their own silent space.

I studied the swaying movement of the trees and noticed that it wasn't a simple back and forth, but more of a circular stirring— clockwise, counterclockwise, diagonal, and sometimes back and forth.

A single cloud floated in front of the low shining sun. The sun lit up the fringes of the cloud, edging it with luminous-yellow beams for a few seconds before the wind whisked the cloud away.

Five crows flew downwind, coal-black birds in a clear, blue sky, only needing occasional flaps of their wings to fly quickly. I heard them *caw, caw, caw* back and forth.

FLOW

I lost track of time. Maybe I had drifted into what in positive psychology is called a *flow* state, characterized by complete focus on the present moment, a letting go of the concerns of the little self, and an opening up to the patterns and purposes of big nature.

Perhaps the sensory awareness circle helped to create this flow state. All I had to do was picture myself as a dot in the middle of a circle on my notebook page, then notice and write down everything I saw, heard, felt, and smelled, near and far for ten-minute intervals. Yet at the same time, the task was challenging enough to draw me in as I listened for more subtle sounds, for changes in sounds, for distant sounds as I looked at levels and layers of trees and branches, grasses and weeds, bushes and shrubs, rocks and mosses.

OLD HANDS

Gazing at the swaying tree tops, I felt myself slipping into that state where I saw more than trunks and branches. I began to see patterns and themes. I noticed how gracefully, how naturally, how comfortably each tree moved with the wind, bending easily to match the strength of each gust, and then settling back to an upright position. The trees, I realized, were old hands at this. They had centuries of experience learning to live with the wind, a potentially destructive force. The fiber and structure of each tree was tuned to coexist with the wind.

Each species of tree seemed to have its own formula, its own style of adaptability. The tall, thick-trunked, thick-branched cherry trees swayed and stirred less than the thinner-trunked maples. The gray birches, with their slender trunks and thick, lacy branches, moved the most of all. The younger and thinner of each type of tree bent and swayed more than the older, more mature trees.

I could feel this awareness of how trees moved shift to the realm of human affairs. We were old hands too. We carried ancient wisdom of how to stand and move with the forces of gravity and wind. And, I thought, in a more figurative sense, we must also have an equally well-honed adaptability to bend and sway in response to the forces of circumstance, fate, and fortune.

WIND CHILL

As I continued to look up at the trees, the wind subsided. I took advantage of the quiet moment to turn and face the sun and take in the warmth of its rays.

According to my weather app, the wind was from the northwest at 17 mph with gusts up to 33 mph. The temperature was 26. The wind chill or "feels like" temperature was 16.

Wind chill is a controversial notion based on the amount of heat transfer of someone walking barefaced into the wind at 3.1 mph over an open field. Also, feeling cold is a subjective experience, and heat loss varies from person to person. I was sitting still, facing the wind on an exposed elevation. I felt cold. The last ten minutes of my hour were going to be hard. I shifted my chair away from the wind to face the sun and take in its warmth. I was determined to make it through the full hour. The wind blew hard, the strongest gusts yet. Chunks of snow flew from the branches. One chunk dropped down, landed inside my coat and slid down the back of my neck. Three crows flew laboriously upwind. The tree shadows lengthened. Blueish, fading, late-afternoon light spread across the peninsula.

The last seconds ticked by. My hour was up. Relieved, I stood, packed up my gear and trudged back through the snow. Feeling chilled, I imagined blasting my car heater at max. I pictured myself at home, sitting by the fireplace, sipping a cup of steaming tea, listening to the gusts of winter wind roar outside the door and beat against the window panes.

CHAPTER 10

Traveling

I N ENGLISH IT'S CALLED THE URGE TO TRAVEL. IN GERMAN IT'S known as *wanderlust,* translated as the deep desire to hike and roam, a term possibly reflecting romantic era fascination with seeking unity in nature. An even more compelling word in German is *fernweh*, the longing for faraway places and for the personal enrichment that visiting such places can offer.

Fernweh may be an innate human desire to explore new lands and discover what lies beyond the next mountain range. One theory holds that because humans were a nomadic species for 99 percent of their evolutionary history, the urge to move and continually seek better conditions is embedded in our DNA.

Another theory focuses on the reward systems in the brain. The idea here is that the human brain scans for novelty, delights in new settings, and searches for unique experiences, all of which light up the reward centers in the brain. Our huge travel and tourism industry, with its cruise ships, guided tours, and vacation offerings, gives testimony to the universality of the urge to seek these travel-induced brain rewards. Some research even suggests that 20 percent of the population may have a specific genetic variation that makes them particularly inclined to seek out the rewards of travel adventures.

Visiting new and picturesque locations can provide moments of beauty, awe, and gratitude—experiences that from the perspective of positive psychology promote psychological well-being. In addition, many travelers love the learning that occurs when we encounter other cultures—learning of history, geography, and much more. And finally, many of us find the organizing, planning, and problem solving that go with traveling to be very satisfying. It is said that travel brings three distinct joys: anticipation, experiences in the moment, and treasured memories.

Traveling may also have implications for self-development. Our concepts of personal growth are structured by the hero/heroine's journey, immortalized in Homer's *Odyssey* and characterized in the narrative template of the restless soul who receives a call to venture out, leaves home, faces challenges, finds a mentor, learns lessons, wins victories, comes to know him or herself, and returns home transformed with new gifts to share with his or her community.

In a number of ways, this urge to travel interfaces with and may be substantially deepened by the sit spot approach to nature mindfulness. First, there is the challenge of finding a promising sit spot location in a new setting. During the first months of my Forest Stillness year, I traveled to Germany, Colorado, and Wisconsin, and I struggled to find a good sit spot. I was unsure of myself, tried different locations, and had several misfires. But in the end, I found good sit spots in each location. Now when I travel, I enjoy the process of finding a sit spot. If possible I like to scout the area beforehand, find a location that meets my edge habitat criteria and feels right. Then, early the next morning I head straight to the spot.

A second area of interface between traveling and sit spot mindfulness involves learning about a new nature environment. It is important to have a home sit spot where you come to know the plants, birds, and animals and where you see how the seasons unfold. This is your baseline of nature knowledge. When you conduct a sitting session in a new location, you have the opportunity to learn about a new environment, discover different flora and fauna, and experience a different climate and different progression in the seasons. This new learning builds on our natural human fascination with and attention to habitat and to the animals, plants, and birds in each environment. It is a particular joy, a uniquely gratifying and intellectually illuminating experience to see the beauty, complexity, and interrelations of all aspects of nature in new ways. Such experiences not only reveal the new but enhance our appreciation of our home sit spot.

There is also a more subjective dimension that comes with

experiencing mindfulness in a new environment. Every habitat is home to a set of plants, birds, and animals that have adapted to that unique environment. Every environment is also a home to and is known and loved by the people who live there, whether it is the Inuits in the Arctic, nomadic Bedouins in the Sahara, or people living in the Appalachian Mountains. Every environment has a unique feel that those who dwell there know.

This unique feel is sometimes referred to as the spirit of the place. It arises when all of the unique aspects of terrain, light, climate, and flora and fauna weave together to form a greater whole. Spirit of the place includes the essence of a location, the energy, and the human, cultural, and experiential history of that location. It may even include consideration of the sacred dimensions of a space.

Connecting with the spirit of a new place is an enriching and grounding experience. It is for just such experiences that I love to express my innate urge to travel, explore new places, and while there, do a sit spot session or wander walk.

The first sit spot experience described in this chapter, **Lost Lake**, occurred under less than ideal conditions. After conducting a daylong training at a school district in the Central Valley of California, I was tired and faced an early flight home the next morning. During the training, when I had asked about good local hikes, several of the participants mentioned Lost Lake Park. Once work was done I jumped in my rental car and drove to the park.

There was no opportunity to scout the area in advance. I had no camp stool, no binoculars, not even a notebook. But when I arrived and walked through the park, I was so struck by the unique beauty of the setting that I felt compelled to deepen my experience and decided on the spur of the moment to do a sit spot session. It turned out to be memorable and a good lesson that even in less than optimal conditions, taking time for nature mindfulness can be worthwhile.

The second selection in this chapter, **Sunrise over the Crawfish River**, took place at the house of my sister-in-law and her husband in my home state of Wisconsin. I had visited their farmhouse often over many years and had always enjoyed my views of Crawfish River, which flowed near their house.

Waking up early and sitting by the bank of the river, I was present to witness the sunrise, to watch another day in nature begin. This sit spot was a homecoming to the state where I grew up. It was also a wakeup call to all that I had ignored and missed in my earlier years before I knew about the sit spot approach to nature mindfulness. It felt as if I was seeing much that was familiar but in a new and deeper way.

The third selection, **The Green Forest of the Blue Ridge Parkway**, is about a wander walk. I squeezed in this walk among many other activities during the busy days before Christmas. Objectively, I wanted to learn more about some plants that were still green in the winter woods that I had seen on a previous short hike. And then I had a dream about the winter greenery that called me to take a slow wander walk through the woods and connect with another environment.

LOST LAKE

The blue water of the San Joaquin River flowed swiftly through Lost Lake County Park—snowmelt on a long journey from the Sierra Nevada Mountains, through the Central Valley, and on to San Francisco Bay to eventually merge into the Pacific Ocean. The current formed surface swirls that spun downstream like miniature whirlpools. Fluffy, white-seed streamers, like milkweed or cottonwood seeds, sailed upstream just above the surface of the water, blown by a steady breeze. Streams of water and windblown seeds were moving in opposite directions, a contradiction that seemed to fit a setting filled with contradictions.

Across the river a bone-dry field of tan grass stretched uphill toward a bare rock-topped bluff. But around me, along the riverbanks, grew a profusion of green willows, shrubs, trees, and reeds—a verdant riparian ribbon winding through dry hill country.

A warm breeze caressed my face, a pleasant sensation as the humidity was low and the temperature a comfortable 85 degrees. The wind carried spicy, earthy fragrances. Every once in a while a gust would dip down, scoop up the chilly air that hovered above the snowmelt river, cool my face, and waft a menthol-fresh fragrance to my nostrils.

Driving out from the city of Madera, California, in the late afternoon, I had traveled through miles of flat bottomland where I saw acres and acres and rows and rows of walnut trees, pecan trees, and grapevines. Then, when I crested a small hill, a completely different landscape came into view, one with rolling fields of dry tan grass, herds of cattle, and ranches with decoratively lettered entry gates. Miles ahead the fields lifted into brown contoured bluffs, which in turn ascended up to rocky hills. Beyond the bluffs and hills and barely visible on the hazy horizon rose the steep, dark-green, pine-covered foothills of the Sierra Nevadas.

This unexpected and stunning panorama created an instantaneous physical effect, best described as sparkling, effervescent, uplifting sensations flooding my heart, chest, and shoulders. It was a vista I had never seen before, never even imagined, a vista completely different from the rounded forest hills of my home in northeast Pennsylvania. With mounting excitement and growing curiosity, I continued the drive to Lost Lake Park.

I sat on the warm ground next to the river and gazed at the current. Two miles upstream stood Friant Dam, the last of four dams. The San Joaquin was a hard-working river, its waters dammed in four locations to create water supply reservoirs, its current diverted to fill the irrigation canals of the fertile Central Valley. It was a thoroughly tamed and domesticated river, yet as I looked around, the river here seemed wild, surrounded by trees, a haven for birds and wildlife, and a home for salmon, bass, and panfish.

I tuned into the sounds around me, the wind swooshing through the leaves, the soft gurgle of the water touching rocks, the hoarse croaks of ravens, the squawk of a mockingbird, the loud rattle of a kingfisher, and the cooing of mourning doves. I had learned to love, even to honor, this process of settling in to stillness, the progression of the senses awakening and taking in more and more of the surroundings. As the minutes flowed I felt myself blending into the setting, the disturbance of my presence diminishing, the life of nature resuming around me.

Above a rock at the edge of a tiny island, I spotted a bird perched at the tip of a dead branch. I had no binoculars and no bird guide for western species. This was an identification challenge, but for some reason I welcomed it. I was on my own west of the Rocky Mountains on the Pacific Flyway where there are many different and unfamiliar bird species.

The bird, smaller than a robin, sallied out over the stream, skimmed the surface, snatched an insect, flew back, and landed on a big rock. It appeared dark on top and light underneath. I plugged this information into my *Merlin Bird ID* app. Black phoebe popped up at the top of the list of possible birds.

Then I saw two of these birds working around the rocky island, flitting out over the water, returning to perch. One flew across the river right toward me and landed in a nearby bush, close enough that I could clearly discern its blackish head, charcoal-gray back, white belly, and long gray tail that it flicked up and down. It looked and behaved very much like the eastern phoebes I knew from home.

Identification confirmed! I felt a smile of contentment on my face and a surge of joy in my heart. Part of this positive reaction probably came from successful problem solving. But there was more to it, and I wasn't sure I could pin it down. Perhaps it was the happiness of meeting a new bird friend, one I had never seen before. Maybe it was the joy of seeing a species perfectly evolved to this setting in its precise plumage and preferred habitat exhibiting classic phoebe behavior.

I watched the phoebes fly and feed above the flowing river. Two Canada geese swam slowly upstream. Near the reeds in the shadows by the far shore, a bird set low in the water paddled and dove, surfaced, paddled and dove. I knew this was a grebe of some kind but without binoculars impossible to identify. I felt a tinge of frustration.

A flock of little birds swept into a tall bush next to me. They were all gray, in constant motion, calling back and forth with short, high-pitched, scratchy calls. They fluttered among the branches and combed the undersides of the leaves with their bills. I focused on the field marks of one bird and put the info into *Merlin*. They were bushtits, another western species and another new friend. I watched them flutter on to the next bush, saw their gray plumage and long tails, heard their constant, cheerful calls, and felt my joy return.

I glanced up and spotted a mockingbird flying toward the bushes with a Cooper's hawk in hot pursuit. My movement or maybe the reflection of sunlight on my glasses must have distracted the hawk for a fraction of a second. It hesitated and swerved. The mockingbird took the opportunity and dove for shelter in a thick bush. It had been a close call for the mockingbird. I realized that even here in this county park with its well-used campground, picnic tables, charcoal grills, and hiking trails, the drama of prey and predator played out as it had for centuries.

The sunlight, angled now as the sun settled toward the horizon, cast a warm golden hue on the panorama in front of me. I looked across the river at the tan fields and stared at the swirling, moving, ever-changing river.

A gust of wind blew the smell of grilled meat to my nostrils.

Walking to my sit spot, I had seen two Latina women, their children playing nearby, skillfully tending a charcoal grill spread with shiny, dark-green poblano peppers. They must have been preparing the meat course now, I thought. The smell of grilled meat brought hunger pangs to my stomach and a surge of saliva to my mouth.

According to my eastern-time-zone stomach, it was 9:30 p.m. and well past my normal dinner time. I was hungry. I was tired. It had been a long day. It was time for nourishment, time for rest, time to head to the restaurant I had discovered yesterday where they served fresh pasta smothered in savory sauces and featured their own blended red wine made from grapes that grew in the surrounding vineyards.

I walked back to my car and hoped I might return to this park someday, maybe early in the morning when the mist hung over the river and the wildlife welcomed a new day. I would sit by the river for a full hourlong sit spot session. Afterward I would drive east, up the high brown bluffs, up into the pine-covered mountains of the Ansel Adams Wilderness, up to find the source of the San Joaquin River.

SUNRISE OVER THE CRAWFISH RIVER

Quietly, I pushed open the kitchen door of the old farmhouse, stepped down two well-worn concrete steps, passed the old stone well house, and walked through a circle of illumination cast by a bright fluorescent farm light. Crunching across a grass-overgrown, gravel driveway, I walked by a dark-red barn and a rounded concrete silo foundation—all of it barely visible in the predawn light. I continued across the dew-wet grass of an abandoned pasture and reached my destination—a faded, white lawn chair I had set up the night before near the bank of the Crawfish River.

I sat down and took in the view. Directly ahead, two silver-gray canoes rested upside down on the grass. In my imagination the canoes looked ready for a paddle on the Crawfish, a river that meanders east and south before joining the Rock River, which in turn merges with the Mississippi. An image of pioneers canoeing and rowing along the river came to mind. Then more images emerged, scenes further back in time: Native Americans in birchbark canoes and dugouts, paddling, journeying, hunting, and harvesting up and down the length of the Crawfish.

This was a river with a history. In the dim morning light it seemed almost as if faint traces and subtle vibrations of all of those who had traveled the river in the past now lingered in the threads of mist floating above the still gray water. I could almost hear the splash of paddles and sounds of voices. I could almost see boats slicing through the water, could almost pick up on the emotional energy linked to the plans, motives, and concerns of past paddlers.

In front of me the river widened into two long parallel ponds, then narrowed to flow under a highway bridge. Trees and bushes of all sizes, shapes, and heights flourished along both banks. Next to and extending into the river grew a thick, green band of cattails, marsh hay, and smartweed. Patches of green duckweed covered the still inlets—quiet water the steady current couldn't reach.

A car, headlights on, sped down the hill and across the bridge on County Road DG, the old road that linked the farm to the village of Fall River, Wisconsin. Another car followed. People hurrying to work, I thought. An airplane, lights blinking, whooshed high above in the sky where the last pinpricks of starlight were slowly fading in the approaching daylight. Far away a train rumbled down the tracks; its mournful whistle pierced the quiet.

I settled back in my chair, took a sip of hot Assam tea, and reflected with a smile that this had been one of the easiest sit spots to reach, just fifty yards from the door across a well-lit yard. Now I reminded myself to keep it simple—no expectations, no activity, just sit still, open my senses—look, listen, smell, and feel.

It was fifteen minutes until sunrise, but I could hear that the birds were already on the move. Far beyond a cornfield, two crows cawed. A flock of geese, honking steadily, flew high overhead. A shadowy blur buzzed low over the open water—a kingfisher, chattering loudly. Nearby a catbird mewed, a blue jay called, a robin tutted, and a white-breasted nuthatch voiced its nasal *ank, ank, ank*. Across the river, I heard red-winged blackbirds calling *chack, chack, chack*. A little band of chickadees squeaked back and forth as they flitted through the trees in front of me.

The still, dry, chilly, 42-degree autumn morning air felt clean and fresh on my face. I inhaled a melange of smells: woodsy fragrances, the fertile odor of mud and marsh, and now and again a whiff of that invigorating, refreshing, negative-ion-laden air that hovers above flowing water.

It was 6:46, the official time for sunrise, but down in the river valley where I sat, beneath the sloping hills of corn and soybean fields, no bright orb appeared. But slowly, inexorably, the presunrise light spread. Slender strands of yellow and orange and pink appeared above the horizon. As the illumination increased, I felt rising, sparkling sensations in my heart and chest, feelings of joy, a sense of resonance with the rhythm of the rising sun.

As the light increased, the tempo and volume of the morning chorus picked up. I heard the mournful *oo-eek* of a female wood duck, the cheerful *per-chik-o-ree* of goldfinches in flight, the loud insistent *wicka, wicka, wicka* of a flicker, the tinny descending rattle of a downy woodpecker, and an unusual and unfamiliar call—the primitive, rolling, bugled, far-carrying *garoo-a-a-a* of sandhill cranes.

Suddenly, the sun surged above the horizon. Bright angled sunlight illuminated the greens of the grasses, reeds, and leaves and revealed the blues of river water and sky. The bird chorus intensified. It was an electric moment. I felt immersed in and surrounded by a vast and powerful vitality, a panorama permeated with life force, a scene filled with hope with the promise of rebirth.

Spurred on by the rising sun, the birds swung into full action mode. Across the river, a flock of twenty or more redwings—the males black with bright red-orange epaulets, the females plain brown—fluttered down from low branches to the cattails where they perched and swayed on the slender stems. I could sense their restlessness, their urge to gather into flocks—flocks that would grow in number, instinct-driven flocks of older and younger birds preparing to make the long and perilous journey south.

The nearby sound of geese honking pulled me from my reverie. I looked up and saw two geese flying above the river. They began to circle over the open pond area, descended slowly, set their wings, and glided down behind a stand of trees. I heard two soft splashes as they landed.

More calls of sandhill cranes carried through the morning air. Eager to see one, I swiveled, scanned, and spotted a trio in flight—large birds with a seven-foot wingspan, long slender necks, spiked bills, and long legs trailing behind them. Spellbound, I watched the cranes fly gracefully on a level line, strong wing strokes, gray sun-lit plumage, winging over a field of tall, ripening, yellow-tan corn stalks.

I didn't feel the wind start up, but when I glanced at a patch of grass, I saw the slender stems sway ever so slightly, heralding the onset of the day breeze. Soon stronger puffs of wind arose that rustled the cattails. Then a steadier breeze from the northwest developed, a breeze that stirred the branches and rattled the leaves, dislodging a few brown and yellow leaves that slowly fluttered down to the ground.

More birds on the move. A pair of cardinals called *tik, tik, tik* as they moved through the trees. A tiny bird darted out of a bush and down into the reeds, maybe a marsh wren. A robin landed in a tree, tutted, flapped over to the next tree and tutted again. A catbird following the robin's path flew and perched and mewed from branch to branch. Two more little birds popped out of the bushes, then dove back down. A single complex song followed. Were they warblers or kinglets?

I was sitting in prime bird habitat. The band of trees and shrubs and reeds bordering flowing water was ideal terrain. And I had a front row seat for a parade of birds moving up and down the river, an avian parade that had been flying, perching, calling, singing, feeding, and mating along the banks of Crawfish River for centuries.

A glance at my watch revealed that my hour was winding down. My hands were cold and numb. It was getting harder to grip the pencil and write my notes. The warmth of the ascending sun had yet to overcome the morning chill.

A school bus, bright yellow in the morning sunshine, rumbled down the county road, rolled over the bridge, slowed, and the sighing of the air brakes came to a stop. The door swung open. The loud, carefree voices of children ready to start their school day carried across the river.

A good time to end my sit spot session, head back inside the farmhouse, build a fire in the woodstove, warm my hands, sip a cup of hot, black coffee, eat breakfast, and think about all the people over the years who had started their day in a bright, cozy kitchen with a view of the tree-lined banks of the Crawfish River.

THE GREEN FOREST OF THE BLUE RIDGE PARKWAY

The first reason to return and complete the climb to the Haw Creek Overlook was a lingering sense of unfinished business. A few days earlier my wife and I had made it halfway up, but then ran out of time. I was left with the feeling of a job half done, a mission uncompleted. And I could feel the pull of those compelling elements of a climb—the pursuit of a goal, and the physical, emotional, even spiritual challenge of an ascent.

The full hike, starting at the Folk Art Center along the Blue Ridge Parkway, proceeded about 2.5 miles along the Mountain to Sea Trail, and up to the Haw Creek Overlook where a stunning view awaited. Depending on what guidebook you read, it was described as a hike of moderate difficulty with nine hundred feet of gain. And it was a popular hike, one of the best close to Asheville, North Carolina.

The second reason to return was less defined, almost ephemeral. I had seen a cluster of green, low-growing plants alongside the trail, an unexpected sight during late December, the dark days of the year, not a time for forest growth. It was a fleeting impression, but that night the plants appeared to me in a dream—a dream infused with a sense of wonder about green growth during dark days. When I woke up with the dream images fresh in mind, I knew I had to go back and understand what I had seen.

A Wild Christmas Tree

I parked in the lot at the Folk Art Center, donned a fleece and a beret—the conditions were mild enough—grabbed my trekking poles, stuck a minibottle of water in the back pocket of my hiking pants and climbed the steps to the Center and found the intersection with the Mountain to Sea Trail. Through the windows of the Center, I could see last-minute Christmas shoppers searching for gifts among the mountain crafts—paintings, carvings, weavings, textiles, and jewelry.

At first the path was wide, covered with fine gravel. There were signs providing information about the trees that grew by the trail—red maple, tulip poplar—trees I knew well so I walked by. But when I came to the sign for the American chestnut in front of a huge decaying log, I stopped. The chestnut, a stately and abundant tree that once provided high quality lumber, generous shade, and plentiful nuts for humans, beasts, and birds, was totally decimated by blight during the early twentieth century. Some four billion chestnut trees died.

I felt a pang of sadness and a sense of loss for these trees that once reigned tall through the forests of eastern North America. Recently, I read that new blight-resistant, hybrid strains of chestnut are being developed. I decided I should get one of these new chestnut trees to plant in my yard and maybe even a second one to plant secretly in the woods, a private act of restoration. I liked the way walking and experiencing things directly guided my decision-making, helped to give me a vision for the future, and generated impulses for acts of conservation.

Further down the trail, someone, perhaps an employee at the Folk Art Center, had hung tiny red ornaments on a small evergreen, creating a wild Christmas tree. I paused, gazed at the little tree, and decided that this was my favorite Christmas tree of the year and that I really liked the person or persons who had come up with this idea and brought it to decorative fruition.

WINTER ORCHIDS

Departing from the environs of the Folk Art Center, I continued along the Mountain to Sea Trail (MST), a narrow trail now, marked by white blazes on the trees, its dirt and rock surface coated with fallen leaves ground fine by countless footsteps. The MST, one of America's famous thru-hiking trails, stretches almost twelve hundred miles from the high peaks of the Great Smoky Mountains to the sandy beaches of the Outer Banks. An image of a solitary hiker came to mind, possessions in backpack, stepping steadily down the trail, cloaked in a sense of forest communion, moving forward on a journey. Maybe I was seeing a vision of myself.

Scanning the ground along the trail, I looked for the green plants. Funny, how faulty memory can be. I thought I remembered where I had seen them, but now I couldn't find them. I kept walking and searching and then—there they were, a cluster of low, broad, spear-shaped, light green, faintly striped leaves.

I knelt down and snapped a photo with my *Picture This* app. The percentage number churned closer and closer to 100%, and after a few seconds, the app revealed its decision—a putty root orchid. "An orchid," I exclaimed out loud. That's a plant for a humid, tropical rainforest, I thought.

I read more. The putty root orchid is common throughout the deciduous forests of North America. And then this sentence blew me away: "The basal leaves die back in summer and grow in winter once the forest canopy has disappeared and it has more access to sunlight."

Here was a plant that had evolved its growth pattern into a remarkable niche. Growing up in Wisconsin and living in northeastern

Pennsylvania, I had the mindset that the forest shuts down in winter. But here things were different, and the putty root orchid had adapted and found a way to take advantage of the milder winter.

I was clearly in a different climate, a more temperate and nurturing forest. I had often felt there was something healthy and vibrant about these Blue Ridge Mountains—the elevation, the clean air, the long vistas, the people who lived here. These forests seemed to have a generous, life-sustaining force.

I also realized once again how nature awareness can leap over the boundary from sensory impressions to emotional insights. I was seeing a manifestation of adaptability and resilience. The putty root orchid found a way to adapt to its environment, found a way to unexpectedly grow and prosper in dark, cold times. I guessed I could do the same.

My steps lightened by what I had seen, I continued down the trail and after fifty yards saw another cluster of plants. These leaves were wider and a solid light green. I took a photo, ran it through *Picture This* and was stunned to have yet another orchid, this time the crane-fly orchid. I read that this orchid grows in clusters, with connected roots holding edible, starchy, potato-like corms. Surely, the Native Americans and early settlers knew this plant. I read further that it offers beautiful summer flowers of white, yellow, purple, and green. I would have to return in the early summer to see these two orchids in bloom, knowing that they use winter sunlight to create summer flowers.

CONNECTIONS

Eyes out for more green, I continued up the MST. Next to the trail in an open area, I spotted a thickly branched short bush still bearing leaves. *Picture This* identified it as dwarf honeysuckle, an invasive plant with origins in Europe and Asia, a robust, disease-resistant shrub with showy, fragrant, white flowers in early summer followed by red berries. Hummingbirds sip the nectar. Bees, butterflies, and flies pollinate the tubular blossom. Tanagers, thrushes, robins, orioles, and phoebes feed on the juicy berries, and the thick foliage provides birds with spring nesting spots and year-round cover.

The word *invasive* has negative connotations and stirs mixed emotions. I read that dwarf honeysuckle competes with native species and the berries are mildly toxic to humans. But on this December day, its green foliage was a welcome sight. I spotted a pair of chickadees flitting within the thick branches. I wondered if and when a plant transitions from the category of invasive to native. Maybe there was some kind of a continuum here, some gentler words to deal with this transition. The chickadees certainly weren't making any distinction.

Heading down a short steep hill, I came to the spot where the trail crosses the Blue Ridge Parkway. As I crossed the road, I saw a man, younger than me, sitting on the back of his SUV, putting on running shoes. I was hiking; he would be running. He was younger; I was older. Yet in that moment it seemed that we both felt a sense of camaraderie. We were partners in being outside enjoying nature, partners in taking on a climbing challenge.

We greeted each other, commented on how good it was to be outside, and in some unspoken way encouraged each other. During the social distancing of the pandemic, such random social encounters took on great value.

I continued on the path, ascending through a stand of pitch pines, an arbor of green boughs that filled the air with aromatic fragrance. I heard steps behind me, edged off the trail, and let my jogger friend pass, wished him a good run while he gave me a thumbs up for my hike.

Ascending

The trail grew steeper, ascending over rocks, around fallen trees, across exposed roots, ever higher. It was hard enough for me to walk the narrow, rocky, root-laden trail even with the help of trekking poles. I couldn't imagine running up the trail.

I climbed for another mile and began to notice those shifting, doubting, dramatic thoughts that always seem to accompany a climb or any daunting task for that matter. I checked my pedometer to see how far I had come and wondered how much further I had to go. Doubts as to whether I would make it began to creep into my mind. The wind was picking up, the temperature dropping. I spoke with a hiker coming down who told me that I didn't have that far to go. He said to look for a marker and then turn left to the overlook.

There were birds around. I saw family groups of crows flying over the tree tops cawing back and forth. I heard the evocative distant hoarse *cr-r-ruck, cr-r-ruck* croak of a raven. A pileated woodpecker, crow-sized, bright red top notch, and long, spiky bill flew across the trail into the woods and landed on a dead tree. I paused, watched it begin to hammer the tree, and heard the loud resonant *tap, tap, tap* of its bill on the trunk followed by its loud *kik-kik-kik-kik* call.

I enjoyed seeing the Carolina chickadees that appeared out of the woods, perched on branches near the trail, and squeaked, twittered, and called *chick-a-dee, dee, dee.* It was role reversal and humbling, for it was the chickadees that spotted and studied me, not me finding and observing them. They were the lookouts and gossips of the forest, sharing their observations and providing commentary for all the other birds and mammals.

SUMMITING

A final steep climb and I reached a hilltop. I could hear cars whooshing down the Parkway and saw hints of an open vista through the trees. Spotting a marker beside the trail, I turned onto a narrow path. Edging down the path, I covered two descending loops and was surprised to arrive at a steep fifteen-foot-high bank that I had to slide down to finally arrive at the open ground of the overlook.

I walked to the edge of the Parkway and took in the full panorama—an open view of a wide, fertile valley sprinkled with clusters of neat houses and bisected by dark lines of roads and highways. In the far distance stood a line of mountains veiled in a blue haze, the Blue Ridge Mountains. The view was as good as advertised.

Nearby a family took selfies. A couple emerged from their car with big smiles and took in the view. At the end of the outlook I found a wider path that led up to a cluster of rocks where more people sat and enjoyed the view. Everyone seems to like an expansive view of valley and mountains, a view that creates a sense of awe, a view that must touch some pleasure center in the brain.

RETURNING

Continuing up the rock face, I found a wide path that joined the Mountain to Sea Trail, stepped back onto the trail and began my return. Descending the trail, I felt less concern about my destination and took more notice of the splashes of green in the forest. I had seen ferns on my ascent and now stopped to take a picture and run it through my app. It was Christmas fern, a native plant that prefers moist, shady woods. Its name comes from the fact that it remains green until Christmas time.

Further down in an open area by an abandoned road, I found a stand of tall, skinny, dark-green, snaky, rough horsetail, another invasive plant, one that is pest resistant and helps to control erosion. A little further along I spotted shiny, pale, striped leaves of spotted wintergreen growing near to the ground. I saw holly trees with sharp-shaped, shiny, dark-green leaves and bright red berries. I passed through stands of lush green rhododendrons with tan flower buds holding the promise of spring blooms.

Continuing down the trail, I came to a damp rock face covered with mosses of various textures and shades of green. *Picture This* informed me that the largest patch was common hairmoss, which thrives in regions with high humidity and abundant rainfall.

Picture This even offered a poem by William Barnes.

Oh rain-bred moss that now dost hide,
The timbers bark and wet rock's side,
Upshining to the sun, between
The darksome storms, in lively green.

Yes, even in winter the forest along the Blue Ridge Parkway was filled with lively green.

CHAPTER 11

Wander Walks

I HAVE ALWAYS LOVED WALKING OUTSIDE SURROUNDED BY NATURE, breathing in the fresh, warm air of spring and summer, the refreshing air of a brisk fall day, and even the bracing cold of winter. The green exercise obtained by walking also helps to keep me physically fit. And increasingly, scientific studies are finding that a walk in nature boosts mood and improves cognitive abilities. There are plenty of reasons for me to strive for a daily walk.

But the quality of my walks changed after my Forest Stillness year. Now, when I walk, I see, hear, feel, and smell more. And what I observe affects me in deeper and more heartfelt ways.

My guess is that my year of hourlong nature intensives turned on a heightened acuity to the sounds and sights of my environment. Now, when I walk in the woods, even if I am with someone and conversing, a part of my hearing is attuned to the birdsongs, to the sound of the leaves rustling in the breeze, and to the rushing of water in a brook. A part of my vision takes in the colors, the varied and subtle hues of the grasses, shrubs, trees, and sky. I pick up on the heady fragrances of meadow grasses growing and the tangy scent of a pine woods. My skin feels the breeze and warmth of the sun.

Given this acquired or perhaps reacquired sensitivity to the sensory inputs of nature and my longstanding love of walking, I began to wonder if I could combine the two. Could I walk in a mindful way and at the same time get exercise? After some experimentation I found that I could.

I named these mindful sojourns wander walks. Over time I have figured out a few things that seem to make them work well. First, I walk more slowly with less concern for miles covered and pace achieved and more emphasis on the quality of the experience. This allows me to put more attention on listening, looking around, and inhaling the air.

Second, I pause from time to time, taking a moment to gaze at a wildflower, watch a rabbit munching grass, or look at a butterfly gathering nectar. Often when I pause, a bird will flutter up to the top of a tree or a rabbit will hop across my path, as if nature is revealing herself. During these pauses, I often see something new, a vista that I hadn't noticed or a plant that I might have walked by previously.

Sometimes I stop to identify a wildflower, stems of grasses, a bush, a tree, a bird perching or flying, or a birdsong or call. Knowing the names of plants and birds makes them seem like new friends that surround me on my journey. This learning about nature is part of what has been called deep walking.

Third, I allow myself to be moved by what I see and hear. I celebrate the multitude of growth buds on a pine tree, cherish the flute-like song of a wood thrush, or feel invigorated by the scent of junipers. I may even get a sense for the spirit or mood of a particular spot—the stillness of a hemlock cathedral or the inspiring panorama of distant hills under a blue sky. Sometimes I'll reach out to pat the trunk of a sturdy beech tree or caress delicate birch leaves.

As I walk and as my sensory awareness deepens, I am more drawn into the present. Whatever self-created worries, anxieties, melancholy, or other dramas filled my mind and heart prior to walking seem to fade away. Open to the moment, I begin to ease into mindfulness, to sense joy, gratitude, contentment, and the illumination of new learning, and to feel the same rejuvenation of mind, heart, and spirit that I feel during a sit spot experience.

From time to time while walking in this slow manner, I find that my breath becomes aligned with my pace. As a result my stamina increases. I can wander walk for miles and miles. Time is more often a limiting factor than physical fatigue.

And there is another practical factor that drew me to explore the wander walk as a vehicle for creating nature mindfulness. I realized that nature sitting experiences, for a variety of reasons, might not work for everyone. Wander walks might offer another and for some people a more approachable pathway to nature mindfulness.

Below are three versions of a wander walk. The first is simply called **The Wander Walk** and describes my initial experimentation with this concept. This walk took place on a nature trail on Cape Cod. I walked the trail once at a typical pace and in a typical manner with my wife and then walked it again alone, slowing down, practicing sensory awareness, and merging into mindfulness.

In the second selection, **Walking to Oneself**, I explore the potentials of a wander walk to encounter a deeper, truer sense of self. This hike with a specific goal in mind was like a minipilgrimage that seemed to tap into the transformational potentials of a trek. The walk took place early in the morning in the Pisgah National Forest near the Blue Ridge Parkway in North Carolina.

The third selection, **eBirding for Mindfulness**, blended bird watching, data collection, and wander walking. I found that listening to, spotting, and identifying birds while walking slowly through forest, field, and marsh deepened my focus, sharpened my sensory acuity, and enhanced my awareness of nuances in habitat. Along the way eBirding pulled me mindfully into the present moment.

THE WANDER WALK

I started near the high sand cliffs facing the Atlantic Ocean, the shoreline a battleground between land and ocean. Low-growing plants and grasses struggle to stabilize and hold the ground against the relentless wind and waves, while tides and storms nibble away inches and feet of shoreline every year.

Standing at the Marconi Beach outlook in the Cape Cod National Seashore, I could visualize the location where in 1903 the first transatlantic telegraph message was sent, an exchange of pleasantries between King Edward VII of the United Kingdom and President Teddy Roosevelt of the United States. The building that housed this telegraph station is long gone, its function replaced by repeated waves of new technology, one of them being the cell phone in my pocket on which I can effortlessly send a text to my son in Berlin or my daughter in Bremen, Germany. Even the spot where the station stood is gone, eaten away by erosion.

Change and more change. The only constant is the ocean waves, long lines of frothy white breakers rolling in and splashing onto the sandy shore below me.

I turned and headed inland, knowing that this walk was going to be an experiment. I had, over the last months, learned that many of my readers, even though they wanted to deepen their experiences with and their connection to nature, simply couldn't, for a variety of reasons, pull off the hourlong sit spot experience that I presented in my book *The Stillness of the Living Forest.*

I thought that I needed to offer a nature experience that was more approachable, more user-friendly. I came up with the idea of a wander walk, a slow stroll through woods or fields while engaging in full sensory awareness. On these wander walks I made frequent pauses to examine, study, gaze at, learn about, even befriend various aspects of nature—the birds, animals, wildflowers, and trees.

Heading through the coastal heathland, I shifted into wander walk mode, looking carefully at the dark-green, low-growing, earth-hugging patches of golden beach heather, broom cowberry, and pink-blossomed sea roses. These were all plants adapted to thrive in the dry, shallow, sandy, windblown oceanside soil. Amidst these low plants I also saw a few scattered, stunted, wind-bent pitch pines, looking like wild bonsai specimens.

I tuned into the soundscape. The soft, steady *shrump, shrump, shrump* of the waves onto the shoreline created a background. I listened for the songs or calls of any birds that might live in this scrubby terrain and heard the whiny mew of a hidden catbird; the insistent, high-pitched, repetitive *tseet, tseet, tseet* calls of a chipping sparrow; and a novel song, one that grabbed my attention, the rich melodious *too tee tee chidididididi* of a vesper sparrow. I tracked the song to its source and spotted the sparrow perched in a low, scraggly, bear oak.

Crossing the mostly empty parking lot, I stepped onto the Atlantic White Cedar Swamp Trail, a one-mile-long path that descends from seaside heath to a swampy glacial depression where a stand of white cedar trees grow. I thought that this trail with its changes in habitat and vegetation would provide a good setting to pilot the wander walk concept.

My sandals crunched on the sandy surface of the trail. A bird darted by, landed in a nearby pitch pine, and sang a loud, clear *drink your te-e-e-e-a.* Binoculars up, I got the bird in focus and was rewarded with a close-up view of a male towhee, a handsome, robin-sized bird with a black head and back, a bright-orange flank, and a snow-white breast. I watched him open his bill and sing *drink your te-e-e-e-a*, his bill quivering as he trilled the final *te-e-e-e-a*.

A moment of beauty. Towhees are typically shy birds, yet this one landed a few feet away, displayed his plumage, and gave a musical presentation. I always feel fortunate and grateful when I witness these moments of nature beauty, moments that fill my heart and transform the way I see the world. I wondered if the easygoing energy of the wander walk was already inviting a different response from nature.

Proceeding down the trail, I observed that the pine trees, now sheltered from the steady ocean wind, grew taller. I paused and inhaled the fresh smell of green pine boughs above and brown, dry pine needles below. This was an open pine woods with spots of bright sunshine and patches of ferns, checkerberry, and wild sarsaparilla covering the ground. I felt the warmth and richness of the vegetative growth rising from the sandy soil. A gust of wind sighed through the pine branches above me. Yes, sighing is exactly the sound the wind makes when it blows through pine boughs!

Chirps and squeaks carried from the pine woods, perhaps chickadees. I stopped and made *pish, pish, pish* sounds, an imitation of an avian scolding call that usually brings birds in to take a peek. Soon two little birds flew closer, flitting from branch to branch. One landed right above me and called out *chickadee-dee-dee-dee*— another close encounter with nature.

I took a few more steps down the trail, paused, and placed my palm on the brown, scaly bark of a thick pitch pine. I felt the warmth of the wood, sensed the plentiful sap and resin within, and pictured its spreading, water-gathering roots.

As the trail descended further down into the glacial depression, I noticed the transition from pitch pines to tall white oaks. At this lower elevation there was even more shelter from the ocean wind, and over the decades fallen leaves, twigs, and pine needles had composted into soil that could hold water and nutrients, creating an environment where oaks could thrive.

It was shadier here, dappled sunlight, a lattice of light and shadow. I placed my hand on the trunk of a white oak, felt the dry, tight-scaled bark, felt the strength and density of the wood, and sensed the depth of the root system.

The breeze picked up and swayed the dense green canopy of oak leaves above me, creating a rustling and swishing, like thousands of strands of paper softly crinkling, a soothing sound that rose and fell with each gust. I guessed it is true that each leaf of each tree creates its own unique wind-song.

I arrived at a gray wooden boardwalk that led through the swamp. Pools of water, surprisingly clear, stood on both sides of the boardwalk. Moisture-loving plants grew here—vibrant, verdant mosses, lacy-leafed ferns. And I saw the tall white cedars, straight trunked, dead lower branches, dark-green, lacy foliage up high reaching into the sunlight.

I took in the atmosphere of the white cedar swamp. It was dark and shady with only small scattered dots of sunlight reaching the ground. I sensed a quality of stillness. The trees, leaves, water, and moss absorbed the sounds, creating a cathedral-like quiet that evoked a reverential feeling.

Stopping near a tall, thick white cedar I reached out and placed my palm on its vertically striated gray-brown bark. I sensed the dry, hard quality of the wood and marveled at how trees growing in a swamp can create wood with such a dry quality to it. I read later that white cedar was prized by the colonists who used it for boards, joists, frames, rafters, and doors, and particularly floors because it could be scoured to a clean, bright white.

Continuing along the boardwalk, I felt the swamp slowly shift in mood. The thick stillness, the daytime darkness, the shifting shimmers of sunlight, the pools of placid water, and the lush dark-green clumps of moss pulled me into a somber mood.

Stopping and peering into a pool of water, I saw the reflection of a tangled matrix of branches and trunks and spots of sky and cloud. A scene from *The Lord of the Rings* came to mind in which Frodo stares into the Dead Marsh, is drawn down, and falls helplessly in. I found myself gazing into a dark maze of alluring reflections. I felt an instant of vertigo, a fleeting willingness to succumb, to let myself drop into the lush, life-taking, life-giving waters of the swamp.

I jerked back, turned, and walked briskly to the end of the boardwalk and felt a tinge of relief when I stepped on solid ground and slowly began to ascend back to the brighter oak woods. When a robin, the first bird I had seen since entering the deep swamp, flew across the trail, landed in a tree, and sang a few bars of *cheerily, cheer-up, cheerily cheer-up*, it seemed as if I had returned to the land of light and life.

Continuing along the trail I spotted a tall blueberry bush, peered into the foliage, and discovered a cluster of ripe blueberries. Reaching in, I plucked five ripe berries, placed them in my mouth, and chewed slowly. The taste, a sun-warmed blend of sweet and tart and fruit, was vastly superior to any store-bought blueberries. The only comparison my mind could generate was that of a vintage Burgundy with subtle tastes of fruit, mineral, and earth.

As I walked back up the trail into the open pine trees, I realized that my stroll was drawing to an end. I could again hear the distant *shrump, shrump, shrump* of the ocean waves. Slowing my pace I noticed a sea rose near the path still in bloom with light pink, tattered blossoms. I bent down, sniffed, and inhaled a sweet floral fragrance.

The trail ended. Stepping back into the parking lot, I reflected on my wander walk. I felt that same lightly euphoric, deeply satisfied, softened personal borders, nature-connected high that I so often felt after an hourlong sit spot session. I had been touched by the beauty and awed by the diversity, vitality, and resilience of the life forms I had encountered. I sensed a shift in my consciousness to a more open, soft focus. And even though I had walked over a mile, I felt relaxed, refreshed, and rejuvenated.

The wander walk worked for me. And now, two weeks later, as I write these words, I can easily call up images, sounds, and sensations of the White Cedar Trail. I can hear the steady sound of the surf, the song of the towhee, and the sigh of the wind through the pine trees. I can feel the warm, dry earth, retouch the trunks of the trees, smell the pine-scented air, and feel that nature-connected shift in consciousness.

Now I wonder if a slow, sensory awareness stroll through nature will work as well for others. Will this description be enough to get others started, enough to help them develop their own version of a wander walk?

WALKING TO ONESELF

"Both friends came to realize that walking over long distances and spans of time is the surest way to find oneself."
—Torbjorn Ekelund

I gazed into the campfire, watched the yellow and orange flames rise and fall, heard the crackle of burning wood, and smelled the wood smoke. Staring at the flickering flames, I made a decision to get up early and take a wander walk. I wanted to better understand this "finding of oneself" through walking.

Adding two final oak logs to the fire, I watched the wood catch and spark and reflected on this phenomenon of finding oneself. It seemed that everyone who took a long thru-hike described a deeper, clearer, truer connection to oneself.

I wanted to learn more about what happens in body, mind, and soul to create such a deeper connection to self. My plan was to hike from my campsite in the Pisgah National Forest up to Sleepy Gap, a scenic pull-off along the Blue Ridge Parkway, a spot that provided both a panoramic view of mountains and valleys, and an intersection with the famous Mountain to Sea long-distance hiking trail.

An Early Start—Mile 0.0 to 0.86

I woke up spontaneously as the first hints of daylight spread through the forest and filtered in the screen windows of the tent.

Silence at all the other campsites. Having learned that it is unwise for me to set off early without caffeine and food, I sat quietly at the picnic table, sipped a bottle of cold, creamy frappuccino, and munched a few Italian milk-and-honey cookies—cookies plain enough to pass for food.

Silence in the woods. I was up before the birds. As I sipped the last drops of coffee, the first bird sang, a Carolina wren, opening the morning birdsong chorus with a loud, clear, jaunty *tea-kettle, tea-kettle, tea-kettle*. A white-breasted nuthatch followed with a nasal *yank, yank, yank* chant. A cardinal whistled its pure *birdy, birdy, birdy* song.

I set off down the road from the campground, a road that I had walked often with my wife, but now I stepped alone. In the quiet of morning, I heard the soft shushing of water flowing along the bottom of the ravine. In the distance, deep in the heavily leafed oak and maple forest, a yellow-billed cuckoo called a mournful *ka-ka-ka-kow-kow*. Fresh morning air touched my face. I inhaled the fragrance of damp earth and fertile forest. My senses were awake.

Stepping off the road onto the Pine Loop Trail, I started on the first segment of my route to Sleepy Gap. This trail ascended up a ravine next to Bent Creek. A sign set next to a thick, mostly decayed fallen tree read Natural Disturbances and described the heavy damage to the forest, including the uprooting of many trees, caused by hurricane Opal in 1995. This sign, with its faded, almost illegible print, covered with a thin layer of mold, was itself an emblem of natural disturbances. The Pine Loop Trail, imposed upon an old road and heavily trafficked by day hikers and mountain bikers, was another well-worn nature disturbance with its bare reddish dirt and its network of exposed roots that looked like arteries coursing through the earth.

Rhododendrons grew in dense profusion in the moist soil along the creek. I gazed at the shiny dark-green leaves and thought about how beautiful this trail must be in the spring when the rhododendrons bloom. I remembered the Rhododendron Park I had visited in Bremen, Germany, where I learned that these plants grow all over the world in areas of dappled sunlight. This moist, shady forest along the banks of Bent Creek was ideal habitat for rhododendrons.

I settled into a rhythm of walking, stretching out the last vestiges of morning stiffness, my limbs finding their way into smooth coordination. I felt the urge to keep walking, knowing how readily walking stimulates thinking. I had read how great thinkers like Darwin, Kant, and Roseau walked to think and problem solve. I had a pretty good idea that as I walked, new layers of thought would cover earlier layers, so I planned to stop periodically to write down my observations. I sat on a log and wrote my first set of observations.

ALONE ON THE TRAIL—MILE 0.86 TO 1.56

Continuing my ascent along the side of the ravine, I emerged from the rhododendrons into a hardwood forest of tall, stately, thick-trunked oaks and maples, a dense canopy of green leaves above, a carpet of lacy ferns covering the forest floor.

I paid very close attention to my surroundings. I was on my own and had to find my way, had to keep track of land marks, read the map correctly, and make the right turns. There would be no group decision, no reassurances from others that the route was right.

Arriving at the first trail intersection, a connector to the Explorer Trail, I stopped and double-checked the map. A few steps down the trail I paused, looked back, and fixed landmarks in my mind that I would need on my return trip.

Hiking alone, finding my way, focused on the trail, I tuned into the present moment. Extraneous thoughts and concerns were pushed to the periphery of my awareness. Maybe this heightened trail focus created by traveling alone and maintained out of the need to survive was one element of finding oneself.

Ascending—Mile 1.56 to 2.49

Reaching the Sleepy Gap Trail, a sign indicated that this trail was reserved for hikers—no mountain bikes or horses allowed. The trail climbed steeply upward with sharp turns, frequent switchbacks, and in the steepest places, steps carved into the earth. A trail crew had been working recently, clearing fallen logs and branches, digging drainage ditches, building steps, and in one spot hacking a seat into a log. I was so tuned in to the trail that I could almost feel the intentions, almost read the minds of the trail crew as they crafted a route for water diversion and built steps exactly where needed.

I heard the birds of the deep high woods—the slow, mechanical metronome *chweeo, cheewup* of a blue-headed vireo; and the continuous *here I am, over here, here I am* of a red-eyed vireo. Looking up the trail, I saw it wind and twist and turn up and up the side of the mountain. Far above I spotted beams of bright sunlight filtering through the trees— an opening perhaps, hopefully my goal, the Sleepy Gap Overlook.

As I gazed up at the trail, I realized that this was a climb each person would need to take at their own pace. Each climber would need to follow the path in their own way. The path suddenly became both literal and figurative. Tangible reality and transformational metaphor merged.

Everyone has a path. I was walking my path. As Torbjorn wrote, "The path is the goal and the goal is the path."

My legs energized, my steps lightened, all other concerns fading away, my purpose singular, my mind focused, I climbed my path toward the summit, feeling how the blend of experience and metaphor brought me closer to self.

Striding to the top of the trail, I stepped into the overlook, into a lush open meadow offering a panoramic vista. Below me I saw wispy-blue morning mist floating above a wide valley and draping across distant mountains. These were the blue ridges for sure. Birds sang around me—chickadees, a tufted titmouse, a robin, and a catbird. Goldenrods bloomed. I felt a sense of elation. I had reached my goal.

As I sat down to write my notes, I noticed a sign with an arrow pointing up a hill to the Mountain to Sea Trail. Maybe this was like the search for self. You reach one level, celebrate briefly, but then in a humbling, sobering moment you realize that the path goes on and another climb waits.

THE MOUNTAIN TO SEA TRAIL (MST)—MILE 2.49 TO 2.90

I followed the Mountain to Sea Trail as it climbed across rocks, between trees, and under branches. Steep steps led the way. I immediately sensed a difference in this trail. It was a thru-hiking trail, not a day-use path like Sleepy Gap.

The MST was narrow, less traveled, less worn, and in places lightly covered, almost camouflaged, by leaf litter. If a trail, as Robert MacFarland contends in his book *On Trails*, holds the voices, thoughts, and feelings, the subtle vibrations of all who have previously traversed it, then this trail sang of long-distance treks, of hours and days and nights of steadily moving forward through sun and rain and wind. It sang of a deeper, longer journey to oneself.

This was an alluring song to me, a siren call to leave everyday life behind and trek in sacred solitude down this long path from the high peaks and deep ravines of the Great Smokey Mountains to the tidal marshes and sandy beaches of the Atlantic Ocean.

Stepping slowly, steadily, silently, almost reverently down the trail, I felt the stirrings of an urge to commit to a long thru-hike. Trails came to mind—the famous Appalachian Trail, the majestic Pacific Crest Trail, the long North Country Trail, or the Ice Age Trail that wound for a thousand miles across my home state of Wisconsin.

It was hard to turn around. But a glance at my watch reminded me that it was time to head back to the campground to meet my wife and daughter for a picnic lunch.

FOREST TREASURES—MILE 2.9 TO 3.59

Descending the steep Sleepy Gap Trail felt more demanding physically than ascending. Gravity pushed me downhill. I used my trekking poles and the muscles of my upper legs as brakes. I could feel the strain on my knees as I picked my way down the steps, over rocks, and around steep turns. I recalled that more injuries occur when hiking down than when hiking up.

As I descended it occurred to me that the descent from the elation of summiting was also fraught with psychological challenges. How do you hold on to the essence of summiting? How do you share your joy and inspiration with others?

I wasn't sure how to manage the psychological challenges of the descent, but I discovered that I could relax into the physical challenge. I evened out my breathing and searched for the sweet spot of balance with gravity and effort, of letting gravity assist me instead of fighting it.

As my body took over the process of descending, I looked around at the forest floor. This was late summer in a North Carolina rainforest where it rained almost every day. Mushrooms grew all around on the forest floor, on the fallen half-rotted logs and stumps. I saw a stunning variety of shapes and colors—round caps, crystal-like forms, indented hats, buttons, umbrellas, gills, and stalks with marshmallow tops. I saw an array of colors—red, white, orange, tan, and brown.

I spotted an acorn that had fallen on the trail. I am not one for collecting souvenirs and don't like to disturb nature as I walk. But this time I stopped, picked it up, held it in my hand, and placed it in my pocket. I would set it on my dresser to remind me of this hike.

JUST WALKING—MILE 3.59 TO 4.79

Back on the Explorer Trail the way was wider, the descent more gradual. I eased into an effortless rhythm of walking, boots padding softly and steadily across the earth, arms and legs moving in synchrony, eyes looking ahead. Walking felt effortless and natural.

I reflected that the human body had evolved for bipedal locomotion, an evolution that probably resulted in losing some mammalian advantages in strength, speed, and climbing ability, but a development that allowed the eyes to gaze ahead, freed up the hands to grab and manipulate objects, and allowed the back to carry burdens. Perhaps this bipedal posture was one factor that stimulated the growth of the frontal lobes and brought the abilities to plan, organize, know time and distance, and above all, to wander.

I felt this core ambulatory experience, felt my alertness to all around me, felt my curiosity to discover what lay beyond each turn in the path. I felt the reassuring comfort of my backpack—my supplies for daily life if needed. I felt the readiness of my arms and hands to grasp, pull, carry, and explore. As I walked I felt fully human. Perhaps this connection with basic human bipedal locomotion was another way of finding oneself on the trail.

RETURN—MILE 4.79-5.71

The trail ended. I rejoined the road. The cool fresh air and soft angled light of morning had been replaced by the bright direct light and rising warmth of midday. Cicadas called. Dragonflies darted. Butterflies fluttered among the goldenrods and Queen Anne's lace. A warm breeze whooshed through the leaves above me.

I arrived back at the campsite feeling satisfied. Sitting down, I unlaced my boots, peeled off my socks, aired out my feet, and thought that most likely there were many ways in which walking leads to oneself. I had learned about a few but surely there was more to learn, more long walks to take, more paths to follow, more discoveries to make.

EBIRDING FOR MINDFULNESS

I couldn't pinpoint the moment when I descended into melancholy, that all too familiar state where I felt discouraged, tired, hopeless, annoyed, and of course, sad. It was most likely a litany of little things adding up—a misunderstanding with a friend, no clear way forward on a task that needed to be done, an appliance breaking down, persistent bad weather, an aching knee. And maybe there were bigger things lurking in the background—a worrisome health problem, a family member struggling.

No solutions emerged for the problems at hand, and even if I had solutions I lacked the energy or enthusiasm to implement them. It was clear to me that I needed to push an inner reset button. And then the idea came to me—get out of the house, get out in nature, go for an eBird walk.

After a struggle to overcome inertia, I laced up my hiking boots, slipped on my binocular harness, opened up the *eBird* app on my iPhone, clicked the box for Start Checklist, and walked out through my backyard. I told myself—just walk, look and listen.

A SHIFT

A *tap, tap, tap* drifted down from the top of a big sugar maple. I looked up, scanned, and spotted a male downy woodpecker using his specialized back toe and tail to hold vertical on the trunk while he picked at the bark for insects and caterpillars.

From high in an ash tree came the nasal *ank, ank, ank* of a white-breasted nuthatch. I followed the sound and saw it descending head first down the trunk, nuthatch style. At the edge of the yard, a gray-plumaged catbird ducked from branch to branch in a thick shrub. Soon I heard its plaintive *mew, mew, mew* call.

Three birds before I even left my yard. Not bad, I thought. I stopped to enter a tally for each on the *eBird* app. I reflected how each bird was in its natural niche, behaving in its natural way, a thought that gave me a scintilla of comfort.

Along the grassy path heading downhill to the beaver pond, I slowed my pace and inhaled the earthy, lush, fertile smell of a late summer meadow and paused to gaze at the wildflowers—butter-yellow sprays of goldenrod, vibrant purple New England aster, creamy-white boneset, and dusky-pink Joe Pye weed.

I continued along the path, feeling my feet touch the freshly mowed grass and press into the faintly yielding ground. A soft breeze caressed my face. Above, in a delft-blue sky, a row of white, cotton-puff clouds floated above a distant line of dark-green forested hills. Two turkey vultures, the golden cleansers of nature, rocked on their V-angled wings and circled effortlessly high in the sky. I added them to my *eBird* tally.

Above me were high-pitched, trilled *zeee, zeee, zeee* calls. I stopped, scanned, and spotted a cedar waxwing perched on a bare branch of a dead tree. I brought up my binoculars and saw its crested head, dainty black eye mask, tan plumage, and yellow-tipped tail—all outlined against a blue sky. Two more waxwings flew into the tree. I gazed as they sallied out into the air, snatched insects, and flew back to perch.

Walking further I heard and then saw a goldfinch looping in front of me, calling its cheerful *per-chik-o-ree, per-chik-o-ree* flight song. At the beaver pond, where the mirror-still water reflected the trees and sky and clouds, a stately, shy blue heron flew up, voicing a loud hoarse squawk. Two wood ducks jumped up from the water, took flight calling a plaintive *jeeee, jeeee, jeeee.* A chattering kingfisher flew along the stream. I added four more birds to my tally.

Continuing along the path I began to notice patterns around me—stands of poplars with their leaves fluttering in the breeze, a patch of purplestem asters, and clusters of butter-yellow goldenrods covered with honey bees harvesting late summer pollen. The burgundy-red leaves of the red osier dogwood announced the approaching shift in the seasons.

I watched a monarch butterfly fluttering gently above the goldenrod. Something caught my eye. A chunk was missing from its left wing, yet it flew on, doing its duty in life—searching for nectar, looking for a milkweed on which to lay its eggs to give birth to the next generation, to continue the migration of the species. If it could move ahead and fulfill its duties with a damaged wing, I thought I could move ahead as well in spite of any chunks missing from my wings.

I realized that I was beginning to feel better. Nothing had changed with any of the life problems and difficulties I faced, but my internal state had begun to shift away from pessimism and negativity toward hopefulness. All I had done was notice nature around me.

Noticing

I reminded myself to slow down and listen as birds are often more readily heard than seen, especially in the late summer months when the trees and shrubs are in full leaf and the grasses stand tall and thick. I let my hearing drift near and far, tried to notice and accept all of the sounds, tried not to filter out the unpleasant whine of a distant truck struggling up a hill or the harsh caws of a crow. And I tried to not give special attention to the pleasant sounds. No judging, just listening. I heard the distant *cr-r-ruck* call of a raven.

I also tried to employ a kind of open, loose scanning to detect birds perching, flitting, flying, hovering, or soaring. This loose kind of scanning allowed me to also take in the vistas, colors, and patterns, further facilitating a shift in consciousness—a calming, a letting go, a change of focus from the little *I* with all of its waves of worries and concerns to the bigger *I*, content to be part of the ocean.

Suddenly, intuitively, I turned, looked up, and in the distance spotted a large bird, wings flat, soaring. Binoculars up, I spotted its bright white head and white tail. It was a bald eagle. I tracked its majestic flight. As it flapped and soared high above the ground, I felt my spirits lift.

MOMENTS

Pausing beneath the sheltering branches of a cherry tree, I looked down the trail and in the top of a pine tree saw a goldfinch, its golden-yellow plumage luminous in the rays of the afternoon sun. It hadn't noticed me. I watched it perched on a dark-green pine bough, turning its head, looking around, peaceful, relaxed in its wild and timeless setting.

I was mesmerized, taking in this moment of beauty. I thought back to a similar moment I had experienced in the spring while on an *eBird* walk with my friend Chris.

We were working our way carefully down a steep muddy trail through shrubs and weeds and second-growth trees, enveloped in a veil of morning mist. Chris paused and murmured, "I think the light is still a little dim for the birds."

And then, as the ascending sun finally garnered enough strength to penetrate and dissipate the mist, we both sensed the morning light increasing. We began to see birds moving in the branches—a warbler flitting from twig to twig. We began to hear birds singing—a catbird mewing, a wren chattering.

Chris hung a Bluetooth speaker on a broken branch of a hawthorn tree. We stepped back about twenty feet. He found an owl mashup on his phone and pushed play. The tremulous, descending whinnying of an Eastern screech-owl filled the air accompanied by an assortment of strident calls, buzzes, and squeaks, a medley of alarm and attention calls. We stood silently, waiting and watching expectantly.

A catbird flew down, perched on a nearby branch and cocked its head in curiosity. Two chestnut-sided warblers flitted into the tree above the speaker. I could see their yellow caps and the beautiful stripe of auburn-colored plumage running beneath their wings. A common yellowthroat with its jaunty black face mask appeared. A slate-gray tufted titmouse arrived. Four more kinds of warblers materialized in the tree and flitted nervously from branch to branch. A pair of chickadees, the gossips of the forests, flew in, always present for any social event.

We stood still, jaws dropping, eyes growing wider, taking in the view as more and more birds appeared—an ovenbird and a veery, a Cape May warbler and a yellow prairie warble, all edging closer and closer to the speaker. We tried to identify and count all of the species that had materialized out of the mist, early migrants needing a morning meal and local birds looking for food. It was a cornucopia of wild birds, a vision of plenty.

The owl mashup came to an end. Quiet returned. Little by little, the birds flew off, fading back into the mist, back into the trees and shrubs. We stood spellbound, silent and still, not wanting to break the magic of the moment. Finally, Chris spoke softly, reverentially, "These are the moments you live for."

Yes, I thought, moments of beauty, moments that on a literal level flood the body with endorphins and positive hormones, moments that on a figurative level fill the heart and nourish the soul.

GENEROSITY

I continued on my walk. My *eBird* tally was up to twelve. I had hopes of reaching twenty or more, which would be a good count for late summer.

And then it all dried up. I walked and walked, but there was nothing to be seen or heard. I even took a detour down a brush-lined road that usually is filled with birds, but all I saw was an occasional bird butt; all I heard were distant squeaks. I couldn't see or hear enough to make an identification. My feelings of discouragement crept back in.

Frustrated, I shifted my attention to the trees and wildflowers. Using my *Picture This* app, I identified a tall, stately American linden. Alongside the trail I spotted a cluster of blue bottle gentians in bloom, a rare wildflower that blooms just for a week in late August and early September.

I looked up at the sky, took in the patterns and shapes of the puffy white clouds, and listened to the wind sighing through the branches of a white pine. I let go of the need to see birds.

A moment later a small bird landed on a limb in front of me. Binoculars up, I saw a black head, gray back, yellowish breast, and a long tail flicking up and down. It was an eastern phoebe, a nice find. Two more flew in and perched in the tree, another landed on a street sign. The phoebes were moving south.

I heard a sweet, slurred, down and up *pee-a-wee*, the namesake call of an Eastern wood-pewee. A few minutes later a group of small brown birds fluttered out of the thick field grass, landed on the road, and began to pick through the mowed grass along the shoulder. They were chipping sparrows—rufous cap, white eyebrow, black eye line, delicately mottled brown and black back, grayish breast, softly calling *tseet, tseet, tseet* as they hopped along the road right in front of me.

Another bird flew into a tree—an Eastern bluebird—bluish back, orange breast, singing a single sweet musical *chur-wi*. I heard a chattering in a bush. Peering in with my binoculars I spotted a dusky-brown house wren. Two mourning doves whistle-winged overhead.

Suddenly, so much seen, so much learned. All I had done was offer time, attention, presence, and then just let go. Nature stepped in and generously provided instruction. I thought of the old saying, "The teacher comes when the student is ready." I felt fulfilled, encouraged, and reminded to patiently wait out the dry times, to use my intervals of melancholy as opportunity for learning and growing.

Resonance

Some of the goals of psychotherapy are to achieve insight, obtain a clearer knowledge of and acceptance of the self, gain a vision of the path ahead, understand and transcend self-imposed doubts, and overcome self-imposed worries and limitations. The trick comes with the timing and readiness. When is the client ready and open to receive the insight?

On this *eBird* walk, in a state of nature mindfulness, some of these just right therapeutic insights came to me. Reflecting on my feelings of fatigue, I noticed vigorous new growth on the tips of wild rose branches. When I thought about feeling stuck and unable to see a path forward, I saw tree roots growing around a rock, finding a way around an obstacle, showing me the meaning of resilience. Filled with doubts about my abilities, I considered how a pair of wood ducks used their natural abilities to find just right food on the perfect habitat of a newly formed beaver pond.

Nature is not random but filled with patterns and meaning, creating a resonance with what Mark Nepo calls, "the mysterious circulation of the healing life force through us and in us."

I made my way back home in a different state than when I left. Returning to my yard, I noticed that my melancholy, my minidepression had evaporated. The gray clouds of my worries had floated away. The sky above was blue and clear and open to myriad possibilities.

I finalized my tally and pushed the submit button for my *eBird* list, a small but positive act of contributing to science, possibly to the well-being of the world, and certainly to my personal well-being.

CHAPTER 12

Mindfulness Afloat

FTER MONTHS OF OBSERVING NATURE FROM THE SHORELINE of Prompton Lake, I wondered what it might be like to conduct a sitting session on the water. As with many initiatives that later turn out to be beneficial, it took several years to progress from idea to implementation. On the day I finally climbed into my kayak, paddled to a secluded location, and conducted my first session on the water, I discovered a number of dimensions of a sit spot afloat that seemed to facilitate nature mindfulness.

The most immediate aspect, one that takes my breath away every time I launch my kayak, is the open vista across the water to shoreline to sky, a vista that must resonate with some primal, comfort-in-nature chord.

The shoreline, with its sand, rocks, grasses, reeds, shrubs, and trees, provides multiple layers of fractals—those repeating, branching visual patterns so soothing and fascinating to human senses, mind, and heart. All of this vegetation is cloaked in palettes of calming colors, changing continually from spring and summer greens to autumn golds and reds to winter grays and browns. On the horizon, the blues, greens, and grays of the water meet the blues, grays, and whites of sky and clouds.

The surface of the water provides its own calming views— sometimes a liquid mirror reflecting trees and clouds, sometimes a tangle of wind-blown wavelets, sometimes a pattern of rolling waves. And the water offers its own palette of pleasing and changing colors—shades of blue, tints of green, and on a cloudy day, hues of gray.

The motion of a kayak in water can also be comforting. I love the feeling of freedom when I push off from shore and glide almost resistance-free across the water. And there seems to be something soothing about the gentle motion of boat upon water, perhaps kindling memories of the comforting watery medium in which both species and personal life evolved—a kind of coming home. Out on the water, the many tactile sensations pull me into the present moment—the feel of the breeze blowing unfettered across open water, the sensation of spray on skin, or the embracing warmth of direct and reflected sunlight.

The fragrances of nature—many of which science has shown act to calm emotions, balance the nervous system, and boost the immune system—waft readily across open water. Pausing while paddling, I enjoy inhaling the fresh, negative ion-loaded fragrance of air above moving water or the bracing scent of a salt breeze. Sometimes near the shoreline I smell the rich, growing plant smell of a cattail marsh or the fragrance of a pine forest.

The soundscape is unique out on water. I can readily hear the bow of the kayak splashing softly, waves lapping against the shoreline, or a stream tumbling into a lake. Across open water I take in the distant cries of the gulls, the calls of shorebirds, the songs of the forest birds, and the croaks of frogs.

The experience of time seems to change on the water. The steady current of a river, the rhythm of the tides, and the rising and falling of the waves all belong to a different sense of time, a departure from linear time to an immersion in circular time—the time of repeating patterns, of *now* time. In these moments it is easy and feels natural to let go of worries of the past and concerns for the future and bring one's awareness into the present moment.

Conducting a sit spot experience afloat also offers ideal, up-close viewing of nature. In a kayak I can paddle close to the riparian zone, that part aquatic, part terrestrial, ever-changing edge between fresh water and upland ground. These zones hold a particularly diverse variety of animals and birds, along with a rich mosaic of plant life. Riparian zones are often transit pathways for animals and birds moving along the zone or from water to upland. The same dynamic variety of life occurs in tidal zones as well.

Edging a kayak next to a riverbank, along a lake shoreline, or into salt marsh affords the opportunity for views of birds and mammals hard to obtain when walking or sitting on shore. Something about a small boat moving slowly or sitting still doesn't alarm the birds and mammals the way a walking or shore-sitting human does.

Drifting silently with the wind, floating with the current under a veil of morning mist, or paddling in the fading light of dusk, I am often able to approach herons, sandpipers, ducks, and shorebirds much closer than if I were on foot. River otters, muskrats, and beaver swim nearby. Dragonflies land on the boat. Water bugs scurry across the surface. Fish jump nearby.

For the purpose of nature mindfulness, water provides both a literal and metaphorical gateway to a present-centered state of mind. Literally, all of the pleasing sensory inputs calm and balance body, mind, and emotions. The deepened sensory awareness offers a crucial element for the transition into nature mindfulness. Metaphorically, floating on a river, lake, or bay is a flow experience.

It is for all of these reasons that I have come to believe there is value in sitting still on the water, observing, and connecting with nature. The sit spot sessions I have done on the water have been unique and meaningful.

Afloat on White Oak describes my first sitting experience afloat. It took place early on a rainy summer morning. I paddled out on an abandoned lake, pushed my kayak onto a mudflat, and after a few minutes of stillness seemed to blend into the setting. I soon felt surrounded by and immersed in up-close views of the life of birds, animals, and plants.

In the second session, **The Gathering Ground**, a spontaneous opportunity to conduct a sit spot session presented itself as I paddled through a coastal salt marsh in Virginia, a good reminder of the importance of intuition in selecting a location for a sit spot. I parked my kayak in a bed of reeds for a long and constantly changing view of the birds and plant life of a tidal marsh.

The final selection, **River Reflections: A Journey down the Lackawaxen**, is a wander-paddle. I set off on an early morning kayak journey down the Lackawaxen River. Drifting slowly with the current and paddling through rapids, I watched a rich display of nature unfolding in and around the river as the sun rose and the day warmed.

AFLOAT ON WHITE OAK

A flock of geese—large and gray, their white chin straps barely visible in the predawn light—paddled slowly away from the stony bank of the abandoned boat launch at White Oak Pond. A quick count revealed more than twenty-five, a flock augmented by a number of almost fully grown goslings.

The geese swam slowly out toward open water, moving steadily and effortlessly, tracing Vs across the still surface. Perhaps they had spent the night in the safety of the deeper water near the old boat ramp. They didn't appear alarmed by my presence, possibly due to the early hour, a time when birds and mammals often seem less afraid, or maybe they had simply seen few humans around the deserted pond.

I unloaded my kayak and dragged it across the rocky, weedy ground to a small inlet in the shoreline reeds. Climbing in, I shoved hard with the paddle, pushed the boat across the black mud, and floated free. I always love that first moment of floating free, low, and level in the water, moving easily with the slightest push of the paddle.

The weather forecast called for a break in the rain. My plan was to paddle across the open water, push the kayak into the edge of a vast marsh, and conduct an hourlong sit spot session afloat. After a brief search I found a small mudbank covered with weeds and wildflowers, backed the stern of the kayak onto it, and settled in with a full view of the open water. In a few minutes it felt as if my presence was ignored, as if I had vanished into and was absorbed by the marsh.

Swallows swirled overhead, lifting, turning, ascending, dropping down, deftly snatching insects from the air. I tried to identify the different species, a challenge because they flew constantly, twisting and turning through the air, difficult to track with binoculars. Gradually, I got them in sight long enough to identify them.

The most graceful were the barn swallows with slender wings, streamlined body, long forked tail, blueish back, cinnamon neck, and buff-colored breast. I watched them fly and glide and listened to their short, sweet *vit, vit* song. There were tree swallows as well with violet-green backs, white breasts, broad wings, and squared off, faintly notched tails, singing more a musical, liquid, twittered *weet,*

weet, weet song. And I spotted a few northern rough-winged swallows, plain in appearance, brownish back, white breast, gray-brown throat, broad wings, squared off, notched tails, voicing their hoarse rising *frip, frip* calls.

The three types of swallows seemed happy to share this prime pond habitat with its abundance of insects. They appeared in waves. For a while there were no swallows, and then suddenly many, some flying a few feet over my head with such quiet wing strokes that I could barely hear their wing beats. I saw immature swallows with indistinct plumage, flying and hunting alongside their elders and parents with what appeared to be full proficiency. I estimated there were at least a hundred swallows swooping and feeding over the pond and marsh.

Ahead on the water swam a lone duck. Binoculars up, I saw a mostly gray duck. Given the distance and the dim light, it was hard to identify. I watched it swim, pause, climb out on a mudbank, pick for food, and waddle back in the water. Somehow it seemed like a young duck on its own. I didn't know why, but I felt a sense of kinship to this duck. Perhaps because we were both alone, both engaged in the tasks at hand. The duck slipped into a patch of reeds and disappeared.

A trio of red-winged blackbirds, chacking emphatically, corkscrewed down out of the sky, set their wings, and landed nearby amidst a thick patch of cattails. Another two flew in and joined them, then another five. I listened to their *chack, chack* calls. Some walked on the mud, picking for food, others clung to vertical stems, and still others perched jauntily on the top of long, dark-brown cattail heads.

More blackbirds flew in. I saw the plain, brownish females and spotted an occasional flash of bright orange from the wings of the males. They seemed restless, probably getting ready to assemble into migratory flocks that included the old generation and the new young birds that would be making their first trek south.

The geese, hidden now behind the reeds, began to honk, hesitant at first, then louder before they suddenly lifted into the air and flew right over me. I could hear their strong wings fanning the air as they steadily gained altitude, honking, climbing, and heading out for a day of grazing in nearby farm fields.

A light mist began to fall that quickly turned to rain, the drops splashing softly onto the surface of the pond, creating impact circles. The rain soaked my shoulders and the pages of my notebook. It was a gentle rain, unexpected, just more water joining this day's watery theme, I thought. I grabbed my life preserver, put it over my notebook to keep the pages dry, lifting it when I made notes.

The lone duck reappeared, much closer now. I was happy to see it again. I brought it into focus with my binoculars and studied its appearance—gray head, short gray bill, and a faint white eye ring. It seemed oblivious to my presence. I watched it feed, saw its bill open and close as it snatched morsels from the mud, saw it strain water with its beak. It was an intimate view into the life of a duck. I felt almost as if I was invading its privacy.

The duck climbed onto a mudbank, offering me a full view. I saw its mottled brownish breast and short gray legs. A quick peak at the photos on the *iBird Pro* app informed me that I was looking at a female wood duck, most likely a juvenile. For a few moments I relished the thrill that comes with a confirmed identification. I wondered if this was simply the satisfaction that follows successful problem solving, or was it based on something deeper, some hard-wired reward circuits from a time when precise knowledge of flora and fauna increased the odds of survival.

My little duck friend disappeared back into the reeds. I wondered why she was alone at this time of year when most birds were gathering into flocks. Was she the sole survivor of a clutch that had been predated? Had she become separated from her nestmates? She appeared energetic, competent, and in possession of a strong will to survive. I wished her well.

A gust of wind swayed the long, slender, green leaves of the cattails back and forth, creating a soft rustling sound. The swaying motion and rustling sounds seemed eternal, a soundscape heard well before my existence and one that would continue well after I was gone.

I listened to the birds around the pond: the electric spark-like *dtzee, dtzee, dtzeet* of a kingbird, the cawing of distant crows, the strident *jay, jay, jay* of blue jays, and the lilting *per-chick-or-ree* of a flock of bright-yellow goldfinches in flight. I heard the croaking of frogs and the loud, harsh squawk of a blue heron taking flight.

Gazing down at the mudflat around me, I saw a prosperous diversity of plant life. Some of the plants I knew: the brown-topped cattails, the pink-blossomed smartweed, the purple-blue spires of pickerelweed, and the yellow cup flowers of lily pads. But there were many, many more plants and flowers—low and tall, spreading and climbing—that I didn't know.

I thought about the history of White Oak Pond. It was formed in 1820 by the Delaware and Hudson Canal Company as a reservoir to supplement the water level for barges carrying anthracite coal from the mountains of Pennsylvania to the Hudson River and on to New York City. When the canal went out of business, the pond was eventually taken over by the state and for almost a hundred years provided a favorite spot for fishermen and boaters. Then in 2015, amidst considerable outcry, the state drained the pond after deciding that the dam was structurally at risk.

For three years now, the pond had gone wild. In the center and around the old boat ramp, there was still an area of open water, now enlarged by recent heavy rains. The rest of the former lake had naturalized into a vast, verdant marsh, an unplanned wildlife refuge for birds, reptiles, fish, and mammals.

I thought about the human perspectives on White Oak Pond, the concept of changing owners, the building and maintenance of the dam, the controversies over the water level, the arguments and plans for restoring the pond, and the various concerns of landowners, the state, and sportsmen and women. All of these perspectives seemed distant and foreign as I sat in my kayak. Out on the water where nature had had free reign for three years, I sensed a very different reality, one characterized by resilience, adaptability, growth, and a primal life force, a force that pulsed within me as well.

The rain picked up. The hull of my boat was dotted with mosquitoes, flies, and other insects. The rain must have driven the insects down toward the surface of the pond. Glancing around I saw that the swallows had also descended and now were skimming the surface of the pond, finding the insects where they were, instantly adjusting their hunting strategy.

I saw movement on a narrow, plant-covered mudbank ahead. Scanning with my binoculars, I spotted a trio of sandpipers crouching and creeping along the mudflat. I honed in on field marks: reddish-brown plumage, short black beaks, legs seemed dark but easily could have been mud-coated. They took flight, rapid wing beats flying low over the water in close formation, bright *preep* calls. It was hard to know for sure with such a brief sighting, but most likely they were least sandpipers, birds that had bred high in the arctic tundra and were now working their way south. From the air they must have spotted wild White Oak Pond, liked the look of it, and settled in to rest and refuel.

Surprisingly, my sit spot hour was already up. I pushed off the mudflat and paddled further up into the marsh, following the narrowing course of the stream that fed White Oak Pond. I saw and heard more ducks, mallards, and wood ducks, and more herons—both great blues and greens. The rain fell harder. I turned around, paddled back to the boat ramp, pulled the kayak out, dragged it up to my car, hoisted it into the rack, and secured it.

I like to reflect on how I feel after a sitting session. That day I was wet but happy, uplifted by the beauty I had seen, and soothed by the sounds I had heard. After an hour observing life on White Oak Pond, I sensed a feeling of attachment, a bond of appreciation to the pond, and I knew that I would want to return. There was something about the rewilding of the pond, something about the power and strength of that process that made me feel simultaneously small and insignificant yet also connected and restored.

THE GATHERING GROUND

In the wind shelter of an island of tall reeds, I pivoted the kayak around and began my return paddle down the Assateague Channel. Now the stiff northeast breeze sailed me down the channel, and the ebbing tide flowed in my favor. An occasional easy stroke with the paddle was all that was needed to move forward and stay on course. The sun broke through the thick, gray, early November clouds. I savored the warmth of the sunshine as it touched my face and chest. The waves splashed against the kayak. A solitary seagull, bright and white, looped lazily over the water and called *kee-ew, kee-ew, kee-ew*.

My kayak glided under the graceful arching concrete bridge that connects Chincoteague Island to the barrier island of Assateague, the home of the Chincoteague National Wildlife Refuge. Once past the bridge I had a full view of the stately, old, burgundy-striped Assateague Lighthouse, a tall sentinel whose light still circles and shines through dark nights and thick fog. Along the shoreline of the refuge stood vast stands of golden-brown cordgrass punctuated by spits of tan sand. On my right, across the channel, stood the developed shoreline of Chincoteague Island, rows of bright-blue, white, and gray condos and colorful and capacious channel-side homes with piers, porches, and docks

Angling into a channel that would eventually take me back to the kayak launch at Memorial Park, I was surprised to see that a tidal mudflat had emerged where earlier there had been open water. An oystercatcher and a seagull walked across the mudflat stepping through upturned oyster shells, searching for food. I knew these emerging tidal flats influenced the rhythm of shorebird life and quickly decided this was a good time and place for a sit spot experience.

I had been planning to do a session of nature observation during my brief visit to Chincoteague, had been searching the refuge for a good location and thinking about a good time—all of this part of my usual deliberate approach. But now, this spot presented itself, and I decided to spontaneously accept what felt like a gift or even a directive from nature.

Paddling over to the far side of the mudflat, I backed my kayak into the reeds. I had not brought a notebook but for some reason had stuffed a notepad from the motel into my pocket, and digging around in my shirt I found an old ballpoint pen. Things seemed to be working out.

I took in the open view around me. The mudflat lay directly ahead, reed banks to the left and right, open water in the channel, and in the distance was the lighthouse, surrounded by trees and framed by a gray sky. The wind rattled and rustled the reeds, wavelets lapped against the kayak, seagulls called.

The oystercatcher walked toward me along the edge of the mudflat. I brought up my binoculars and got it in focus—a big, handsome, boldly-patterned shorebird, jet-black head, long, strong red bill, bright-white breast, tall pale legs. Its bill was mud-stained, its legs mud-streaked. It probed its bill into the mud, shook its head vigorously, withdrew its bill holding a chunk of soft gray flesh at the tip, lifted its head, and swallowed the morsel. That morsel must have been an oyster, I thought with a smile. And it looked very much like the fresh oysters I had enjoyed the night before.

A few minutes later three more shorebirds stepped along the edge of the mudflat—long legs, rounded bodies, long necks, and long bills. They moved closer. I studied them through the binoculars— bright-yellow legs, long, dark bills, mottled brown-and-white breast plumage. The birds walked slowly and gracefully, picking delicately into the mud and then suddenly broke into a frenzied dash through the shallow water, scooping and spearing with their beaks. These were a type of shorebird known as greater yellowlegs.

A large-winged, slender bird flew over me, set its long wings, and glided silently to a landing on a thin strip of mud at the edge of the reeds. Binoculars up, another striking close-up view—nature generously teaching me about shorebirds. This was a heron with slate-blue plumage, dark-purplish head, a blueish spear-shaped bill, and dull-dark legs. A check on my *iBirdPro* app confirmed that it was a little blue heron, a first ever sighting for me.

I'm not a compulsive life-lister, but there is something satisfying about seeing a bird for the first time, something exciting about seeing it alive and moving, something compelling about observing and naming another unique creature, another brightly colored tile in the mosaic of life. And this heron was behaving exactly as expected; it was in a marsh, at water's edge, standing stock still, neck extended, sharp bill poised at a 45-degree angle, coiled and ready to spear a fish in the tide-drawn shallows.

I glanced back at the original mudflat and saw that two more mudflats had emerged, a reminder of the rapidly changing landscape of a tidal channel. More birds arrived—gulls, terns, and sandpipers. I thought about the cycle of the tide and about the birds' time awareness. It wasn't like they were sitting up in a tree watching and waiting for their feeding grounds to emerge. They had a way of knowing, an awareness of the tide, a way of sensing the emergence of the flats, and they flew in and arrived right on time.

A ring-billed gull foraged amidst the shells and debris. It grabbed a shell in its beak, flapped up in the air, higher and higher, hovered, released the shell, and flutter-followed it back down to the mud, seized the now shattered shell, picked it open, and swallowed a morsel. How it found that shell amidst a jumble of shells was a mystery to me.

A minute later the seagull repeated the maneuver a second, third, and fourth time. The whole process fascinated me; the most beautiful part was the down-following flight—white wings fanning the air, and the impeccable finding of the shell. More avian skills, more avian ways of knowing revealed to me.

I looked at the reeds surrounding the kayak—green and tan, narrow and tubular, smooth cordgrass adapted to grow in saltwater, evolved to thrive in the twice daily tidal immersion, a rapidly growing opportunistic plant that protects the shoreline. The stalks of cordgrass rattled with each gust of wind, a rustling chorus, rising and falling, softer and louder.

I heard the seabirds calling up and down the channel—gulls, sandpipers, and willets. Each had its own signature call, but all were resonant, full toned, far-carrying calls, calls I suddenly realized were designed to carry through the noise of wind, waves, and rustling reeds.

A flock of sandpipers flew down the channel—fighter-jet sleek with pointed, angled wings, fast wing strokes—slicing through the wind, banking, whirling, setting their wings, gliding in unison, and landing on the far mudbank. Once on land they looked so different—small, rounded birds, walking delicately on slender legs, heads down, probing the mudflat with long beaks, moving in concert. It can be a challenge to identify sandpipers. My best guess was that these were dunlins, birds known to fly in flocks and feed on mudflats.

More birds appeared, feeding at the splendid table provided by the receding tide. Gulls flew in to pick for food among the upturned shells. A snowy egret winged over the channel, landed along a far reed bank and immediately assumed its statue-like hunting pose. Common terns arrived, flapping over the shallow water, plunge-diving down to snatch the increasingly vulnerable fish in the shallowing water. Cormorants, big and black, with fast, regular, duck-like wing strokes zipped down the channel. Two cinnamon-colored, winged, long-beaked shorebirds flew above the mudflat, marbled godwits perhaps. High above, a trio of turkey vultures glided in large circles. A flock of honking geese climbed and after arranging themselves into a V, flew toward the refuge.

I gazed upon the mudflat. The little blue heron stared steadily into the water. The lighthouse watched over the channel and the islands. Three watchers we were. I was surely the least skilled. The little heron more focused, especially at low tide. But the lighthouse saw it all—the tides ebbing and flowing, the storms rolling in, the cloud banks drifting by, the seasons cycling, the boats and ships plying the ocean and channel, and the flocks of birds coming and going, calling and crying, flying and feeding.

It was I who broke focus first. My hour was up. The kayak seat wasn't designed for a long periods of sitting, and I felt stiffness spreading into my legs and back. I pushed the kayak free from the reeds out into deeper water and paddled back to the park, ceding the channel and the mudflats to the true watchers.

....

RIVER REFLECTIONS:
A JOURNEY DOWN THE LACKAWAXEN

....

A push of the paddle against the bank and the kayak floated free into narrow Dyberry Creek. Another stroke brought the boat to midstream where the fluid fingers of the current wrapped around the hull and began to carry it downstream. Dim, early morning light surrounded me. Wispy gray mist floated above the water. The temperature hovered at a chilly 45 degrees.

Suddenly, a clump-island of tall grass with narrow channels on either side loomed menacingly ahead. Quick decision made, I aimed for the gap on the left where tiny wavelets roiled the surface, hopefully offering enough depth and flow for a safe passage. I shot through the gap millimeters above the rocky bottom. Another patch of frothy water emerged. I studied the surface, picked my path, and zipped through again, but this time heard and felt soft thumps against the bottom of the boat.

I encountered more rapids to thread through, narrow spots to navigate, overhanging tree limbs to duck, and even two bridges to paddle under—all of it challenging kayaking demanding full focus. This wasn't the peaceful drifting downstream that I had imagined.

Gradually, I settled into a pattern of paddling and picking my course. Slowly, the stream widened, the challenging spots came further apart, and I had the freedom to look and listen. Lush green weeds, grasses and reeds grew in profusion along the banks. Further up the bank, thick, dense bushes merged into tall trees. Sometimes tree branches stretched across the creek, creating a green leafy tunnel. I heard traffic on the nearby highway and occasionally saw the back of a house, yet I knew this wild stripe of river land was ideal bird habitat.

Yellow warblers, luminous saffron-feathered darts, flew across the creek, flitted from branch to branch, and sang their musical *sweet, sweet, sweet, a little more sweet.* Brown-tan song sparrows hopped along the shoreline and chanted, *maids, maids, put on the tea kettle-lettle-lettle-lettle.* Crows cawed, blackbirds and grackles chacked, blue jays jayed, mourning doves cooed, and from a quiet eddy a great blue heron squawked into flight. Ahead, a bald eagle flew silently and majestically, long wingspan, strong wing strokes, bright-white band across its tail feathers.

The Lackawaxen River flowed in from the right, absorbing little Dyberry Creek. I was paddling on a real river now, wider, a greater volume of water, flowing insistently downstream to the Delaware River, on to Delaware Bay, to finally merge with the Atlantic Ocean. This was a dynamic river constantly scouring its bed and changing its channel.

The Lackawaxen wound through the little town of Honesdale. Houses and backyards appeared along both banks, but only a few had walkways to the river or chairs along the bank. It was a mostly underdeveloped and underappreciated river. Beyond the riverbank I saw old brick shoe factories and tall church spires piercing a pale-blue sky in the distance.

There was refuse in the river—cans, plastic bottles, a bright-red fishing bobber, and an old, black, half-buried tire. I looked ahead and with alarm saw two storm-downed trees splayed across the river completely blocking the channel.

I jammed my paddle in the water, slowed the kayak, bumped softly into the trunk of the first tree, and carefully stepped out onto the rocky, slippery bottom. Crawling, climbing and crouching over and under tree trunks and between branches, I dragged my kayak forward while the current pushed, slapped, and swirled against the boat and around my legs. I managed to just squeeze through the tree barrier. With a sense of relief I climbed back in the boat and once again floated free.

The temperature remained in the forties. A chilly mist lingered above the water. My fingers were numb, my torso chilled, my butt wet. I hadn't dressed warmly enough—no vest, no gloves. I glanced up and saw bright sunlight illuminating the spires of the church steeples. Warmth and sunshine would eventually find its way down into the river valley. There was nothing to do but paddle on.

I drifted into a wide, quiet stretch of river sided by wooded backyards and brush-covered banks. On a little stony point, two fawns stepped exploratively, almost playfully into the shallow water. They were improbably small, like perfectly sewn stuffed animals come to life; light-tan fur, delicate white spots, dainty black hooves, black button noses. They spotted me, froze, backed up, cowered, and watched me warily with soft brown eyes as I drifted by.

Once past town I saw the back of the commercial sprawl that stretched down the highway—metal buildings, auto repair shops, tire stores, gas stations, and warehouses. I heard the steady hum of traffic along the highway. But the river remained a hidden swath of wild nature.

Ducks swam on the water—a half-dozen green-headed drake mallards and a brown hen mallard followed by a trio of ducklings, most likely the survivors from a larger clutch. A mother common merganser with her reddish, tufted, punk feather-do led a convoy of fuzzy brown ducklings. Robins, catbirds, orioles, and yellowthroats sang. A dark-brown muskrat slithered off a large rock, slid underwater, and swam away.

The river reached an open area, grassy, with gently sloped banks. The rising sun finally shone upon me. I pulled over, beached the boat, stepped out, opened my thermos, and poured a hot steamy cup of coffee. I clutched the cup with the numb fingers of both hands, trying to extract all the warmth. I sipped the hot black coffee. Every morning cup of coffee tastes good, but this cup, sipped alongside the river while surrounded by tall green grass and luxuriating in the warmth of the sun, was an especially good cup.

Warmed by the coffee and sunshine, I continued my journey downstream, settling into an easy and efficient rhythm of paddling and drifting. In a stretch of wide quiet water surrounded by tall hemlocks, ashes, and maples, I spotted a green heron perched on a snag just above the water—a crow-sized bird, greenish back, chestnut neck, greenish-black crown, short spear-like bill—a solitary bird of rivers and swamps. It fluttered up to a higher branch, and then as I came closer, flew right over me and landed halfway up a tree, perching deftly.

Ahead, along the stony shoreline, a small animal stood near the water. What was it? A big cat, a little dog? I held my paddle still, floated silently closer, and realized that it was a gray fox pup—pointy ears, gray fur, long fluffy tail, alert posture. The young fox stood its ground as I drifted by, proud predator bearing, gazing at me openly, even a bit defiantly.

As my journey continued, the river revealed its ever-changing personality. There were serene stretches with wide calm water, overhanging trees, sun-speckled shade—a peaceful side of its personality. Then suddenly, the river was filled with roiling water, swirls and waves and dark dangerous rocks piercing the surface as the river showed its dangerous and challenging face. Then, just seconds later I drifted into an open stretch with gently sloping sand banks, surrounded by meadows of grasses, milkweed, and goldenrods where blue-green tree swallows skimmed over the water and circled above chirping musically—a welcoming, friendly river.

I looked at the water. Large and small chunks of brownish foam speckled the surface and floated downstream. Patches of tiny insects squirmed on the surface, sometimes a hundred or more, sometimes a dense mat of a thousand or more. I peered down into the clear water and saw moss-covered rocks and patches of a seaweed-like plant anchored to the rocks with stems and lacy leaves undulating in the current. In a shallow area the seaweed edged to the surface and slender stems topped with tiny white flowers reached up into the air. Water flowers in bloom, a remarkable and lovely adaptation I thought, one that I had never seen before.

On my left, old stone walls stretched along the bank. These were the walls of the Delaware and Hudson Canal, which for many years was a vital and thriving commercial artery for shipping Pennsylvania anthracite coal to the markets of New York City. The rectangular fitted stones, the product of hundreds of man-hours of hard labor, still stood firm, but were being steadily reclaimed by nature, by mosses, weeds, and seedling trees. For a moment I imagined the canal the way it had been—the coal-laden barges, the tow path with mules and guides, the workers tending the canal, the crews upon the barge, the creaks and groans and rattles of the wooden craft and the leather harnesses, and the yells, curses, and conversations of the crews.

On my right another stone wall, this one bracing the right of way of the Delaware and Hudson Railway that in its day had been equally busy and noisy—steam engines chugging, steel wheels rolling on steel tracks, bells clanging, whistles tooting. These days the only trains that travel the tracks are weekend and holiday excursions.

My mind drifted back further in time, and I pictured Native Americans paddling down the river in hollowed-out dugouts. And further back in time, perhaps there were peoples who walked the easier terrain near the river, who hunted and fished along its banks. And now, it was just me paddling silently downstream, hearing the voices and feeling the lingering energy of all who had plied this river previously.

I checked Google maps to track my progress on this twelve-mile trip. I had to be alert for the pullout spot located behind a restaurant. The map showed that I was getting close, closer than I thought and truth be told, closer than I wanted to be.

My journey seemed almost like a miniature lifespan. I was born under the bankside branches in dim morning light. I fought my way down the narrow creek channel. Then, with adolescent energy I paddled hard, eagerly faced the challenges, fought through the rapids, and muscled my way through fallen trees. As the river widened and deepened, I settled into a more mature rhythm of efficient paddling and drifting, going with the flow. And now, feeling a bit of fatigue, I paddled on, bathed in warm sunshine, surrounded by green growth, wanting the journey to continue.

I drifted past the landing spot, had to paddle my way back upstream, eventually beached the kayak, and dragged it up the steep bank through thorny brambles and thick stems of Japanese knotweed. I called home for a ride and then sat down in a chair near a pagoda the restaurant owners had built, a scenic spot for photo-ops and outdoor weddings.

I watched the river flow along and listened to its soft song. Usually after a nature adventure, I felt excited and energized, but today after being alone with the river, I felt quiet, focused, and humbled.

CHAPTER 13

Nearby Places

F OR MOST OF MY LIFE I BELIEVED IN THE MYTH OF THE REMOTE
wild, the idea that to connect with nature I had to journey to the
far forest and trek to some distant and pristine wilderness. The
further I traveled the better. The harder it was to get there and the more
challenging the conditions, the more profound the experience would be.

Family life was one source for this myth. My dad happily drove us
in a Nash Rambler six hours to "up north" Wisconsin where we headed
down a narrow dirt road to an isolated log cabin that was off the power
grid, three miles from the nearest neighbor, and surrounded by thousands
of acres of national forest. When we stepped out of the car, the only sounds
we heard were the sighing of the wind through the pine boughs, the calls
of ravens and Canada jays, and at night the howling of the coyotes.

This was the real wild. This was true nature. Even though at
home we lived within sight and sound of Lake Michigan and were
surrounded by prairie, meadows, and woods, we dismissed these
elements of our regular environment as "nature-lite."

The myth of the remote wild creates limitation. One is ignoring
the opportunities for nature connection that are all around us. Given
the crucial importance of time spent in nature to our well-being, it
makes sense to take advantage of any and all nearby locations that
might provide a dose of nature.

Second, the belief that we have to travel, that we have to
dedicate extra time and make special preparations in order

to interface with healing nature creates yet another obstacle, another reason to procrastinate, another justification to wait until "everything has settled down" or "we have enough time." Having the option to experience nature that is convenient and close to home reduces this obstacle.

A third consideration is that the myth of the remote may exclude some people from purposely spending time in nature. Not everyone feels comfortable in the wild. Not everyone feels safe or physically able to trek to and sit in a remote location. Having the option to engage with nature in a backyard or nearby park makes the process more accessible to more people.

Finally, opening up sit spot options close to home is an acceptance of human individuality. For each of us our relationship with nature has context and is a product of our life experiences. Taking into consideration our individuality is part of the fine-tuning needed to develop our relationship with nature.

With all of these considerations in mind, I chose the four sit spot experiences described in this chapter with the hope of breaking the grip of the myth of the wild in my own mind. I wanted to nurture the idea that nearby nature is just as exciting, interesting, rewarding, restorative, and transformational as any far away, wild location.

In the first selection, **A Backyard Sit Spot**, I present an early morning sit spot session in my backyard. I did it as an experiment, and it turned out to be a very good experience, revealing much that I had missed, changing forever the way I see my immediate surroundings, and subsequently encouraging me to take frequent, brief, slow wander walks around my yard.

Koppenplatz, the second selection, occurred while I was visiting my son in central Berlin. Surrounded by an urban environment and needing some time in nature, I walked to a small nearby park for a sit spot session where I felt the residues of history, watched people using the park, and observed ever-present nature. This experience convinced me that even a small urban park could be a good place for a mindful sit spot.

In the third selection, **A Feederwatch Sit Spot**, I discuss how I took the concept of nearby places to its most convenient level by conducting two bird-watching sessions from the warmth and comfort of my home office. From behind a divided light window, on two bitter cold winter mornings, I was able to observe, learn from, and experience nature.

The fourth selection, **A Vacant Lot at the Beach**, took place while I was on vacation. A trio of warblers darting into a clump of thick bushes drew my attention to a vacant lot that I had walked by many times and ignored. The next morning I conducted a sit spot session seated on the edge of the lot and discovered interwoven communities of plants and birds thriving in this small abandoned plot. I learned about the rich life in a unique old dune habitat. Nature is truly all around.

A BACKYARD SIT SPOT

The question in mind as I walked across the yard was: Could I experience a deep nature connection right in my backyard? I thought the answer was yes, given that nature was most likely just as rich and complex in my backyard as in some remote forests. But, I had doubts as well. Maybe my backyard sit spot would turn out to be a big dud—boring, nothing happening, too tame, no real experience of nature. Maybe it was necessary to journey to a wild setting to truly experience nature.

First Light Chorus

Setting up my camp stool atop the elevated sand mound that stood in the middle of my backyard, I sat down, pulled out a notebook, and drew a circle for my first ten minute observation.

It was 5:07 a.m. Brutally early, I thought, but necessary if I wanted to be present for the summer sunrise. Fortunately, it was convenient to tumble out of bed, put on layers against the morning chill, stagger down to the kitchen for a glass of orange juice, grab my gear, and step a quick ninety seconds across the yard to reach my destination.

I had heard distant birdsongs wafting in through my screen window when I woke up at 4:45, a reminder that birds begin to sing at first light, which begins a full half hour before sunrise. Now, as I settled in and listened with full attention, I was amazed by the sheer volume, intensity, and variety of the morning chorus. The busy lilting chatter of the house wrens nesting in the garden set the tone. A Carolina wren added its loud, pure *tea-kettle, tea-kettle, tea-kettle* song. A robin voiced its cheerful *cheerily, cheer-up, cheerily, cheer-up*

A cardinal sang a clear whistled *purdy, purdy, purdy*. A catbird sang its jumbled medley of song snippets, and a phoebe sang its namesake, raspy *fee-bee, fee-bee*.

Crows cawed in the distance. A goldfinch looped over the yard singing *per-chik-o-ree*. Then two chimney swifts—those usually high-flying, insect-catching birds often described as flying cigars due to their blunt-shaped body and sickle shaped wings—flew right over me, voicing their unmistakable twittering chirps. A mourning dove cooed softly. A red-eyed vireo sang its robin-like song over and over.

The many birdsongs—eleven different species—blended, over-lapped, cascaded, intertwined, and rose and fell in volume. It occurred to me that this first light, presunrise part of the morning chorus might just be the best part. And I made this discovery right in my backyard.

WHOSE PROPERTY?

Sensing a presence, I turned to my left and spotted a deer grazing peacefully in the corner of the yard near an old stone wall. Spellbound, I watched the deer—attired in its summer brown-tan coat—step slowly forward on graceful slender legs, bend its long neck down and nibble at the green grass, a mystically beautiful scene in the soft morning light.

Entranced with the view and eager to capture it with a photograph I foolishly jerked my camera up. Then, when I tried to snap a photo, it was too dim for the autofocus. As I struggled to adjust and re-aim the camera, the wary deer, probably surprised, maybe annoyed to have an intruder on its morning grazing ground, lifted its head, stared at me, turned, and quietly slipped back into the woods. I coached myself to let go, relax, breathe evenly, and return to an open focus. Then I spotted movement in my peripheral vision. Turning slowly, I spotted a small brown creature moving across the yard.

What was it? Binoculars slowly up, critter in focus, I saw the neat black eye mask, the bushy-ringed tail, the pointy ears, and the gray-brown fur of a raccoon. Oblivious to my presence, it ambled across the yard, paused to check the ground, and on two occasions dug into the ground with its crafty finger-like paws. Preoccupied with its morning feeding, the raccoon ignored me, continued across the yard, and scuttled off into the brush.

Glancing toward the garden, I spotted two rabbits peacefully munching grass. A minute later a gray squirrel ran in front of me, skittered up the trunk of a big maple, paused on a branch, and let out a loud challenging chatter. Were his comments directed at other squirrels or at me? Two more deer edged into the yard and began to graze peacefully.

I had lived with the assumption that this yard was *my* property. After all, I paid for it and I had a deed to prove it. I mowed the yard, raked the leaves, and picked up the fallen branches. But witnessing this early morning parade of animals, my assumption of ownership seemed tenuous. The real owners and users seemed to be the animals that in the privacy and quiet of the early morning exercised their rights of ownership.

TIME

I drew a circle for my third ten-minute interval. As often happens during a nature sitting session, time perception began to change— slowing down, allowing me to take in more details, yet simultaneously flying by, as I became present-centered, creating a sense of timelessness.

The animals, the deer, raccoons, rabbits, and squirrels belonged to this timelessness. They had been using this land long before my house was built. I glanced at the house, a two-story colonial, built in 1811 by Connecticut carpenters. I considered it old, but in this moment, in the presence of this perennial parade of animals, the house seemed recent, like an upstart. And I, who had lived in the house for a mere seventeen years, was even more of a recent arrival.

My gaze centered on a grape vine growing on a trellis near the kitchen window. Ah, I thought, I have a picture of that same grape vine from 1935 when depression-era, unemployed architects were hired by the federal government to do studies of historic homes, make drawings, and take photos. The grapevine was at least eighty-seven years old. I tended the grape vine now. Somehow this felt like my connection to a greater time scheme.

CHANGES

The sun, hidden beyond the ridges, valleys, forests, and fields, had officially risen. I couldn't see it, but I did see a steady increase in illumination—a pale-blue sky filled with cotton-puff clouds and a spreading tint of pink to the southeast.

The morning bird chorus changed, less loud and insistent, making it possible to pick out a few new performers. I detected the mournful *pee-a-wee* song of the an eastern pewee, the nasal *ank, ank, ank* call of a white-breasted nuthatch, the sharp volley-like *tsee, tsee, tsee, tseeo* of an American redstart, the insistent *teetcha, teetcha, teetcha* of an ovenbird, and the descending whinny of a downy woodpecker.

I thought there might be even more singers out there, so it was a good time to turn on my *Merlin* app and run a sound recording. I watched the sonogram of the calls and songs unfurl across the screen of my phone in real time. I listened and saw the song of a robin, Carolina wren, catbird, and cardinal light up in yellow each time they sang.

And then Merlin detected the song of the wood thrush. I listened carefully and there it was, from the woods beyond my property, the beautiful, flute-like, *eee-o-lay* song, one of my favorites, a true forest song, and another nature gift right in my own backyard.

Catbird on a Tin Roof

The leaves on the trees hung motionless. There was no wind. And then I noticed that the old rope swing hanging from a big sugar maple was swaying back and forth. What was going on?

I spotted a catbird on the ground near the swing. I knew that again this year catbirds had a nest somewhere in the thick privet bushes along the edge of the yard. Occasionally, I saw one fly up from the ground when I walked through the yard or heard them sing when I worked in the garden. Now, I had a chance to watch a catbird in action.

Catbirds are one of my favorite birds, plain charcoal-gray in appearance, members of the mimic family along with mockingbirds and brown thrashers. And while these latter two are more disciplined songsters, accurately reproducing song and sound snippets, catbirds are the free jazz members of the family, taking all kinds of sound snips, jumbling them together, never repeating phrases, and punctuating the medley with cat-like mews.

The catbird in front of me had most likely wintered down south along the Gulf or Caribbean coast, flew north, and selected my yard as its home sometime in early May. I watched it hop along the ground, flutter up to a table, and then flit over to a chair as if it owned the yard furniture. And then, sure enough, it flew over, landed on the swing, and set it in motion. I couldn't help but smile.

Whimsical characters, these catbirds, with personalities to match their free jazz song style.

Looking across to the metal roof of a barn next door, I saw a catbird perched at the peak of a metal roof joined a few seconds later by yet another catbird. What were they doing? Maybe this was an important part of patrolling the boundaries of their territory, or maybe they were just enjoying the view.

TREES

My gaze settled on the line of tall trees edging the driveway, trees that I had walked and driven by hundreds of times, trees that I had mentally labeled simply as big trees. But now, as often happened during a sit spot session, I began to see things more vividly. Each tree had a different shape, different branching system, different configuration of leaves, and even leaves of different shades of green.

To the right stood a big black cherry with a thick mass of dark-green, narrow leaves. The cherry tree had an oblong shape with irregular zig-zagging branches that at the tips were laden with small green cherries. These would ripen into burgundy berries much beloved by the birds, fruits that in former times would have been made into tart-tasting jellies to bring a reminder of summer warmth to cold winter mornings. Next to it a tall American elm with its distinctive high-divided branches offered a lovely vase shape. Its dense leaves were dark-green. This was a survivor tree, one that had somehow eluded the Dutch elm diseases. Next to the elm stood a pair of white ash trees—tall and oval-shaped with trunks divided low and high, criss-crossing branches holding a thick mantle of grass green leaves. These were two healthy ash trees, not yet affected by the spreading emerald ash borer, but surely at risk.

To the left, closest to the garage, stood a medium tall, round-topped butternut, with open Y-shaped branches and yellow-green leaflets. In late summer it would drop big butternuts to the ground, nuts that would be quickly grabbed by the patrolling gray squirrels and buried for later eating.

The shape and foliage of each tree stood out, each telling a unique story of growing, blooming, propagating, providing shelter and food, and contributing to the greater story of nature.

Reflections

The sit spot session had zipped by. Sitting in stillness for a full hour, surrounded by a vibrant community of birds, animals, plants, and trees, I felt content, grateful, and fully alive.

I folded up my camp stool, stepped down from the sand mound, and headed to the kitchen to brew a cup of morning coffee. I had been able to experience a full nature connection in my backyard. And I realized that my view of the backyard had changed forever.

KOPPENPLATZ

Koppenplatz, a postage stamp-sized park in the Mitte section of Berlin, like most plots of urban land, has a history of reinvention and repurposing. In Berlin's early history, this was an area for cattle barns set up outside the city proper. Later it was dedicated as a burial ground for the poor. Next it became the center of a neighborhood for poor Jewish and Eastern European immigrants, and when full urbanization arrived, it was designated and then carefully redesigned as a city park.

During the Nazi reign, Koppenplatz was used as an assembly point to deport Jews to death camps. Also during WWII, French POWs were forced to build two air raid shelters. And in the era of East Germany, the Platz continued as a drab urban park, although a playground was added. Now in open, free, tolerant Berlin, it is a green, tree-filled, well-trafficked park tucked into a hip neighborhood surrounded by desirable apartments, inviting sidewalk cafes, aromatic coffee bars, fashionable boutiques, and cozy restaurants.

I came to the park for the greenery, the birds, the wildlife, and the people. Practically speaking it was the nearest nature area where I could duck away for an hour while visiting my son. And I was curious to conduct an urban sit spot session.

An Empty Table

It was 6:00 p.m. when I sat down on a slightly graffitied park bench. Church bells chimed and pealed—three different bells from three different directions. A light wind whooshed and rustled the leaves of the trees in front of me. Behind me, hidden within thick green foliage, a chorus of house sparrows chirped tunefully. An amsel, a black robin-sized bird, a member of the thrush family, hopped along the ground nearby, piping its musical whistle.

The loud, excited, happy voices of children carried from the playground at the far end of the park. From the sidewalk behind me came the voices of two women walking by, absorbed in conversation. High on a tile rooftop across the park, a pair of rock pigeons cooed. In the distance I heard the sound of a street car clacking steadily along its tracks.

Most of the park benches were occupied—Berliners pausing, resting, and relaxing for a few minutes in nature. A young man in a white T-shirt sat on the bench to my right, a young woman on the bench to my left, her bike next to the bench, a book in her hand. Straight ahead, just beyond the paved walkway that ran through the park, a line of rose bushes were decked out in a profusion of white blooms. Past the park stood a row of newer apartment buildings, four stories high, painted in subdued yellow and beige shades, red or black tile roofs, rows of windows looking down on the park. In the far distance stood the high spike and bulb of the TV tower at Alexanderplatz, the East German modern, high-tech statement.

Two young women rode in the main entrance, parked their bikes, and set their back packs on a bench. One, with short, bright, blond hair, took off her jacket, fluffed her hair, smoothed her simple white dress, and walked over to a bronze sculpture of a table. She sat on the corner of the table and assumed various poses while her friend snapped pictures. After a number of shots, the friend approached, they reviewed the pictures, conferred, and then the blond returned to the table to make more poses while more pictures were taken. Perhaps this was a school project for the photographer or portfolio material for the model. Photo shoot concluded, they sat down, talked, laughed, sipped sodas, and munched on snacks.

The table that they innocently used as a prop was in fact a memorial to the Jews of the neighborhood who had been rounded up during the Holocaust, deported, and executed. Titled *The Abandoned Room*, the sculpture features a chair standing behind the table and another chair tipped over on the floor, elements that evoke the image of a forcefully emptied room. A poignant poem on a bronze plaque begins with the line *"O die Wohnung des Todes,"* which I translated as "Oh the apartment of the dead."

There are more reminders of the Holocaust around the park—brass plaques embedded in the sidewalk in front of the homes of the deported. Each plaque, shined up by the passage of footsteps, notes the name, birth date, deportation date, and the location and date of death.

No fault to the two young women for using the table as a photo prop, I thought. Perhaps the best art is adaptable enough to mean different things to different people and to invite different uses. These two young women were born after the Berlin Wall came down, after the fall of East Germany, well after the end of sixty particularly dark years in the history of Berlin.

Avian Life

I studied the birds of the park. Some were familiar—the pigeons and sparrows—while others were new to me. I spotted a pair of rooks flying into the thick foliage of a tree—birds similar in size to a crow but with soft gray-blue plumage upon their back. A black-billed magpie, black and bright-white with a long back tail, darted out of a tree down to the ground, picked through the unmowed grass and flew back into the branches.

Gazing up, I saw a pair of pigeons moving from rooftop to rooftop. Then further up, barely visible, three swallow-like birds circled high above the park. I noticed forked tails, a chunky body bigger than a barn swallow. Quick research on my phone revealed that these were common swifts—skilled, high-flying insect hunters—known in Germany as *mauerseglers* or wall-gliders due to their habit of constructing nests on the upper reaches of city buildings

I was stunned when I looked at their range map—summers across Europe, Asia, and the Middle East; winters in equatorial and subequatorial Africa—a completely different range map from the birds I knew at home, a range that included a long, perilous flight over the Sahara desert.

Human Life

A parade of people and their dogs proceeded through the park. A man led—or more accurately was led by—a large, muscular black Lab. A grandmother and her young daughter walked two cocker spaniels, the young girl dragging her dog and chatting constantly at the grandmother, who seemed to be quietly soldiering on.

An older man led a small white dog that jumped up on the bench next to me to greet and be petted by the quiet man in the white T-shirt. A few words on the pleasant weather were exchanged between dog owner and park sitter. I thought Mr. White T-shirt must be a park regular. Across the park three young men sipped beer from brown bottles, talked loudly, jostled, teased, and bumped against each other, looking like playful bear cubs.

A woman jogger with a chocolate Lab ran past a young man with a black German shepherd on a leash. The dogs froze in place, halting the humans midstride. The canines shifted into wild wolf mode, tails and ears up, circling and sniffing before allowing their owners to continue on. A few minutes later a large brown- and gray-striped cat padded cautiously through the park, a miniature tiger on the hunt.

A young woman rolled her bike up to the bench on my left to the woman reading. She quickly set aside her book, and the two women greeted each other, hugged, laughed, sat together on the bench, and settled in to a warm conversation. Friends meeting as planned in the park. Gathering and greeting in a green space.

URBAN ADAPTABILITY

I saw a woman rolling by in a wheelchair, wearing a bright-green tank top revealing muscled, tanned arms. She wheeled quickly and steadily. At her side a young girl on a scooter kept pace, both of them on wheels, moving together. Their destination was the playground. The mother parked in the corner, the daughter set down her scooter, and ran to the swing set. Adaptability, resilience, and the strength of the mothering instinct were the thoughts that came to my mind.

It was after 7:00 p.m., and my allotted hour for observation was up. The daylight had softened, but this far north it would be well after nine before the sun finally set. I glanced up and spotted a flock of swifts circling low over this city park. I saw their brown breasts and heard their high-pitched wheezy calls. As they swirled above, I pictured a map of their long migratory route and thought about the recently discovered facts that they may stay aloft for as long as ten months, may ascend as high as 10,000 feet, and then sleep as they slowly drift down. Something about the circling of the swifts created a swirl of inspiration in my heart.

Departing

I strolled around the park, past the somber evocative table and chairs, past an older couple on a bench smiling and petting their three miniature bulldogs. This urban sit spot session had revealed a continuum of life from plants to animals to birds to humans and had shown the strong pulse of nature amidst the city, a pulse to which I felt connection and membership.

I headed back to my son's apartment. We planned to walk to a restaurant with sidewalk tables where we could sit outside, enjoy the lingering light of a long northern day, watch the shadows lengthen, feel the shadows of history, take in the excitement of the present, and talk about prospects for the future.

A FEEDER WATCH SIT SPOT

For the majority of enthusiasts; however, birdwatching simply provides a personal and very special entrée into the natural world.

—Graeme Gibson

Day 1

Faint first light, swirls of yellow and orange edging above the southern horizon, the excitement of an early morning winter sitting experience—this all felt familiar. The difference was that I didn't have to layer up, drive on icy roads, and trudge through deep snow to get to my destination. Instead, I was seated in my office, wearing comfy old sweat pants and a warm flannel shirt. A thermos of freshly brewed Brazilian coffee sat at the ready on my desk. This was going to be an inside, stay home and stay warm sit spot session.

I had several purposes in mind. First, I wanted to explore, hopefully verify, and then share the idea that you can sit inside your house and still have a deep, nature-connecting experience. You don't have to venture out to some far away, isolated, idyllic wilderness location. Just dedicate an hour, sit quietly by your window and observe nature around you.

Another objective was to combine a sitting session with FeederWatch bird-tallying. Project FeederWatch is a citizen science initiative administered by the Cornell Laboratory of Ornithology. Thousands of participants all over the US and Canada count birds at their feeders for two consecutive selected days separated by at least a five-day interval and then submit the data online to the Lab. FeederWatch season runs from November through April. The data collected has been extremely valuable for scientists tracking trends in winter bird populations along with documenting the occasional and exciting irruptions of finches from the far north. Participants benefit by becoming better birders.

Even though I have been a loyal FeederWatcher for twenty-four seasons, most of my observations have occurred in brief intervals—while reading, sipping coffee, sending emails, or just checking on my feeders as I walk by the window. I wanted to see what it would be like to get up well before sunrise, watch the birding day begin, and observe nature unfolding at and beneath my bird feeders. Would I see more? Would I learn something new? Would doing a sit spot session deepen my FeederWatch experience?

FIRST VISITORS

The temperature was 7 degrees below zero with a winter weather advisory in effect, the kind of conditions when birds need the supplemental food available at my array of feeders. I peered through the storm window into the dim gray light. Something moved beneath the feeder—a rabbit scanning the snowy, icy ground, nibbling seeds, hopping a few feet, searching, nibbling more—a member of the night shift cleaning up. I don't think of rabbits as seed eaters, but free food is good food.

The rabbit hopped away as a deer stepped warily into the scene, a doe; with a thick, dark-brown coat; lovely, big brown eyes, long delicate ears swiveling to scan for sounds; slender dancer legs; and neat black hooves. Seemingly feeling safe, the doe dropped her head and began to vacuum up the seeds on the ground that I had spread earlier. Well, they would soon be all gone.

The doe found a remnant of frozen suet, bit off a chunk, chewed it thoroughly with her molars, grabbed the rest, and chewed it up. I don't think about deer eating beef fat, but once again, in winter, any food is good food.

I gazed at the deer, at its thickest, just-right coat for winter. Its flag tail was tucked tightly to its butt for a bit of extra warmth. The doe looked up and gazed in my direction. I felt that she knew I was there. We were only fifteen feet apart, separated by a thin pane of glass. But I was sitting still, my intentions peaceful and respectful, and the doe was hungry. It bowed its head and resumed feeding.

AVIAN ARRIVALS

I watched the daylight slowly and steadily increase, saw the details of my surroundings come into focus. I loved witnessing this turning of darkness into light, this daily reveal of the world of forms—the tree trunks, shrubs, weeds, an old stone wall set against a backdrop of snow-covered ground.

It was 7:16, only ten minutes until sunrise and still no birds. Then, in the low branches of a cherry tree, I spotted two small birds perching—dark-eyed juncos, ground feeders, waiting for the deer to depart. Sure enough, as soon as the deer stepped away, the juncos fluttered down to the ground and began to pick for seeds. Soon, two more landed, another three, then four more—a winter flock foraging.

It was fitting that the juncos were the first to arrive. They are, according to data collected by Project FeederWatch, the most common feeder bird in the mid-Atlantic region. They are also a lovely winter bird, slate gray on top, pale-pinkish bill, gray breast, white belly, and white edged tail feathers that flash when they fly.

These juncos were on their version of a southern vacation. They breed far to the north in Canada and Alaska, and in high elevations in the US. They always seem to appear just before the start of FeederWatch season and head back north when the season ends.

A female cardinal flew in, landed amidst the juncos, searched for seeds, then flew up, perched on a black oil sunflower seed feeder, plucked out seeds, cracked them open, and extracted the seeds—a delicate task accomplished easily with its stout nut-cracking bill. A bright-red, male cardinal—a visual highlight—flew in, perched on an adjacent feeder, and began to feed on the protein and fat rich seeds.

A chickadee—a backyard regular—fluttered in, landed on a feeder, plucked out a seed, and flew off to eat it. Through the glass I heard its familiar and cheerful *chick-a-dee-dee* call. Then there were three chickadees flying in, plucking seeds, fluttering off, returning for more.

MORE ARRIVALS

It was 7:35. The first rays of warm, copper-colored sunshine illuminated the tree trunks in front of me. The world of color returned—tan goldenrod stems, gray tree trunks, and dark-green bittersweet vines. I could almost feel the warmth of those first beams of sunshine.

More birds arrived, a red-bellied woodpecker and a downy woodpecker, both landing on the suet feeder, drilling away for chunks of fat and seed. I saw two tree sparrows amidst the juncos, small sparrows with reddish caps, delicate brown plumage and a dark splotch on their breast. Three white-throated sparrows joined the growing crowd of ground feeders. These sparrows, with their bright-white throats, yellow swatch above their eyes, and their lovely whistled *Old Sam Peabody, Peabody, Peabody* springtime song are a personal favorite. Interestingly, over my years of FeederWatching, they have become regular winter visitors.

Mourning doves—plump, rounded, delicately marked plumage of beige and tan and brown—fluttered down from the trees—five, then seven, then fifteen in all. Some fed on the ground while others perched on the hopper feeders. The doves on the ground waddled around, ducking down and plucking seeds in a very pigeon-like manner. A trio of starlings arrived. A gray tufted titmouse appeared. A pair of house finches landed on the sunflower feeder and fed steadily.

I heard a volley of loud *jay, jay, jay* calls as a trio of blue jays buzzed in and landed on the feeders. The jays can be feeder bullies, pushing the other birds away and squabbling among themselves. I had loaded the peanut feeder and now watched the peanut-loving jays fly down and deftly snatch peanuts, displaying astounding eye-bill-wing coordination. Peanut in bill, they would zoom off to hide the treasure.

As I sat watching the birds come and go, the time extending well past an hour, certain impressions came to mind. I sensed an atmosphere of mutual reassurance. The birds, a variety of species, shared the space peacefully and seemed to gather comfort and a sense of security from each other's presence.

They also shared the task of constant vigilance for Cooper's hawks that have learned to stalk bird feeders. On several occasions the birds scattered suddenly. But no hawk was seen, and gradually the birds filtered back down.

I also saw what I called the personality of each bird on display, the unique nature that came to expression before my eyes. The juncos travel in winter flocks, calling softly back and forth to stay connected. The cardinals travel in pairs, staying in touch with *tink, tink, tink* calls. The blue jays travel in boisterous family clans. The woodpeckers come singly. The chickadees flitted in and out. Each bird seemed totally free to express its true nature. I wondered, *What is my true nature?*

Adaptability was on display. The juncos, normally ground feeders, occasionally popped up to the hopper feeders where the seeds were more plentiful. The blue jays had figured out how to snatch the prized peanuts from the feeder. The starlings found the feeder filled with mealworms. The chickadees sampled all food sources—sunflower seeds, mixed seeds, and suet. The titmouse snatched a peanut. The deer fed on seeds and suet. I wondered if I had the same adaptability.

As I watched, it also seemed that the birds came and went in waves. A dozen doves fed, then faded away, then drifted back down from the trees. The finches, now six of them fed steadily, disappeared, and then minutes later reappeared. The blue jays came and went, the chickadees too.

Watching these waves and pulses of life that I sensed were not random, but somehow purpose driven, I felt a connection, felt part of these waves of being.

DAY TWO

A winter storm warning was in effect, steady, heavy snow falling, a fine day for feeder watching. No deer this morning. At 7:09 I heard the soft *stip, stip, stip* calls of dark-eyed juncos, the earliest of the early birds approaching. Suddenly, in the dim predawn light, little gray shapes fluttered down to the ground, five juncos, the return of life into a gray and white lifeless world. Watching the juncos, I felt a tiny jump of joy.

I heard the *tink, tink, tink* companion calls of cardinals. A female and two bright-red males landed on the feeder and began to munch seeds. The bright-red cardinals contrasted with pure white snow, more bright life returning to the world.

Three chickadees arrived and resumed their snatch and fly and return routine. I studied one as it grabbed a black sunflower seed in its tiny beak and flew away. Soon the doves appeared. I watched them flutter gracefully down from the trees to the ground—doves of peace, doves of delicate beauty.

The two tree sparrows returned. I watched them carefully, noticed the buff and tan plumage on their back, the bright-white wing bars, and in particular the straight long tail, a true sparrow tail, a detail I hadn't noticed before. Nearby, a white-throated sparrow searched for seeds.

I was glad that I had returned for day two. Maybe yesterday had been a practice day, a work through the novelty day. Somehow I was more tuned in today, was seeing and feeling more.

I heard crows cawing. A red-bellied woodpecker flew in, its name a misnomer as the bright orange-red plumage is on its head and throat. The woodpecker displayed its assertive nature by shooing a starling away from one of the suet feeders.

A petite downy woodpecker landed on another suet feeder. I looked with appreciation at its black and white ladder-pattern back and the bright splotch of scarlet on the back of its head. A bigger but similar looking hairy woodpecker flew in and tried its luck at a mesh sunflower seed feeder.

Suddenly, a new bird appeared—small, long tailed, russet on top, tan breast, and a distinctive beige eyebrow—a Carolina wren. A busy bird, that picked away on one suet feeder and switched to another, tail bobbing, moving with purpose and intensity. This wren is another personal favorite perhaps due to its cheerful *teakettle, teakettle, teakettle* song sung all the months of the year.

An Aviary

There must have been more than forty birds on the feeders and on the ground—little sparrows and juncos and chickadees; medium-sized blue jays, starlings, and cardinals; and the bigger mourning doves. I saw them hop around on the ground, jockey for position at the feeders, and flutter in and out of the trees. I felt as if I was visiting an aviary.

The birds fed busily but not frantically. They seemed to take this winter weather in stride as if it was just another day. Clearly they hadn't heard the dire storm warnings, the urgent admonitions to rush out and buy bread and milk that had filled the airwaves and media the last two days.

Two gray squirrels scampered down a tree trunk. One, its fur dappled with white snowflakes, climbed to the end of a branch. The second followed. The first jumped to another branch and ran back to the trunk of another tree. The second followed. The first ran down to the ground near the feeders. The second followed closely. The first ran off and the second followed. It looked like intense courtship behavior, which was clearly more important to them than feeding—another example of business as usual amidst a winter storm.

I watched the snow falling. It became heavy, then lighter, then almost stopped—then picked up and in a few minutes was heavy again. More waves I thought, waves that I was able to witness by sitting still.

My coffee was cold. Once again I had been sitting for more than an hour. The time flew and I felt fortunate to have seen the activity of another day beginning in nature. I set my tally sheet aside. Duty to science done, I headed to the kitchen to prepare a hot breakfast and brew a fresh cup of coffee.

I felt a deep sense of satisfaction. Greater depth of understanding, enhanced acuity, and a heightened appreciation had arisen from my FeederWatch experience. As Graeme Gibson wrote when watching birds: "you never know what to expect. You might even discover some unanticipated aspect of self."

A VACANT LOT AT THE BEACH

Down three flights of stairs, a few steps across the yard, and I arrived at the edge of the vacant lot. I had often walked by this lot while staying at my timeshare when on vacation. Usually, I was on my way to the beach and had paid scant attention to what looked like an overgrown, neglected property.

Then, two days ago, on my way for a beach walk, I heard faint *seet-seet-seet* calls, turned and spotted three small birds flying over and then dropping down into the vacant lot. Curious, I stepped to the edge of the lot and was surprised to look down into a bowl-like sand dune edged with thick brush.

Merlin Sound ID identified the calls as yellow-rumped warblers. Scanning the shrubs with my binoculars, I caught a confirming sighting of three small, active, brownish birds, with the distinctive bright-yellow patch above the tail, the field mark that gives this warbler its common name—butter butt.

Satisfied with the identification, I continued on my way to the beach. Yet an impression of the lot lingered in my mind, some sense that this vacant, forgotten lot was a place of vibrant life. The impression grew into curiosity, into questions, and finally evolved into a call to go to the lot to conduct an hourlong sitting session, to explore this tiny chunk of nature.

CONDITIONS

First light peeked through the window on the last day of my timeshare week. Now or never I thought. I was reluctant to get out of a warm comfortable bed before sunrise, but over time had learned about overcoming inertia. I knew it was important to heed the call of intuition. If I didn't explore this place, I would regret it. And I had an agenda. I wanted to confirm that opportunities for nature connection were available in nearby and even neglected spaces.

I sipped a quick half cup of hot coffee, layered up, grabbed a boat cushion—as I had no camp stool—walked to the lot, sat down, settled in, and began to engage in sensory awareness.

Above me a gray dome of clouds. A chilly, steady, strong, gusty northeast wind made the 64 degrees feel much colder. The wind whooshed by my ears, rattled the stems of the dune grasses, and carried the sounds and hectic energy of morning traffic on Fort Macon Road.

In front of me I viewed a bowl of sandy terrain covered with slender grasses, bright yellow wildflowers, and even a low-growing cactus plant. Extending out from the base of the bowl grew bushes that in turn were edged by dark-green taller bushes and trees. Past the rim of the bowl stood a row of beach homes and then a vast gray sky reaching out over the Atlantic Ocean.

I noticed the faint impression of a trail that coursed diagonally down and across the dune. Some animals, maybe rabbits or raccoons, had made and traversed this trail. This was I realized a place of life, a community of plants, birds, and animals. I began to feel as if I was sitting inside a life-sized terrarium.

From behind, to the left, and from the bushes in the hollow ahead, I heard the harsh, emphatic *chack, chack, chack* calls of three mockingbirds, seemingly egging each other on, taking their job as the morning sentinels seriously. Further away came the *wreeet,*

wreeet, wreeet calls of a Carolina wren, and from somewhere back on the timeshare property, I heard the cheerful *chirp, shillip* song of house sparrows.

DESIGN

Settling my gaze on the sand at my feet, I noticed the surface was dimpled by raindrops that had fallen overnight. I studied the blades of beach grass emerging from the sand—slender, flat, slightly waxy surfaces, green, moist, and growing at the base, tan to withered brown at the top. This plant, American beachgrass, was, I learned later, the ultimate dune pioneer, an intrepid dune stabilizer with intricate rhizomes penetrating three feet deep and webbing out beneath the sandy soil to help hold it in place. Clusters of yellow daisy-like flowers bloomed atop low-growing, slender-leafed plants—camphor weed—another dune native. I spotted another wildflower, with bright golden sprays—seaside goldenrod—shorter than the typical goldenrod and with waxy leaves, an adaptation to seaside life.

Spreading across the sand, beneath the wildflowers and grasses, almost serpent-like in appearance grew low prickly pear cactus with light-green sections, sharp white spines, and here and there a few fading red flowers. To my right I spotted a cluster of orange-yellow beach blanket flowers.

All of these plants offered a natural, flowing, soil-solidifying, wild life-nurturing, visually pleasing landscape design. It was, I reflected, a stark contrast to the manicured yards and planted palms around the houses beyond the vacant lot.

MOTION

The wind blew harder. According to *Dark Sky* weather app, the gusts were up to 25 mph. I watched the wind rise and fall as it blew through the leaves and branches of the bushes and trees edging the lot. The gusts flipped the leaves of a thorny olive, creating a shivering display of silver. The low, stiffer leaves of the wax myrtle moved slowly, ponderously, and in unison.

The branches of a loblolly pine swayed and sighed. The blue-green sprigs of a red cedar swung back and forth. The leaves and twigs of the live oaks rippled in the breeze. Each shrub and tree had its own unique way of responding to the wind. It was, of course, out of necessity that each of these beach plants adapted to the ever-present coastal breezes, but in this moment as I watched the branches and leaves sway, I saw a troop of free-spirited wind dancers, each creating its own interpretive performance.

Movement in the sky caught my gaze, a solitary mourning dove flying and then landing on a utility wire where it sat motionless. A few minutes later, three stubby-winged starlings flew in and landed on the wire near the dove. Four more starlings arrived and landed nearby. I watched as the starlings grouped and then regrouped. Two flew up and moved further down the wire. Then five lifted up and formed a new group. The purpose of this movement, I knew not.

Were the birds merely restless, were they reinforcing flock structure, or were they engaging in social alignment? I know that wild birds don't waste precious energy. There was some purpose to the movement.

In the sky, beyond the houses, over the ocean, I spotted a big flock of birds in flight. Binoculars up, quickly in focus. It was a flock of cormorants—black compact bodies; strong, rapid wing strokes—perhaps fifty in the flock. I watched as they formed and reformed, spread and bunched, ever in unison, coherent motion, a murmuration before my eyes.

PROVIDE

Soft *seet-seet-seet* calls of yellow-rumped warblers came from the thick shrubs at the bottom of the dune. After scanning with my binoculars for more than a minute, I eventually spotted three of them fluttering in and out of the shrubs and along the branches. Then I heard sharp *teee, teee, teee* calls, followed the sound and located an Eastern towhee, black head and back, dusky orange flanks perched on a branch of a live oak. Listening carefully, I heard soft, sweet *tchep, tchep, tchep* calls—song sparrows—and then spotted them, chunky brown-streaked birds hopping between the stems of grasses.

There were lots of birds living in this little protected sand dune. Perhaps they found shelter and cover in the thick brush and trees from the wind and predators. But then I wondered if there was more to the story.

Looking down at a wax myrtle or southern bayberry plant next to me, I saw dark-blue berries clustered along the stem. I plucked a berry, crushed it between my fingers and inhaled the fragrance. A fine fragrance for Thanksgiving candles but these seeds were also good food for birds. Ahead I saw seed plumes atop little bluestem grasses, more food for birds. I gazed again at the patch of bright orange-yellow beach blanket flowers near, a provider of pollen for the bees and butterflies and another source of seeds for the birds.

The bordering live oaks dropped tiny acorns, still more food. The goldenrods and camphor weed offered seeds, and the viny dune greenbriers that slithered across the ground offered still more berries. This little lot, this tiny patch of coastal dune was an avian smorgasbord. No wonder the birds found and dwelled in the vacant lot.

SCALE

Through a gap between the houses I saw a trio of pelicans—strong-winged, flying in a line, perfect choreography—flap, flap, glide, flap, glide. Two ring-billed seagulls flew high overhead, white torsos against a gray sky; long, slender black-tipped wings, making easy strokes through the air.

I was writing down observations for each ten-minute interval, an exercise in linear time, yet as I gazed around the dune I began to feel a sense of timelessness. I was surrounded by eternal cycles—the increasing illumination of the day, the flowering of the fall plants, and the seasonal rhythm of the birds feeding on seeds. Looking at the sloped dune, I felt the even longer time cycle of wind and plants forming and shaping the sand. I sensed the slow and steady progression of growth from beach grass and little blue stem to bayberry and thorny olive to pine and juniper and live oak—the journey from sand to dune to maritime coastal forest.

My sense of size-scale began to shift. The vacant lot that previously had seemed small and insignificant grew in size, seemed large and expansive, filled as it was with varied and vibrant communities of plant and animal and bird life, decorated with myriad textures and forms of trees and bushes, each swaying with the wind.

The world beyond the dune, with its rows of trim, rigid, multistoried rectangular houses, circumscribed paved driveways and schemed landscaping grew smaller, became less significant in my eyes. The houses, shuttered and empty for the winter, stood separate and isolated. No sense of community there.

When I had entered the vacant dune, I had felt like the big

human surveying a little property, but now as I perceived the long waves and cycles of time and the dynamic life processes surrounding me I felt small. Not bad small, more good small.

VISION

As the final minutes of my last ten-minute interval ticked by, I felt a sense of relief. The wind was relentless and chilly. I wondered if the coffee in the coffee maker might still be hot. Glancing up at a beach house in an adjacent lot, I suddenly noticed that there were stickers on the windows. It was a new house.

A pang of sadness gripped me. Was this lot next? Most likely the opportunity for profit dictated that someone would buy and build. I pictured the scene—bulldozers leveling the land, vegetation yanked up and cleared, another three-story house surrounded by a groomed yard. What a loss!

Then, being hopeful, probably overly optimistic but impossible to suppress, another image came to mind. A bench placed where I sat, maybe another bench or two scattered around the edge of the lot providing places to sit, watch, enjoy, learn, and connect with nature. This little lot could be a tiny nature reserve, a place to experience balance, restoration, and rejuvenation.

Unlikely perhaps, but who knows what the cycles of time will bring. Who knows how and when and if a vision might come to fruition. I did know that I would carry a vision of this vacant lot, this tiny chunk of coastal dune, this rich vibrant nexus of nature within me.

SIT SPOT GUIDANCE

CHAPTER 14

How to Do a Sit Spot Session

❧

A SIT SPOT IS A PLACE IN NATURE THAT YOU HAVE CHOSEN where you go frequently to sit still, observe your surroundings, take in the sounds, inhale the fragrances, and feel the sensations. The purpose of a sit spot is to have a consistent place where you can practice dedicating your attention and time to being in and connecting with nature. If you are like me, after a sit spot session you will most likely feel relaxed, restored, and rejuvenated, and will have learned things about nature and yourself.

When I first read about the sit spot in Jon Young's book *What the Robin Knows,* I thought right away that it was a way to deepen my relationship with nature. Soon I selected a home sit spot along the shoreline of a nearby lake and visited my spot an hour a week for a full year. At first I followed the guidelines offered by Young, but gradually began to make modifications that worked for me.

Similarly, each reader should feel free to make their own adjustments to the guidelines offered below. The sit spot experience, once initiated, takes on a life of its own and seems to be imbued with self-correcting dynamics. In other words, once you start the process you can only go right.

In the sections below, I offer suggestions on selecting a sit spot, deciding what equipment you might need, staying safe in the outdoors, structuring an observation, allotting time, and dealing with resistance and challenges. I also offer suggestions for how to reflect on and process your observations. These are not hard and fast rules—just guidelines.

Selecting a Sit Spot Location

A good sit spot location is usually near diverse habitat that includes the elements of water, forest, and field. A single dimension environment such as a dense pine forest may not offer as much wildlife and plant diversity as a location near a stream running through second-growth forest and next to open meadows.

Places where different habitats intersect, so-called edge habitats, often attract the greatest variety of animals, birds, insects, amphibians, plants, bushes, and trees. This greater variety of life will provide you with more interest, more nature lessons, more awe-producing moments of beauty, and promote faster, deeper nature learning.

It may sound like a challenging assignment to find both edge habitat and water, but such locations are often nearby. They can be found where a backyard ends and a wooded area or field starts, or even where two backyards are separated by a line of shrubs. The water source might be a tiny trickle down a shallow creek bed or a reedy remnant of a pond. If you can't find a spot with all of these elements, any spot with some of these elements will do. And remember to select a spot with a clear, open view of your surroundings.

A backyard, a city park, or even a vacant lot can provide just as suitable a setting for a sit spot as a local nature reserve, state park, or national forest. Nature is all around us, and in fact, birds and plants are opportunistically repopulating urban and suburban areas.

Convenience is an important consideration. You want a place you can get to quickly and easily. My sit spot at Prompton Lake was a ten-minute drive from home. I have another favorite spot near a beaver pond that is an easy ten-minute walk from my house, and I recently set a bench in a corner of my yard, so I can step out my back door, walk a few paces, and sit down to observe nature.

Ultimately, you will obtain the benefits of time in nature when you put in what Jon Young calls "dirt time," or time spent in nature. The easier it is to get to your sit spot the more likely you are to visit. Frequent visits in turn will allow you to observe nature during different times of day, under different conditions, and through the cycles of the seasons.

Finally, your sit spot should "feel right." When I first searched for a sit spot, I relied on objective criteria, became overloaded with information, and ended up paralyzed by indecision. Soon I developed a more intuitive sense for finding the right spot. This sense included a feeling and an inner voice. I would be heading to a spot and some feeling or inner voice would tell me to move twenty feet to the right or left or fifty yards to a little hill, a move that usually would be rewarded with new sights, sounds, and discoveries.

Gradually, I began to acquire the ability to "see" locations that both looked and felt right. This didn't feel like acquiring a new skill, but more like uncovering a latent ability to register both the various elements and the full Gestalt of a favorable spot. Now, even when I travel, I quickly recognize good sit spot locations.

Equipment

Equipment needs vary individually and may change over time and through the seasons. The following suggestions reflect my current preferences.

Seating

I take a small, lightweight, three-legged camp stool with a carrying strap that I can sling over my shoulder. The stool allows me to sit up and is more comfortable for my back than sitting on the ground, especially in wet and cold conditions. Also, I can see more. Lightweight camp stools are readily available at most retail and online sporting goods stores. Some people take a small cushion and some like to sit on the ground or on a log or rock, which also works fine.

Clothing

Blending in with nature doesn't come from camouflaged clothing but more from your inner attitude and external demeanor, so wear comfortable, warm clothing. When you sit still, you may need extra layers to keep warm. If rain is in the forecast, remember to bring raingear. Earth tones such as browns and tans and grays are usually most compatible with a nature setting. If your sit spot is near water or if it has rained recently, you may need waterproof footwear. It is uncomfortable to sit with wet feet. A ball cap, hiking hat, or a stocking cap can help to keep you warm on a chilly day and shade your face and neck on a sunny day

GEAR

I like to bring binoculars to view birds and mammals up close. I recall an early morning sitting session when I used my binoculars for a close up view of a male song sparrow singing on a misty morning and watching the water spray off of his feathers as he belted out his oratorio. Binoculars allow me to see beautiful and awe-inspiring scenes up close. Sometimes I use my binoculars to identify a bird or an animal from a distance. I often carry field guides for trees, birds, and wildflowers in my backpack in case I want to identify something or get detailed information.

NOTEBOOK

I take a 6.5-by-9.5-inch spiral bound notebook. Each page is big enough to hold two ten-minute observations. This size notebook is convenient to carry, rests securely on my leg, and has enough backing to allow writing. I bring along a mechanical pencil and make sure that I have extra lead and a backup pencil. Ballpoint pens can freeze up in the cold, run out of ink, and smear in rainy weather.

SMARTPHONE

I use an app on my smartphone to get a compass reading on the direction I'm facing. I also check a weather app for the temperature, wind direction and speed, forecast, relative humidity, and the times of sunrise and sunset.

There are smartphone apps that can help with bird identification such as the free *Merlin Bird ID* or the reasonably priced *iBird Pro*. I also use *Picture This* to identify plants and trees. Importantly, I put my phone on silent mode and refrain from checking or responding to emails, texts, and calls.

I take a camera to photograph anything unusual, unique, or beautiful. Usually, I do my photography after my session ends.

FOOD AND DRINK

Initially, I brought along a thermos of tea or coffee and a snack. As time went on I found this distracting. Now I just bring water to stay hydrated.

SAFETY

Always, always, always respect nature! Be prepared and stay safe. I keep a pack of matches, a multi-tool knife, and a water bottle in my backpack just in case I need to respond to an emergency or assist someone else in need. I let a family member or friend know when I depart and where I am going. I monitor the weather forecast for extreme conditions such as thunderstorms. I take along my cell phone in case I need to reach out for emergency help.

It is also important to be prudent regarding insects and ticks. In insect season cover yourself, maybe use bug repellent or wear tick-resistant clothes. Check yourself for ticks afterward. Also be aware of animals that could become aggressive. Where I live bears can be a problem.

HOW TO OBSERVE

Once you are seated at your spot, the next step is to settle in and engage your senses. This sounds simple but initially may be challenging. Start by noting objective measures—temperature, wind direction and speed, cloud cover, data that will help you tune in to the day's conditions. Look up at the sky and note the colors and clouds and quality of the light, conditions which may change substantially during your session.

Then, start with your vision, your normal "go to" sense. Take in the colors and shapes around you. What do you see on the ground? Notice the leaves, moss, rocks, sand, and soil. Look at the plant life—grasses, weeds, wildflowers, trees, and bushes. Look for birds, mammals, amphibians, and insects.

Listen to the sounds around you, the wind sighing through the leaves, the water lapping and flowing. Listen to the songs and calls of the birds. Notice human-caused sounds, the cars and trucks, dogs and cows and roosters, even the jetliners whispering high across the sky. Listen to the sounds near and far, soft and loud, the sounds that arise and those that fade away. Over time you may find that listening becomes your most important sense in nature as it provides information from all 360 degrees. It tells you what is near and what is far. It allows you to detect what is moving and in what direction.

Often our sense of hearing is underdeveloped or even atrophied due to living in a world of constant mechanical noise. To function in everyday life, we learn to ignore many surrounding sounds. Consequently, you may need to learn to turn off your normal auditory filters and suppressors. Initially, quiet may be novel, even unnerving. Soon, your acuity will increase and you will begin to hear new sounds, more sounds, all of the sounds of nature around you.

Inhale through your nose to take in any smells wafting through the air. Notice the pleasant smells—the scent of the earth and composting leaves, the smell of air and water, the subtle fragrance of wildflowers, the tangy aroma of pine trees. Notice any unpleasant smells—the reek of rotting plants, the stink of decaying animals, the smell of smoke, and the biting odor of combusted gas. You may need to sniff several times to reawaken this sense.

Pay attention to your sense of touch, to the tactile receptors on your face, neck, arms, and hands. Notice the sensations created by the air against your skin, by the temperature, the humidity, and the wind. Notice the feeling of warmth if the sun is shining. The skin is our largest sensory organ, yet the myriad of tactile sensations coming into the brain are typically ignored. In the woods, our sense of touch can help us to gain a literal and figurative feel for the conditions.

It will help to have a system for keeping track of what you notice. Young suggested observing fully for ten minutes and then jotting down your observations. I tried this but felt like I was missing a lot of information, drifting off during the intervals, and struggling to record everything.

I adopted a system of drawing a circle to represent my surroundings and putting a dot in the middle to represent my location. I call this the sensory awareness circle. During each ten-minute interval, I note the location of all of the sensory input around the circle and jot down quick notes for each impression.

After ten minutes I draw a new circle, note the time, and begin to record impressions for that interval. I continue through six of these intervals. Sometimes I get fascinated or distracted and lose track of time. Not a problem. Each new circle provides an opportunity to start over with your attention.

Develop your own system of notation using words and arrows to note the direction, force, and sound of the wind; the sight and color of leaves falling; the sounds of water; the shapes and textures of bushes and bark. Note the presence and sound of birds, insects, and mammals.

The notes you take are not intended to be scientific data; they are simply your way of continually noticing sensory impressions, your way to keep your attention on nature and on the present moment.

It may seem contrary to the spirit of nature observation to impose this ten-minute recording structure, but I found the sensory awareness circle to be very helpful. The act of recording through timed intervals kept me engaged, brought me more and more into the present, and reigned me in from daydreaming and dozing.

Be prepared to gradually notice more and more. As I settled in and as nature adjusted to my presence, the world came alive and I saw and heard more. Most people conducting a sit spot session realize that as time goes on they see things they missed at first. The more you look, the more you see. Similarly, you may hear more sounds and notice more smells and sensations.

Another advantage of the ten-minute intervals is that it allows you to track changes and movement in nature. Sometimes, during the first several intervals, it seemed to me that very little was happening. Often by the third or fourth interval, the wind direction and strength might have changed. Different birds and animals might have appeared. I gradually realized that each ten-minute interval told a unique nature story.

I sometimes used the blank facing page in my notebook to make notes or drawings about nature. These notes might include insights that occur to me or might be questions that I need to pursue further. Young also recommends making sketches of your surroundings as a way to deepen your observations. I'm no artist, but I have found that making a sketch helps me to see more.

Time

Scientific research indicates that any amount of time sitting and observing nature will benefit your well-being. It could be ten minutes, thirty minutes, or an hour. Select a length of time that sounds right to you. Give it a try and see how it goes.

I followed Young's guideline and chose an hour for my sit spot sessions. People may find this daunting. I did at first but then embraced the challenge. An hour allowed me to blend in and to shift to a state of nature awareness. Consequently, I recommend starting with or working your way up to an hour.

Jon Young also talks about a forty-minute threshold, which is the amount of time that it typically takes for people to settle in and to let go of any previous perceptual conditions or mood states. Young also thought that forty minutes was how long it took nature to recover from your intrusion and return to baseline.

I found the forty-minute threshold to be valid. Around the forty-minute mark, it often seemed like a whole new world unfolded before me. From the perspective of mindfulness, it may take that long to let go of the created world of thoughts and merge fully into an open and mindful state. I slowly got better at this blending in and opening up process. By the last months of the year, it sometimes only took ten minutes for nature to reappear and for me to tune in.

How often should you go to your sit spot? Jon Young went to his spot every day for seven years, a remarkable accomplishment that yielded profound learning and deep personal transformation. I went to my sit spot once a week for a year, and it changed my life. Several times a month will certainly be helpful. Some regularity in conducting sit spot sessions will help to create cumulative effects. Frequent visits also allow you to observe changes in nature, changes in the progression of seasons, and changes from week to week.

Another time consideration is the minutes before and after your sit spot session. I call the time before the session starts the "zero interval." I keep track of my impressions as I approach my sit spot. These include my inner state, my thoughts about the upcoming session, what the mood of nature seems to be, and what I notice as I walk to my sit spot. I call the time after my session the "+1 interval;" this is when I more readily notice changes in the environment and within me. I use the facing blank page of my notebook to write down any impressions, thoughts, and feelings from these two intervals.

STUDYING LIFE

The flora and fauna, all the living things that surround you during your sit spot session can be deep sources of interest, learning, beauty, and inspiration. Different people are drawn to different life forms. Some study the trees or wildflowers, the mosses, the insects, or the mammals. I try to notice and learn about all of these life forms, but for me, birds are a particularly important avenue of connection to nature.

Birds are the story and tell the story of nature. Their presence, arrival, and departure tell us about the seasons. Bird vocalizations provide a supersensitive and far-reaching radar, a picket line of early warning stations to inform us about what is going on around us. And birds provide ample opportunities for nature awareness.

Following Jon Young's suggestion, I developed a system of notations to keep track of avian activity. I noted flying birds with a line, and if I saw a pair or flock, I added the number. When I recognized the bird I used an abbreviation—American Robin = AmRo. If I didn't recognize the bird, I wrote something like "lbb" to stand for little brown bird.

The three main kinds of bird vocalizations—territorial songs, flock calls, and alarm calls—became rich sources of information for me. Territorial songs, like the familiar *cheerily cheer up, cheerily, cheer up* of a robin, told me what birds had set up a home breeding territory nearby. Flock calls, such as the metallic *tik, tik, tik* of cardinals or the soft *tchep, tchep, tchep* of song sparrows, told me what birds were in or passing through the area around my sit spot. Alarm calls told me about possible bird predators in the area.

My growing awareness of birds and gradual learning of their songs and calls added much to my sit spot experience. Through practice, study, and using the *Merlin ID Sound* app, I slowly learned more songs and calls. I also learned the names of the various trees, wildflowers, ferns, bushes, and mosses.

A progressive process of learning about birds or about any flora or fauna is an integral part of the sitting experience. The variety of life surrounding your sit spot tells you much about the unique slice of nature that you are observing.

THE STAGES OF OBSERVATION

SENSORY AWARENESS

I came to recognize stages in the sit spot experience. The first is sensory awareness. This includes time for settling in, sitting still, and taking in your surroundings. The longer you sit and the more times you sit, the more acute your senses become. Sensory awareness is the gateway to nature mindfulness.

BLENDING IN

The next stage is blending in. Usually, when we walk through the woods we create a disturbance. The birds and mammals scatter and hide. But when we sit still, nature slowly recovers, the animals and birds resume their lives, and nature begins to reveal itself.

Inner attitude may be an important aspect of blending in. After my very first sit spot session, I felt a deep appreciation for all that I experienced. Carrying an attitude of gratitude into the woods combined with feelings of openness are key elements for blending in. These attitudes most likely affect your nonverbal behavior in a way that allows birds and mammals to see you as non-threatening. More on this topic in the next chapter.

MINDFULNESS

Gradually, you may move into a state of "mindfulness," a state of being fully in the present, a condition of being open to all sensory input. In this stage your mind stops creating its own world and simply begins to take in what is there in the moment. In mindfulness the world of nature may become vibrantly alive, and you feel part of it. You see and hear things, notice vivid colors and soothing sounds that you just didn't see and hear before.

In mindfulness you begin to feel refreshed and rejuvenated. Positive emotions such as happiness, contentment, and joy emerge spontaneously. In mindfulness you may also become more aware of internal states. Memories, associations, and insights may emerge, all of which allow you to know yourself better.

Deep Learning

Mindfulness opens the door to the next stage—deep learning. I came to feel over the course of the year that when I offered my attention, nature responded with generous teaching. When I made the effort to sit and learn, nature revealed lesson after lesson. For example, I learned the life story of skunk cabbage, discovered the late-blooming bottle gentian, and saw the mating behavior of cedar waxwings.

Transformation

I have tentatively labeled the next stage transformation—the time when the lessons offered by nature are felt deeply. When I saw an ovenbird feeding on suddenly appearing flood debris, I grasped the principle of adaptability. When I watched warblers glean insects from branches and phoebes dart out and snatch insects from the air, I understood the principle of gifts differing, of how each animal has its niche, and how each available niche in nature is fully used. These lessons weren't an academic accumulation of facts but insights that transferred into my being and changed the way I saw myself and the world around me.

Processing Your Observations

Review and edit your field observations after your sit spot session. When I returned home from a session, I would look over my notes and make changes, additions, and corrections using a differently colored pen or pencil. Sometimes I added details and explanations that I missed because at the moment there was so much going on. Sometimes I made corrections. I may have tentatively identified a bird only to realize later that it was a different bird.

The purpose of this review is to make the field notes as descriptive as possible; to enhance the quality of the objective observations; to address the question of what information the senses gathered, what was seen, felt, heard and smelled; and to circle back through and reinforce your learning.

Often when I reviewed my notes, I realized I needed to conduct follow-up research to answer questions that had emerged. I might have seen or heard some bird that I had never seen before. I might have observed a familiar bird or animal behaving in a different manner. I might have noticed a plant, wildflower, or tree that I hadn't noticed before. In short, I noticed something that made me curious, something that made me want to learn more, delve into facts and details, and expand on the learning that occurred during my session.

Sometimes, I had to recognize that my observations exposed what I didn't know. For example, I found that I didn't really know much about seasonal variations in the wind, about the manner in which bodies of water freeze and then melt, about the previous uses of land where I sat, and about the progression of trees in a second-growth forest.

I also liked to consider the stories that nature revealed. I recall a session when I noticed how crows communicate across distance. I remember learning how chipmunks and squirrels forage and then hid seeds, some of which are forgotten about and sprout into seedlings. Sometimes the true story of my sit spot emerged several days later.

One good way to further process your observations is to keep a journal; write up an entry for each session that includes the objective information, the learning, and your personal insights.

Sharing your observations with like-minded or fellow observers is another good way to process your experiences. You might also report your findings to a mentor, someone who has traveled further down the path of nature observation, who might see what you haven't seen, might understand what you have yet to understand, and can guide you with questions or comments.

CHALLENGES

The biggest challenge is carving out time to get to your sit spot. Putting in minutes or an hour at your sit spot increases the probability of experiencing the benefits of time in nature, including physical rejuvenation, the contentment of solitude, the fascination of new learning, and the satisfaction of better knowing yourself.

Yet in spite of all of these positive outcomes, it seems that there is always some strange resistance to overcome, some difficulty in actually dedicating a period of time, in actually getting out the door to go to your sit spot. It is hard to break the gravitational pull of the daily routine.

How does one overcome this resistance? The answer, of course, will be different for different people. For me the structure of a commitment to go once a week for a full year provided an initial impetus to overcome resistance. Now, since I know how restorative and interesting each session can be, a part of me is always looking forward to my next sit spot session.

Physical discomfort can also pose a challenge. You may find it hard to sit still. Your back or legs may start to ache. You may feel stiff and yearn to stand up, move, or stretch. You may feel the need to go to the bathroom. All of these things happened to me. If I needed to move or stretch, I did.

But gradually, something almost miraculous happened. It became easier and easier to sit still as my year progressed. By the end of the year, I was able to sit for a full hour. I think I became used to sitting. More importantly, I believe the experience of an hour absorbed in nature became so engaging and so rewarding that it made sitting still easier.

Internal challenges can also arise. It can be hard to keep your attention on nature. You might find yourself thinking about things you need to do, projects you need to finish, or people you need to contact. Sometimes inner worries or a lingering bad mood may make it hard to attend to nature. There may be intervals with very little going on and your mind may drift off. These reactions are typical and normal. When they occur, simply take a few breaths, hit the internal attention-refresh button, reengage your senses, and scan around your sensory awareness circle. Look for what you have overlooked. Listen for the sounds within the silence. Notice subtle sensations of touch and smell.

Sometimes there is so much going on—multiple birds flying, singing, and calling; animals on the move; intense or rapidly changing wind and weather. Just keep track of what you can. I found that making notes for a ten-minute interval made it all more manageable.

You may get frustrated when you can't fully see or hear things due to dense foliage or interfering noises. You may feel annoyed by human caused noise such as airplanes flying over or nearby traffic. You may feel cold when the wind blows and the temperature drops. You may get wet when a sudden rain shower arrives or when a snow squall blows through. All of these happened to me, and there were times I thought about packing up and heading home, but I was able to talk myself into staying put and finishing my hour. Such perseverance and patience would then be rewarded by some remarkably beautiful or entirely new sight or sound. Ultimately, time and attention are the two resources we have for connecting with nature and enhancing our well-being.

PLEASANT AND INTERESTING

Allow the sit spot experience to be interesting and enjoyable. Consider adding pleasing elements of ceremony. For example, forest bathing sessions begin and end by passing over a Threshold of Connection, a physical step-over or step-through that serves as a transition into the world of nature and into a mindful state.

When I stepped from the parking lot onto the forest trail, and in particular when I stepped across a seep running through the woods, I felt that I was physically, mentally, and emotionally entering the world of nature.

After an early morning sitting session, I would usually return home and reward myself with a full hot breakfast, a kind of physical parallel to all of the nature nourishment I had taken in. Similarly, in forest bathing, each session concludes with a tea ceremony.

Sharing circles that encourage participants to speak from their heart about what they have noticed is another key element in forest bathing sessions. The circles are a social ceremony that allows each person to better understand their own experiences and to learn by hearing about the experiences of others. When I conducted shared sit spot sessions, I found sharing to be deeply meaningful—both sharing done in person and done subsequently in writing. The inclusion of such ceremonial elements seems to touch on core human characteristics and adds depth to the sit spot experience. The ceremonies are imbued with a sense of playfulness, feelings of respect, and a spirit of openness—attitudes that encourage getting the most out of your time in nature.

❧

I have given you my thoughts on how to conduct a sit spot session. But, as usual I am left with a question. How do others experience the sit spot? Let's take a look at what two of my sit spot friends had to say.

CHAPTER 15

The Sharing Circle

I CLEARLY REMEMBER THE EVENT THAT MOTIVATED ME TO conduct shared sit spot sessions. It happened after I had finished an hourlong sit spot at the Rachel Carson Preserve in Beaufort, North Carolina. Having enjoyed the session, I was reluctant to leave and decided to linger for a while. I climbed up to the observation deck to take in the view of the vast salt marsh and gaze out at the terns, pelicans, and gulls gathering as the tide ebbed. I watched the seabirds flap, glide, and plunge into the shallow water, frequently emerging with silvery, wriggling fish clutched in their bills.

Transfixed by this example of timing in nature, by the birds sensing and knowing exactly the right time to arrive over the tidal pools, I reflected on the importance of timing in my life. I wondered how aware, open, and responsive I was to the timing clues around me.

A couple joined me on the deck—bird watchers, I thought, given their multi-pocketed khaki vests and expensive-looking binoculars. After an interval of compatible silence, I heard the woman say to her partner, "When I see the terns flying high and free over the water, it reminds me that when you stick to your principles, when you follow your beliefs, you rise above the surface turbulence. It's as if your values lift you up."

It was a stunning moment for me. We were two people gazing at exactly the same nature scene, both deeply engaged in the view, but each of us experiencing very different reactions and insights.

For days I thought back on that moment. Slowly, two explanatory terms came to mind—projection and timing. A nature view, I thought, might be somewhat like a projective personality test, like the famous Rorschach Test, where a series of neutral but evocative stimuli are presented that allow the examinee to place, that is to project their own inner thoughts, concerns, emotions, issues, and unconscious conflicts onto the picture. But I also thought that there might be something fundamentally different about viewing nature scenes with the shades of green and blue, the branching fractals, and the sounds of wind, water, and bird song. These inputs not only induce a state of mindfulness but seem to pull for positive emotions, thoughts, and insights.

Mulling this over, I came across a social psychology study that found that when subjects viewed nature scenes as opposed to city scenes, they set a much higher value on intrinsic aspirations related to personal growth, core psychological needs, a sense of community, and relationship connections. In contrast, those viewing the city scenes placed more emphasis on extrinsic aspirations such as money, recognition, and acquisition of material goods.

I began to wonder if sitting and observing nature provided a particular palette that facilitated the observer projecting or expressing aspirations linked to their personal growth, to their emotional and spiritual development.

I also began to consider timing, why certain insights emerged at certain times when observing nature. Timing is, of course, one of the greatest challenges in the helping professions.

In counseling, for example, the therapist encourages reflection or free association then listens and observes carefully in order to provide helpful insights or guidance at just the right time, at the moment the client is open, has the information needed to see patterns in their life, and is ready to view new ways forward. When trying to follow the dictum to do no harm, it is a delicate issue for the therapist to not rush the insight, yet not miss an opportunity, to ultimately facilitate the right insight at the right time.

Perhaps, I thought, when one sits still in nature, engages in sensory awareness, and progresses into mindfulness, the just right insights arise at the just right time. Whatever feelings or insights emerge fit with where we are and what we are ready for. Timing when viewing nature scenes may be inherently timely.

When I reflected back on my year of weekly sit spots, this made sense to me. But I wanted to find out if these processes of positive projection, timing, and just right nature insights worked for others as well. I wanted to see if the hourlong sit spot experience had therapeutic implications for others as it did for me. I decided to invite others to join me for a sit spot and then ask each of them to reflect on and write up their experiences.

I also decided to help them process their experiences by inviting them into a sharing circle, by providing them with an opportunity to articulate their reflections and insights. Since my shared sit spots were conducted at different times and in different places, I created a virtual circle by conducting interviews with each of my friends. Drawing on my background as a psychologist, I devised a structured interview designed to be inclusive, not miss any key themes, and yet not pull too hard for specific reactions.

I hoped to answer my questions about positive projection and just right timing. In addition I wanted to find out if doing a sit spot started a developmental process? Did each of my sit spot friends begin to develop their own individual ways to do a sit spot?

Finally, I wanted to collect feedback on what worked and what didn't work in my sit spot instruction and guidance. I hoped to find ways to improve my presentation, ways to make the sit spot experience more approachable and user-friendly.

These shared sit spots turned into very special experiences for me. I learned much from each of my friends. I saw how quickly sit spotters began to adapt, adjust, and individualize the session. And I thought that each friend was in certain ways more eloquent than me in describing the heart of the sit spot experience and in touching on the main themes of this book.

I have included two of the interviews below. Let me begin by introducing two of my sit spot friends—Jerry and Pat.

My first shared sit spot session was with Jerry, a civil engineer, entrepreneur, musician, outdoorsman, and a tech enthusiast. He brought many useful attributes to the sit spot experience. I was relieved when he "got" and enjoyed the hourlong session.

After conducting several sit spot sessions with men, I wanted to get a woman's perspective. Pat, a close friend, a board member of the local Audubon Chapter, an avid hiker, and a dedicated gardener seemed like a good candidate. We sat in silence right next to each other for the full hour, overlooking a small lake at daybreak. Some of our perceptions, reflections, and insights overlapped and some were entirely unique.

JERRY

As you look back on our shared sit spot session, do you have any general thoughts to share?
I think anyone who does a sit spot will really enjoy it. The problem is that sitting alone out in the woods for a full hour is a foreign concept. People will read about it, be intrigued, think about doing it, but may never get around to it.

What motivated you to do a sit spot?
I read your book and I read *The Nature Fix* by Florence Williams, so I was definitely interested in doing a sit spot. For me the tipping point came when you extended a personal invitation. And along with the invitation, you gave me helpful step-by-step instructions. It might work best for people to go on their first sit spot with someone who is experienced and who can lead them through the process.

What were your impressions and reactions while doing the session?
During the first ten to fifteen minutes, everything seemed quiet. But around twenty minutes into it, a lot of small birds started to appear all around me in the trees and bushes. I figured that my arrival had created a disturbance, and it took a while for all the wildlife to get back to their business, back to their natural activity.

After twenty minutes, I heard a stream flowing that was about two hundred feet away. The sound had been there the whole time, but it took that long for me to tune in and hear it.

I also realized that sunrise is an incredibly active time of day. As the sun came up, the birds were singing loudly and flying around, and the wind picked up and rustled the leaves and branches. I've often been up at sunrise to drive to work, take a run, or make breakfast, but I never thought about sitting still and experiencing all the activity, all the sights, sounds, and sensations of a new day beginning.

Was the experience different than you thought it might be?
It was a lot colder than I anticipated. I had checked the forecast and thought I had the right layers of clothing, but I realized that when you are sitting still, not burning calories, not moving around to warm up, and the wind is blowing, it can be "damn cold." Next time I will know how to dress.

What were your reactions, thoughts, or reflections after doing the sit spot?
I noticed that when I was sitting in the woods, I could hear a lot more than I could see. I would hear the wind approaching before I felt it, and I would hear the birds singing or calling before I saw them. I also realized that when you are sitting still, you have a much better chance to hear the 360 degree world around you. I thought then that if you are hiking or biking and not tuned into this auditory input, you are missing half of the experience of being in nature.

I was also surprised at how much I tuned into the wind. Part of that probably stemmed from my experience sailing, but I think another part was that I was sitting still. I noticed that when the wind first picked up, I looked out at the lake and could see ripples approach me. I felt the gusts of wind against my face and was aware of how each gust arose and then abated. I heard the sounds of the leaves and branches moving above me.

Have your thoughts about the sit spot experience changed or developed over time?
Beforehand I thought that doing a sit spot session would be pretty relaxing, kind of like sitting in a La-Z-Boy chair and drifting off. Actually, I was very alert and engaged. The structured observation of scanning the circle around me for all the sights and sounds kept me focused and in the present. The end result was that I felt refreshed, but not relaxed in the sense I had anticipated.

Did the sit spot experience change you in any ways? If so, in what ways?
It gave me a greater appreciation for the original observers and discoverers. People like Newton, Galileo, and Aristotle didn't have textbooks and instruction manuals to rely on. They had to go out

and observe; and then things occurred to them that they might not have even been looking for.

Newton was probably going out looking for apples, but when he got into a deep observational state, he was able to figure out the laws of gravity. The Native Americans weren't given a guide to the stars, but when they sat night after night, season after season, watching the night sky, they were able to understand the constellations and the passage and cycles of time.

It occurred to me when I was doing my session that with focused attention, these original observers were able to see patterns, piece things together, and understand phenomena for the first time. It made me realize what a powerful tool observation is.

Have you done any subsequent sit spot sessions on your own or done any variations that you created?

I've given people a copy your book, *The Stillness of the Living Forest.* I gave one to my brother-in-law who loves to be out in nature, and I encouraged him to leave it in his shed and to pick it up and read the week that matched the current week. I think it is valuable to trace the flow of the seasons week by week and to see how your location matches up with what was going on in northeast Pennsylvania that same week.

I haven't done any formal, hourlong sit spots, but I find that if I'm out in the yard, I'll pause and sit on a bench and take in the sounds and sights. I think I do more what I call "pensive walks" where I move slowly and let my mind wander freely, let ideas and concerns in one ear and out the other. But even though these walks take place on a forest trail, it's not the same experience as a sit spot. Focusing only on the terrain that is in sight with the added structure of the notebook and a fresh circle every ten minutes is a much different experience.

Do you have any other thoughts, impressions, reflections or recommendations to share?

For me, the key is the notebook, the circle, and the ten-minute intervals. That structure is what kept me engaged, kept me seeing and hearing more, kept me connecting more deeply with nature around me. The ten-minute intervals are really valuable as they give you a fresh start every ten minutes. If you miss some sounds or if you drift off or if you think about tasks at home, when a new interval arrives, you get a fresh opportunity to do it again. It reminded me of when I was in a band, and we had a list of songs for a set. If you screwed a song up, once it was over, you could let go and use the opportunity to do great on the next song. The past song—or the past ten-minute interval—doesn't influence, doesn't affect the next song or the next interval. It's a new circle, a new start.

Pat

As you look back on our shared sit spot session, do you have any general thoughts to share?
Our early morning sit spot at Browning Beaver Meadow was a special experience for me. I felt then and still feel grateful. It was memorable and intense. Even though I spend a lot of time in nature, this was different. There was something about paying attention and then becoming mindful. I saw the whole scene in front of me in a new way. My ability to observe expanded out and seemed dynamic. As the hour proceeded, I noticed more and more details. The whole experience remains embedded in my mind and heart.

What motivated you to do a sit spot?
I heard you speak about your Forest Stillness year and read your book, and it sparked my interest in doing a sit spot. I'm a big nature fan so this seemed like a great idea. I was intrigued with the prospect of spending an hour in nature and really paying attention.

What were your impressions and reactions while doing the sit spot?
It was interesting and fun. I became hyperalert and started noticing the sound of wind through the trees, birds singing, and the feel of the air on my face. It was actually quite a sensual experience.

I also noticed how the scene opened up. I remember looking across the pond at the trees and not registering much, and then later I began to clearly see the trees, each tree, its shape and colors. I had seen something blueish along the shoreline and had dismissed it, but later as my vision opened up, I saw that it was a great blue heron standing still in its hunting pose.

As the time quickly slipped by, I also began to understand the structure of drawing a new circle every ten minutes and starting anew with my observations and notes. Spontaneously, my circle began to change in shape, reflecting my experience as the scene in front of me expanded in detail and richness while the area behind me shrunk in size.

Was the experience different than you thought it might be?
Beforehand I was a little worried about whether I would be able to do it right. I was anxious about passing the sit spot "test." Once I got going it was much easier than I had expected. I became absorbed in the experience and process.

My typical mental world of thinking about things I needed to take care of like laundry, shopping, and meals just vanished. The outside world was gone. I felt simultaneously super alert, yet very relaxed. I was busy and engaged yet felt peaceful.

What were your reactions, thoughts, or reflections after doing the sit spot?
Since doing the sit spot I think I have been more attentive when I am out in nature. I have always enjoyed my walks, but now I just seem to be noticing more and taking it in more deeply. Maybe the deeply embedded impressions from the sit spot session have sensitized me to notice more. I think I feel more peaceful, and I have a greater sense of gratitude as well. I feel like I have received a gift of indelible experience.

I've also thought about whether or not I would want to bring my smart phone with me in the future. It was helpful to check the Merlin sound ID for birdsongs, but maybe it took me out of the moment. I also wondered if taking photos was an interruption that broke the flow. On the other hand, I did think it was good to have photos to recall certain moments and impressions.

Another thing is that as I look back on the experience, I see the value of the ten-minute intervals. I saw how it provided structure and helped to refresh and refocus my awareness.

Have your thoughts about the sit spot changed or developed over time?
I've thought about how perception can deepen and change when you put yourself in the right situation and offer up your full attention. I've realized that seeing and hearing and feeling are dynamic and that the brain has a lot of plasticity.

When I'm out walking, I've started to notice good places to do a sit spot—places with a nice view, with interesting terrain, or near a river. It just comes to me.

Did the sit spot experience change you in any ways? If so, in what ways?

One big change is that I was never a big fan of the Browning Beaver Meadow Preserve. I thought the trails were difficult and that the whole place just wasn't that interesting. Now, it is one of my favorite places in nature. I often think about going back and seeing it at different times of day, in different weather, and in different seasons.

I like this preserve so much now that I went through the effort of putting it on Google Maps so that others could find it and enjoy it. Maybe I wanted to share my joy.

In addition, since doing the sit spot I feel calmer and more attentive.

Have you done any subsequent sit spots on your own or done any variations that you created?

I guess I did an accidental sit spot. On one of the last sunny, warm days of the fall, I grabbed my Kindle and walked to a favorite place in the woods, planning to sit and read for a while. When I arrived I discovered that my Kindle battery was dead. For a minute I was disappointed, and then I came up with the idea to walk to a nearby favorite spot in nature where two streams join. I sat and watched and listened for a full hour. This was a bit unusual for me because usually when I'm out in nature, I'm actively hiking or biking or doing something. Now, I have the option of sitting still and doing a sit spot.

It turned out to be a lovely hour. I gazed at the swirling patterns in the water where the two rivers merge, patterns that kept changing and rearranging. I saw fish rise to the surface. I took in the soft yet bright illumination of the late afternoon sunlight and saw the colors of the sunset in the sky. I didn't have a notebook so I didn't use the structure of the ten-minute intervals, but the session still worked out great.

Do you have any other thoughts, impressions, reflections or recommendations to share?

Now that I've done a sit spot session with you and one on my own,

I feel like I can do it. Plus, I have this new ability to notice good sit spot locations. And I've realized since I read your blog post, "The Vacant Lot" that I don't have to be too fussy about the location.

The result is that I have a desire to share the sit spot experience with others. I came up with the idea to create a holiday gift certificate for a guided sit spot that I would conduct. I even have several people in mind to whom I will give this gift.

CHAPTER 16

Deepening Nature Mindfulness

❦

GRATITUDE

S ITTING IN MY OFFICE, GOING OVER MY FIELD NOTES, AND attempting to journal my sit spot experiences, I was suddenly flooded with feelings of gratitude. Surprised by the intensity of the emotion, I tried to figure out its source. Looking down at my notes—descriptions of the sky, wind, trees, snow, the browns and grays of the tree trunks, and the winter birdsongs—I realized I was thankful for all I had noticed in nature.

Noticing details in nature and experiencing gratitude may be linked. Giving close attention to little things in nature directs us to see, hear, feel, and smell more and to more deeply notice the beauty, richness, and complexity of nature, and this attention can bring forth gratitude.

Gratitude became a part of my sit spot routine. Sitting alone and still for an hour, I discovered that little things mattered and gave me pleasure—a clear sky, soft morning sunlight, the arrival of migratory birds, or new wildflowers in bloom.

Over time I came to see gratitude as a process. I noticed more in nature, felt gratitude; noticed even more, and felt more gratitude. Gratitude created a positive feedback loop.

Research has revealed there may be a neurochemical basis to this loop. It seems that when we feel thankful, our brain releases serotonin and dopamine, two feel-good neurotransmitters, chemical rewards that encourage us to have the experience again. No wonder as the year went by that my motivation for my weekly sit spot steadily grew stronger.

Gratitude is also a foundation of positive psychology. Consciously feeling and naming gratitude is seen as essential to building a healthy lifestyle. Within the practice of positive psychology there are many techniques for increasing gratitude, ranging from writing in a thankfulness journal, to dropping notes into a gratitude jar, to keeping a daily list of things for which to be thankful. My experience suggests that being out in nature works well to facilitate feelings of gratitude.

Blending In

Taking a short cut across a golf course fairway to get to a lake shore, I approached a flock of Canada geese feeding peacefully in the grass. As I came closer the sentinel goose extended its neck and watched me carefully. The rest of the flock, alerted by the sentinel's change in posture, began to nervously edge away. At that moment I averted my gaze to the ground, relaxed my body, slowed my pace, and made a slight detour, angling away from the flock. Immediately, the sentinel relaxed; the flock of geese got the signal and resumed their peaceful feeding.

Jon Young has said that if you look directly at an animal or bird, the animal interprets this to mean that you either want to eat them or mate with them. If you avert your gaze and continue on your way, the bird or animal feels less threatened and can resume its activity. Birds and mammals vitally depend on being able to read the "body language" of other animals. At the same time, birds and mammals run on a strict energy economy, avoiding wasted effort and reactions at all costs.

As soon as I shifted my gaze away from the geese, I also shifted my inner attitude to something like, "Hey, I'm just doing my thing so you can go ahead and do your thing." Message sent and message received. My encounter with the geese was an object lesson in the principle of nonviolence. Since that day I have had numerous peaceful encounters with birds and mammals.

Now when I head out for a bird walk or a sit spot visit, I try to cultivate an inner sense of acceptance and respect toward all the fauna and flora around me—albeit with variable success. On days when I am in a peaceful space, I'm surprised at how readily the animals and birds reveal themselves. On other days, when I feel agitated or impatient, I receive immediate feedback as the birds and mammals are nowhere to be seen. Feedback received. I pause, take a few breaths, relax, let go, and adjust my inner state.

Ultimately, it is your inner attitude that allows you to blend into nature. No amount of camouflage clothing, face paint, or stealthy sneaking up can help you to blend in as much as a peaceful mind.

Settling In

Settling in was the name I gave to the process of transitioning from typical everyday consciousness to a state of nature mindfulness. The process began as I drove to my sit spot and began to tune in to the weather and conditions around me. The process became more serious as I walked from my car through the woods to my sit spot, a stage I called the zero interval, a time to open the senses and notice the mood and state of nature.

Settling in began in earnest when I arrived at my sit spot, set up my camp stool, sat down, drew my first sensory awareness circle, and began to scan the full circle of surrounding sounds, sights, smells, and tactile input. Initially, settling in was challenging and took some time. My mind was distracted by things that needed to be done—thoughts about the future—by how I had done recent tasks—thoughts about the past—and by what I needed to be doing now—judgmental chatter. I would talk to myself about my gear, whether I had the right clothing, what others might think of what I was doing, and exactly how well I was recording events. I worried about time. An hour seemed like such a long time to sit in the woods. I questioned the whole idea of giving up valuable time to just sit. I would shift position, get up, stretch, walk around, or sip tea from a thermos. It would take twenty to thirty minutes for me to settle in.

Gradually, all of this mental and physical fiddling faded away. The experience of nature mindfulness became so rewarding that I was motivated to get out earlier and stay longer. I believe that I gradually formed new neurological pathways of sensory awareness that made it easier for me to settle in within the first few minutes.

Then at least three things happened. First of all, my perception of time changed. The ten-minute intervals flew by. Time progressed in waves and cycles. An hour, which initially had seemed daunting, started to almost seem like too little time.

Simultaneously, I began to realize that what I had previously thought of as doing nothing was in fact doing everything. Sitting still in nature and shifting into mindfulness became the most dynamic, restorative, and instructive hour of the week.

And finally, I needed less time to settle in and blend in to the forest baseline. At the beginning of the year. it took thirty to forty minutes before the birds and mammals would resume their natural activity around me. By the last few months, the birds and mammals would appear within five and ten minutes.

TRUST

Halfway through my sit spot year I realized that I was seeing, hearing, and learning something entirely new every week. It might be listening to a jazzy, blue jay songfest in the trees above me, seeing the touching berry-sharing rituals of cedar waxwings, hearing the grunts of cormorants as they sunned themselves on a log, or viewing the secretive behavior of a forest chipmunk. I began to have the feeling that nature was actively teaching me, that there was a kind of student-teacher relationship going on. If I offered my time, attention, and interest, nature in its benevolence gave me new knowledge and new insights.

But then I got greedy. I began to expect a new lesson each week. As the ten-minute intervals ticked by, I began to wonder, even worry about when I would get to see or hear something new. One week my hour was up, and I had seen nothing novel. I thought: *so much for my theory about the nature-teacher thing*, and let go of the concept. But at that very moment, a green heron flew in, perched on a branch fifteen feet away, and used its long bill to preen its blue-green back feathers as the sunlight glistened on its chestnut neck plumage. For a full five minutes, it revealed itself to me before it flew off with a loud *skeew* call.

Trust restored. Now, when I go into nature, I simply offer my attention and trust that experiences and new knowledge will come on their own schedule. As for the learning, I try to help that along by using field guides and apps to identify plants, trees, birds, and animals. I don't do this obsessively but have discovered that knowing a living thing's name brings me more into relationship with it.

Trust in the process of nature mindfulness may also be an expression of openness. Openness is one of the Big 5 personality traits, defined as being imaginative, creative, insightful, and willing to try new things and entertain multiple viewpoints. Traits like openness are thought to be inborn and hardwired. I think it is possible that mindful time in nature creates openness.

A CONSERVATION ETHIC

One of my favorite books, one I reread every several years, is *A Sand County Almanac* by Aldo Leopold. I like the book because it takes place in Wisconsin, my home state, and the nature scenes described are familiar to me. I also like the book because it beautifully, even poetically, describes changes in nature across the months and seasons. And I like the fact that the book, while published in 1948, still seems current, relevant, even prescient.

Rereading *A Sand County Almanac* while writing this book, I was particularly struck by the third section, "The Upshot." In the past I raced through this section, but this time I slowed down as I noticed how much the author's words resonated with my recent experiences.

Leopold advanced what he called a "land ethic," a view in which humans are part of the community of nature and not separate from it. Ethics, he wrote, have over the centuries evolved to help individuals see themselves as interdependent parts of a community and to offer guidance for how to participate sustainably in that community. A land ethic in which humans see themselves as integral parts of the greater community of nature and then act and live in ways to protect, foster, and sustain that community was, in Leopold's vision, a needed next evolutionary step.

Leopold's vision grew in part from his love for and deep connection to nature. His heart, soul, scientific work, and vision for a holistic and healthy future were fueled by his experiences of awe and moments of beauty such as seeing and hearing the early March honking return of geese, spotting tiny spring *Draba* wildflowers bloom, and watching woodcock perform their mystical and magical mating sky dance at dusk.

I developed similar thoughts and feelings during my sit spot year. Sitting still in the forest, merging into mindfulness, and feeling connected to and part of nature, I felt a spontaneous and strong urge to care for nature. I noticed that this urge had a unique quality as it was propelled by love and connection and not by worry and fear. Just as I am naturally inclined to care for my family, friends, and community I began to feel the same motivation to care for nature.

I called this urge a conservation ethic. It started small by wanting to do little things: pick up litter, cultivate the flowers and trees in my yard, reintroduce native species, and feed the birds. But gradually, I noticed that the reach of this heartfelt urge began to expand.

Leopold did not have the advantage of access to all of the contemporary scientific verification of the benefits of time in nature. This new science informs us that a conservation ethic is not only an ideal but is also eminently practical and smart. When humans connect and engage with nature, they are healthier, happier, smarter, and more productive. Following a conservation ethic makes good economic, health, and social sense. It is wise and ethical policy.

Taking a policy perspective led me to consider environmental justice. Engagement with and securing the benefits of time in nature shouldn't just be for those who have the time and money to enjoy it. Nature should be available to people of all economic, social, educational, ethnic, and geographic backgrounds and circumstances. Building and maintaining a nature infrastructure is crucial for individual, community, national, and planetary health.

I find myself increasingly drawn to issues beyond my yard. I happily help to maintain and protect nature areas in my community, county, and state, and I support organizations that provide such opportunities. I sense that in the future I will, with the resources I have, be drawn to even larger policy initiatives.

For me, as it may have been for Leopold, the strength and creativity of my conservation ethic is powered by spending mindful time in nature where I can absorb beauty, experience awe, and better know myself. As John Piccolo wrote in his celebration of Leopold, "One must know thyself to know the world." Recognizing oneself as part of a matrix of interdependent relationships in nature spontaneously engenders a conservation ethic.

In her book *Birding to Change the World*, Trish O'Kane tells her personal story of how connecting to nature through bird watching led her to a path of heart-powered environmental activism. She shared the idea that seeing beauty in nature, advocating for social justice, and protecting the environment can be mutually supportive activities.

Individual experiences with nature can be the building blocks of a conservation ethic. The active expression of this ethic can then deepen the experience of time in nature. My hope is that this book will give you the background information, practical tools, and inspiration to help you connect mindfully with nature and to develop and express your own conservation ethic.

Now

Together we have looked at the science on the benefits of time in nature, considered ways to be in nature, and examined the question of how much time in nature is needed. We have learned about nature mindfulness and explored how sensory awareness provides gateways to mindfulness.

We have also explored a variety of sit spot experiences in different settings, with different people, organized around different themes, revealing a range of mindfulness-based insights.

We have also reviewed specific guidelines for conducting a sit spot. And we have considered the attitudes that can strengthen the benefits of time in nature and deepen mindfulness.

By now you should have a good idea of the value of spending time in nature. You may have ideas and options on how to spend that time. And, hopefully, you may feel motivated, even inspired to budget some of your time and attention to nature mindfulness.

Author's Notes

Introduction: *A Nature Mystery*

Forest Stillness
Harvey, J. *The Stillness of the Living Forest: A Year of Listening and Learning.* Brunswick, Maine: Shanti Arts, 2019.

Nature Fix
Williams, F. *The Nature Fix: Why Nature Makes Us Happier, Healthier, and More Creative.* New York City: Norton, 2017.

Benefits of Time in Nature
Huynh, L. T. M., Gasparatos, A., Su, J., et al. "Linking the Nonmaterial Dimensions of Human-nature Relations and Human Well-being through Cultural Ecosystem Services." *Science Adv*ances 8, no. 31 (2022): 31. https://doi.org/10.1126/sciadv.abn8042; PMID: 35930638; PMCID: PMC9355367

❧

Chapter 1: *Nature and Human Well-Being*

Effects of Forest Bathing (*shinrin-yoku*)
Cheng, X., Liu, J., Liu, H., et al. "A Systematic Review of Evidence of Additional Health Benefits from Forest Exposure." *Landscape and Urban Planning* (August 2021): 212. https://doi.org/10.1016/j.landurbplan.2021.104123

Stress Reduction Model

Ulrich, R. S., Simons, S. T., Losito, B. D., et al. "Stress Recovery during Exposure to Natural and Urban Environments." *Journal of Environmental Psychology* 11 (1991): 201–230. https://doi.org/10.1016/S0272-4944(05)80184-7

Benefits of Nature

Weir, K. "Nurtured by Nature." *Monitor on Psychology* 51, no. 3. https://www.apa.org/monitor/2020/04/nurtured-nature

Phytoncides and Immune System

Chae, Y., Lee, S., Jo, Y., et al. "The Effects of Forest Therapy on Immune Function." *International Journal of Environmental Research and Public Health* 18, no. 16 (2021): 8440. https://doi.org/10.3390/ijerph18168440; PMID: 34444188; PMCID: PMC8394293

Seventeen Minutes

Nisbet, E. K. and Zelenski, J. M. "Underestimating Nearby Nature: Affective Forecasting Errors Obscure the Happy Path to Sustainability." *Psychological Science* 22, no. 9 (2011): 1101–1106. https://doi.org/10.1177/0956797611418527; PMID: 21828351

Nature and Emotions

Bratman, G. N., Anderson, C. B., Berman, M. G., et al. "Nature and Mental Health: An Ecosystem Service Perspective." *Science Advances* 5, no. 7 (2019). https://www.science.org/doi/10.1126/sciadv.aax0903

Capaldi, C. A., Dopko, R. L., and Zelenski, J. M. "The Relationship between Nature Connectedness and Happiness: A Meta-analysis." *Frontiers in Psychology* 5 (2014): 946. https://doi.org/10.3389/fpsyg.2014.00976

Positive Psychology

https://positivepsychology.com/what-is-positive-psychology-definition

Biophilia
Barbiero, G. and Berto, R. "Biophilia as Evolutionary Adaptation: An Onto- and Phylogenetic Framework for Biophilic Design." *Frontiers in Psychology* 12 (2021). https://www.frontiersin.org/journals/psychology/articles/10.3389/fpsyg.2021.700709/full

Attention Restoration Theory
https://en.wikipedia.org/wiki/Attention_restoration_theory

https://positivepsychology.com/attention-restoration-theory

❧

Chapter 2: *How Much Time in Nature?*

Look to the Green
Lee, K. E., Williams, J. H., Sargent, L. D., et al. "40-second Green Roof Views Sustain Attention: The Role of Micro-breaks in Attention Restoration." *Journal of Environmental Psychology* 42 (2015): 182–189. https://doi.org/10.1016/j.jenvp.2015.04.003

Green and Blue Spaces
Geary, R. S., Thompson, D. A., Garrett, J. K., et al. "Green-blue Space Exposure Changes and Impact on Individual-level Well-being and Mental Health: A Population-wide Dynamic Longitudinal Panel Study with Linked Survey Data." *Public Health Research* (Southampton) 11, no. 10 (2023): 1–176. https://www.ncbi.nlm.nih.gov/books/NBK597114

Time in Nature
Meredith, G.R., Rakow, D.A., Eldermire, E. R. B., et al. "Minimum Time Dose in Nature to Positively Impact the Mental Health of College-aged Students, and How to Measure It: A Scoping Review." *Frontiers in Psychology* 14, no. 10 (2020): 2942. https://doi.org/10.3389/fpsyg.2019.02942; PMID: 31993007; PMCID: PMC6970969

White, M. P., Alcock, I., Grellier, J., et al. "Spending at Least 120 Minutes a Week in Nature is Associated with Good Health and Wellbeing." *Scientific Reports* 9 (2019): 7730. https://doi.org/10.1038/s41598-019-44097-3

Tyrväinen, L., Silvennoinen, H., Korpela, K., et al. "Importance of Nature and Its Effects on Psychological Well-being." In *Nature Based Tourism, Forests and Well-being*, Metla's working papers 52, edited by Tyrväinen, L. and Tuulentie, S. (2007): 57–77.

Williams, F. *The Nature Fix.* [see Introduction]

Three-day Effect
Atchley, R. A., Strayer, D. L., and Atchley, P. "Creativity in the Wild: Improving Creative Reasoning through Immersion in Natural Settings." *PLOS ONE* 7, no. 12 (2012). https://journals.plos.org/plosone/article?id=10.1371/journal.pone.0051474

Hopman, R. J., LoTemplio, S. B., Scott, E. E., et al. "Resting-state Posterior Alpha Power Changes with Prolonged Exposure in a Natural Environment." *Cognitive Research: Principles and Implications* 5, no. 1 (2020): 51. https://doi.org/10.1186/s41235-020-00247-0; PMID: 33108586; PMCID: PMC7591649.

Nature Pyramid
Easler, M. "The '20-5-3' Rule Prescribes How Much Time to Spend Outside." *Men's Health* (24 June 2021). https://www.menshealth.com/fitness/a36547849/how-much-time-should-i-spend-outside

Hopman-Droste, R. *Get Outside: How Environment Influences Your Cognition.* https://www.youtube.com/watch?v=B5LqZjrn9M0

❧

Chapter 3: *Higher Realms*

Going In
Muir, J. *John of the Mountains: The Unpublished Journals of John Muir.* Edited by L. M. Wolfe. Madison, Wisconsin: University of Wisconsin Press, 1979.

Eudemonic Effects
Bratman, G. N., Anderson, C. B., Berman, M. G., et al. "Nature and Mental Health: An Ecosystem Service Perspective." *Science Advances* 5, no. 7 (2019). https://www.science.org/doi/10.1126/sciadv.aax0903; PMID: 31355340; PMCID: PMC6656547.2019

Something Spiritual
Huynh, L. T. M., Gasparatos, A., Su, J., et al. [see Introduction]

Mindfulness Definition
Kabat-Zinn, J. *Mindfulness for Beginners: Reclaiming the Present Moment and Your Life.* Boulder, Colorado: Sounds True, 2016.

Mindfulness-Based Stress Reduction (MSBR) https://en.wikipedia.org/wiki/Mindfulness

Mindfulness and Personal Growth
Kabat-Zinn, J. [see previous note]

Mindfulness and Joy
Feldman, C. and Kuyken, W. *Mindfulness: Ancient Wisdom Meets Modern Psychology.* New York: Guilford, 2019.

Intrinsic Positive State
Hanh, T. N. *Silence: The Power of Quiet in A World Full of Noise.* New York, Harper One: 2015, 50–53.

❧

Chapter 4: *Mindful Time in Nature*

Power Trails

Kalevi K., Eira-Maija S., Suvi A., et al. "Enhancing Wellbeing with Psychological Tasks along Forest Trails." *Urban Forestry and Urban Greening*, 26 (2017): 25–30. https://doi.org/10.1016/j.ufug.2017.06.004

https://hikingresearch.wordpress.com/2013/12/16/kalevi-korpela-discusses-finlands-power-forests-for-well-being-and-emerging-research

Ornitherapy

Merker, H., Crossley, R., and Crossley, S. *Ornitherapy: For Your Body, Mind and Soul.* Crossley Books, 2021.

Forest Bathing

Clifford, M. A. *Your Guide to Forest Bathing: Experience the Healing Power of Nature.* Newburyport, Massachusetts: Red Wheel Books, 2021, 61–83.

Sit Spot

Young, J. *What the Robin Knows: How Birds Reveal the Secrets of the Natural World.* New York: Houghton-Mifflin, 2012, 48–79.

❧

Chapter 5: *Sensory Awareness: Gateways to Nature Mindfulness*

Sounds in Nature

Williams, F. [see Introduction]

Salubrious Trifecta

Williams, F. [see Introduction]

Four Types of Bird Calls

Young, J., pp. 1–18. [see Chapter 4]

Coming to Your Senses
Young, J., p. 182. [see Chapter 4]

Green and Blue Spaces
Triguero-Mas, M., Dadvand, P., Cirach, M., et al. "Natural Outdoor Environments and Mental and Physical Health: Relationships and Mechanisms." *Environment International* (April 2015): 35–41. https://doi.org/10.1016/j.envint.2015.01.012; PMID: 25638643

de Vries, S., Verheij, R. A., Groenewegen, P. P., et al. "Natural Environments—Healthy Environments? An Exploratory Analysis of the Relationship between Greenspace and Health." *Environment and Planning A: Economy and Space* 35, no. 10 (2003): 1717–1731. https://research.wur.nl/en/publications/natural-environments-healthy-environments-an-exploratory-analysis

Geneshka, M., Coventry, P., Cruz, J., et al. Relationship between Green and Blue Spaces with Mental and Physical Health: A Systematic Review of Longitudinal Observational Studies. *International Journal of Environmental Research and Public Health* 18, no. 17 (2021): 9010. https://pubmed.ncbi.nlm.nih.gov/34501598; PMID: 34501598; PMCID: PMC8431638

Landscape Preferences
Moura, J. M. B., Ferreira Júnior, W. S., Silva, T. C., et al. "The Influence of the Evolutionary Past on the Mind: An Analysis of the Preference for Landscapes in the Human Species." *Frontiers in Psychology* 9 (2018): 2485. https://www.ncbi.nlm.nih.gov/pmc/articles/PMC6292944; PMID: 30581407; PMCID: PMC6292944

Bennett, K. "Savanna Hypothesis and Landscape Preferences." *Encyclopedia of Evolutionary Psychological Science.* Edited by Shackelford, T. and Weekes-Shackelford, V. Springer, 2021. https://doi.org/10.1007/978-3-319-16999-6_3726-1

Fractals
Taylor, R. "Fractal Patterns in Nature and Art Are Aesthetically Pleasing and Stress-Reducing." *The Smithsonian.* (31 March 2017).

Williams, F. and Aeon. "Why Fractals Are So Soothing." *The Atlantic* (26 January 2017). https://www.theatlantic.com/science/archive/2017/01/why-fractals-are-so-soothing/514520

Landscape Perception
Franěk M. "Landscape Preference: The Role of Attractiveness and Spatial Openness of the Environment." *Behavioral Sciences* 9, no. 13 (2023): 666. https://doi.org/10.3390/bs13080666; PMID: 37622806; PMCID: PMC10452013

Visualisation Techniques for Landscape Evaluation: Landscape Preference and Perception
https://macaulay.webarchive.hutton.ac.uk/visualisationlitrev/chap2.html

Forest Fragrances
Chae, Y., Lee, S., Jo, Y., et al. [see Chapter 1]

❧

Chapter 6: *Beyond the Five*

Proprioception
https://en.wikipedia.org/wiki/Proprioception

Interoception
Robson, D. "Interoception: The Hidden Sense that Shapes Wellbeing." *The Guardian* (15 August 2021).

More Senses
Clifford, M. A., pp. 48–55. [see Chapter 4]

Mirror Neurons
Sutton, J. "Mirror Neurons and the Neuroscience of Empathy." (7 September 2023) https://positivepsychology.com/mirror-neurons

Felt Sense
Clifford, M. A., p. 54. [see Chapter 4]

❧

Chapter 7: *Nature Healing*

Window View
Ulrich R. S. "View through a Window May Influence Recovery from Surgery." *Science* 224 (1984): 4647. https://doi.org/10.1126/science.6143402; PMID: 61434021984

Inspiration for Healing
Merker, H., Crossley, R., and Crossley, S. *Ornitherapy.*

Healing Power of Nature
Selhub, E. M. and Logan, A. C. *Your Brain on Nature: The Science of Nature's Influence on Your Health, Happiness, and Vitality.* New York: Collins, 2012, 206.

Rewilding
https://rewildingeurope.com/what-is-rewilding

❧

Chapter 8: *Returns*

Biophilia
Barbiero, G. and Berto, R. "Biophilia as Evolutionary Adaptation"

40 Minutes
Young, J., pp. 64–70. [see Chapter 4]

✤

Chapter 9: *The Seasons*

Impermanence
Mortali, M. *Rewilding: Meditations, Practices, and Skills for Awakening in Nature.* Boulder, Colorado: Sounds True, 2019, 98.

✤

Chapter 10: *Traveling*

Wanderlust
https://en.wikipedia.org/wiki/Wanderlust

Evolution and Travel
Thorpe, J. R. "There's Actually A Scientific Reason You Feel The Urge To Travel." *Bustle* (26 June 2018).

Peikon, M. "The Desire to Travel Could Be Genetic." *Wanderlust.* https://wanderlust.com/journal/the-desire-to-travel-could-be-genetic

Spirit of the Place
Mortali, Micah., pp. 98-99. [see Chapter 9]

https://en.wikipedia.org/wiki/Spirit_of_place

✤

Chapter 11: *Wander Walks*

Walking to Self
Ekelund, T. *In Praise of Paths: Walking Through Time and Nature.* Vancouver: Greystone, 2020, 33.

The Path
Ekelund, T., p. 197. [see previous note]

Trail Vibes
MacFarland, Robert. *The Old Ways: A Journey on Foot.* New York: Penguin, 2012, 13–33.

eBirding for Mindfulness
eBird app. Developed by the Cornell Laboratory of Ornithology eBird is a worldwide online data base of observations providing scientists with real-time information on bird distribution and abundance. eBird is user-friendly, great fun, good science, and in my opinion can promote nature mindfulness. https://ebird.org

Healing Life Force
Nepo, M. *The Book of Awakening: Having the Life you Want by Being in the Life You Have.* San Francisco: Conari Press, 2011, 262–263.

❧

Chapter 12: *Mindfulness Afloat*

Riparian Zone
The Role of Riparian Areas. https://www.adfg.alaska.gov/static/fishing/pdfs/sport/byarea/interior/publications/ripariandisplay.pdf

❧

Chapter 13: *Nearby Places*

Koppenplatz

Common Swifts
https://avibirds.com/swift

A Feederwatch Sit Spot

Gibson, Graeme. *The Bedside Book of Birds: An Avian Miscellany.* New York: Talese/Doubleday, 2021, xi.

❧

Chapter 14: *How to Do a Sit Spot*

Sit Spot
Young, Jon., pp. 48–79. [see Chapter 4]

Merlin Bird ID: https://merlin.allaboutbirds.org

Picture This: https://www.picturethisai.com

iBird Pro: https://www.ibird.com

❧

Chapter 15: *The Sharing Circle*

The Share Circle
Mortali, Micah., pp. 205–207. [see Chapter 9]

❧

Chapter 16: *Deepening Nature Mindfulness*

Neurobiology of Gratitude
Chowdhury, M. R. "The Neuroscience of Gratitude and Effects on the Brain." https://positivepsychology.com/neuroscience-of-gratitude

Fox, G.R., Kaplan, J., Damasio, H., et al. "Neural correlates of gratitude." *Frontiers in Psychology* 6, 1491. https://doi.org/10.3389/fpsyg.2015.01491; PMID: 26483740; PMCID: PMC4588123.2015

The Science of Gratitude and How It Can Affect the Brain
https://www.calm.com/blog/the-science-of-gratitude

Positive Psychology
https://positivepsychology.com/what-is-positive-psychology-definition

Openness and the Big Five Personality Traits
Annabelle G. Y. Lim, "Big Five Personality Traits: The 5-Factor Model of Personality." *Simple Psychology* (20 December 2023). https://www.simplypsychology.org/big-five-personality.html

Simply Psychology
Annabelle G. Y. Lim, "Big Five Personality Traits" [see previous note]

Big Five Personality Traits
https://www.psychologytoday.com/us/basics/big-5-personality-traits

Land Ethic
Leopold, A. *A Sand County Almanac and Sketches Here and There.* New York: Oxford University Press, 1979, 201–226.

Piccolo, J. J. "Celebrating Aldo Leopold's land ethic at 70." *Conservation Biology*, 34, no. 6 (2020): 1586–1588. https://conbio.onlinelibrary.wiley.com/doi/10.1111/cobi.13526

Beauty and Justice
O'Kane, T. *Birding to Save the World.* New York: Harper Collins, 2024, 214–241.

About the Author

JOHN HARVEY, Ph.D. is a naturalist and consulting psychologist who resides in the Pocono Mountains of northeast Pennsylvania. He is the author of the nature book *Stillness of the Living Forest: A Year of Listening and Learning.* As a psychologist, John works with children and adults with developmental and acquired challenges of learning and memory. He has a long-standing interest in relaxation training, stress management, and personal development, and is the author of *Total Relaxation: Healing Practices for Body, Mind and Spirit*; *Deep Sleep: Complete Rest for Health, Longevity and Vitality*; and a contributing editor for *The Quiet Mind: Techniques for Transforming Stress.* John obtained his doctorate from the University of Wisconsin-Madison. He served for many years as Director of Psychology at Allied Services in Scranton, Pennsylvania, and was an adjunct faculty member at the University of Scranton. John enjoys writing, biking, hiking, kayaking, gardening, bird watching, and supporting conservation projects.

SHANTI ARTS

NATURE · ART · SPIRIT

Please visit us online
to browse our entire book catalog,
including poetry collections and fiction,
books on travel, nature, healing, art,
photography, and more.

Also take a look at our highly regarded art
and literary journal, *Still Point Arts Quarterly,*
which may be downloaded for free.

www.shantiarts.com

www.ingramcontent.com/pod-product-compliance
Lightning Source LLC
Chambersburg PA
CBHW071735270326
41928CB00013B/2689